Real Wages in 19th and 20th Century Europe
Historical and Comparative Perspectives

Real Wages in 19th and 20th Century Europe
Historical and Comparative Perspectives

edited by
Peter Scholliers

Berg

New York / Oxford / Munich

Distributed exclusively in the US and Canada by
St Martin's Press, New York

First published in 1989 by
Berg Publishers Limited
Editorial offices:
165 Taber Avenue, Providence, RI 02906, USA
150 Cowley Road, Oxford OX4 1JJ, UK
Westermühlstraße 26, 8000 München 5, FRG

© Peter Scholliers 1989

British Library Cataloguing in Publication Data

Real Wages in 19th and 20th century Europe:
    historical and comparative perspectives.
    1. Europe. Personnel. Remuneration. Related
    to prices, 1750–1988
    2. Europe. Prices. Related to remuneration
    of personnel, 1750–1988
    I. Scholliers, Peter
    331.2'94

    ISBN 0–85496–273–5

Library of Congress Cataloging-in-Publication Data

Real wages in 19th and 20th century Europe.
    1. Wages —Europe—History. 2. Prices—
Europe—History. 3. Purchasing power—
History. I. Scholliers, Peter.
HD5014.R43   1989   331.2'94   88–35074

Printed in Great Britain

Contents

Tables, Figures and Appendices

Tables

Figures

Appendices

Preface

The Centre for Contemporary Social History of the Free University of Brussels (VUB) organised an international symposium on 'Real Wages in Historical and Comparative Perspective' in March 1988. This conference aimed at contributing to methodological, theoretical and empirical aspects of the comparative study of real wages in the nineteenth and twentieth centuries, thus covering broad economic, social and institutional developments.

It is not by chance that this Centre has organised a conference on this theme. For quite a few years, the Centre has studied the course of wages and prices, first researching prices and wages in the city of Ghent in the nineteenth century, and then wages and prices during the interwar years in Belgium. This research was supervised by Professor Etienne Scholliers, who was the driving force behind the ground-breaking publication *Documents pour l'histoire des prix et des salaires en Flandre et en Brabant* (edited by C. Verlinden, J. Craeybeckx and E. Scholliers, 4 vols, Brugge, 1959–73), which contained over 2,000 pages of figures and graphs of wages and prices, mainly dealing with the early modern period. The Centre and the conference form the logical sequel to the work of E. Scholliers, focusing on the nineteenth and twentieth centuries. Yet the conference was much more concerned with international comparisons.

The present volume contains the revised papers presented by historians and economists at the Brussels symposium. It also contains the contributions made by commentators, which generally proved to be very substantial. Undoubtedly, the significant discussions which arose during the conference (opposing students of different countries, with different experiences and using different sources and methodologies) will continue after the publication of both the papers and comments. One article was written especially for this volume, focusing on places and periods which were somewhat neglected during the symposium.

The proceedings of a symposium show particular qualities and deficiencies. Obvious qualities are the sometimes detailed data, the in-depth analysis, the collection of different views and methodologies and their confrontation. On the other hand, the heterogeneous character of the papers often prevent the emergence of a coherent whole. To cope with this, 'Introductory Remarks' and 'Some Conclusions' complete this volume, aiming at situating all papers and comments within the broad and complex field of the study of real wages.

The publishing of this volume owes a lot to a lot of people. In the first place there are, of course, all those who wrote and presented a paper, all those who made comments and all those who participated in discussions during the conference. Second, Martin Daunton, who was one of the commentators, was so kind (when probably unaware of the amount of work!) to agree to look at all papers by non-native English speakers. Frank Winter also read some of these contributions. Third, the Belgian National Foundation of Scientific Research, the Vrije Universiteit Brussel, the Centre for Contemporary Social History and the publishing house of Berg Publishers Ltd are sincerely thanked for their very valuable assistance in the publication of this volume.

Brussels, Vrije Universiteit
November 1988

P. SCHOLLIERS

1. Introductory Remarks: Comparing Real Wages in the 19th and 20th Centuries*

The Relevance of the Subject

Real wages, the result of a simple division of wages by prices, are at the centre of historical and social-economic research. This is due both to the intrinsic importance of the subject and to a number of debates in which the question of real wages plays an important part. The debate on the standard of living during the industrial revolution in England, the debate on the development of income distribution, and the debate on the relationship between unemployment and real wages, have kept the interest in real wages to the fore. As well as these 'Great Debates', real wages are important in many other research fields, such as domestic demand, labour relations, patterns of consumption, foreign competition, and investment strategies. The relevance of investigation into real wages does not, however, stop here. Real wages reflect two fundamental economic and social factors: prices and wages. The study of real wages, therefore, inevitably involves attention to the history of prices (including business cycles, economic policy or the profit rate) and the history of wages (including productivity, the labour movement or the cost of production). Finally, some economic theories devote considerable attention to prices, wages and purchasing power. The above debates and fields of research explain why real wages are still a major source of interest and why this topic will probably continue to occupy a central position in historical, social, economic and other research.

Though real wages are widely used, this does not preclude a discussion of their development, methodology, nature of the sources and calculations involved, and — above all — their exact meaning. In fact, studying real wages has proved to be an extremely fruitful field for controversy. Discussions emerged because neither the computation nor the significance of real wages is at all clear. Questions put by the very first researchers of real

* Thanks to Jan Craeybeckx, Martin Daunton, Jules Hannes and Etienne Scholliers for commenting on the first version of this introduction, and to Frank Winter for translating it.

wages are still being dealt with nowadays: whether to use wholesale or retail prices as a deflator, whether unemployment and work frequency should be incorporated into the wages series, whether averages should be preferred to disaggregated data, and whether the course of real-wage indices is a satisfactory measure for living standards. The contributions to the present volume stress new kinds of questions: whether non-monetary and non-wage earnings should be incorporated into calculations, whether individual wages or the family income should be considered, and whether the family life cycle is to be taken into account.

Moreover, discussions grew more complicated, as the real wage is, to a certain extent, an ideological issue. Indeed, since the beginning of the study of real wages, clear political-ideological messages were carried by this research, aimed at approving or disapproving economic policy, or at proving or rejecting the success of one or another political regime and/or economic system. In fact, statistics and ideology form one integrated whole. This combination seems to lead not only to controversy, but also to very fruitful investigation, which is constantly in need of new source material, more sophisticated statistics, alternative methodologies, new explanations, etc. As shown in the present volume, old and, above all, new questions are being dealt with in an extensive way. The articles bear testimony to the challenging and fascinating character of the study of real wages, which proved to be livelier than ever during the past decade.

International comparisons are enriching real-wage investigation. It is obvious that such comparisons lead to relevant findings: national experiences of the evolution of real wages can be put in a broad framework; explanations of national experiences can be tested; methodologies' validity and sources' representativeness can be criticised. Nevertheless, why then are international comparisons so seldom made? Real wages have been studied mostly from a national starting-point, involving the construction of average price and wage index figures, and using proper yardsticks for measuring prices and wages. So, when looking at the real-wage series of various countries, it is possible that rather different statistics have been constructed, thus making comparisons hazardous. The present volume is concerned with this international comparison of the rich results of recent study, pointing to difficulties involved with source material, methodologies and explanations.

Some Landmarks in the Research

It seems appropriate to consider the means by which previous researchers coped with the problems of comparing real wages. This will be done through a brief survey of the development of the study of real wages, first by looking at national research in Great Britain, Germany and France, then by looking at international comparisons. Thereafter, some particular questions of real wages will be focused on.

The very first British articles date back to the last decade of the nineteenth century. A. L. Bowley and G. H. Wood published a large number of articles in the *Journal of the Royal Statistical Society* between 1898 and 1909.[1] They compiled abundant series of wages for all categories of workers for the second half of the last century. The main characteristic of these series is their extremely detailed and accurate information, covering different occupations in different regions. This was pioneering work with unique results, and today the figures are frequently referred to. Both researchers were also involved in the history of prices. Initially, this was done in order to be able to deflate the wages series. However, it was very difficult to find a proper price index figure because of the lack of sufficient research. Wood calculated a totally new price index figure based, for the first time, on retail prices. This index figure was not entirely satisfactory and Wood himself wrote that 'the result is frankly experimental'.[2] This did not prevent him combining this index figure with the wages series in order to compute real wages. His main goal was to evaluate the development of the standard and pattern of living. It appears that the 1909 article by Wood was the very first to present real-wage series from the nineteenth century.

In the methodological field, their work was innovatory. Bowley was the first to use index figures in order to accommodate fluctuations in wages. Following this, the use of index figures became the usual means of doing research into real wages. Wood also included employment figures in order to obtain 'wages allowing for unemployment'. Finally, both researchers tried to calculate global, weighted wage averages, enabling a comparison with American real wage statistics. Even before the war, Bowley and Wood's work led to similar studies in other countries.[3]

German research into prices and wages differed from British research in these pioneering days. Of course, prices and wages statistics first had to be collected. This was often done by the regional statistical bureaux of the Reich. The Germans showed more interest in the development of real wages in foreign countries, and did some research based on unpublished sources. A good example of this is the book by R. Kuczynski in which sectoral wages in Germany, the United States, Great Britain, France and

1. A. L. Bowley & G. Wood, 'Statistics of Wages in the United Kingdom during the Last Hundred Years', *Journal of the Royal Statistical Society*, 1899–1909.
2. G. Wood, 'Real Wages and the Standard of Comfort since 1850', *Journal of the Royal Statistical Society*, 1909, p. 95.
3. E.g. E. Mahaim, 'Changes in Wages, and Real Wages in Belgium', *Journal of the Royal Statistical Society*, 1904, pp. 430–8.

Belgium were compared.[4] C. von Tyszka used wages series from this book for a comparative and highly original study of the development of disaggregated real wages in Europe.[5] He combined the results of Kuczynski's wage investigation with his own original enquiries into the cost of living, resulting in many new findings. This comparative approach stressed the importance of situating prices, wages and purchasing power in an international context.

When we turn to French research into prices and wages during the 1900s, it is striking how the greatest attention was paid to the history of prices. Indeed, the only wage series available were those for coal mining and the Paris building trades,[6] apart from a few very short and/or incomplete series. The French ministry of labour published data on the development of the cost of living with regard to four spending categories from 1875 to 1910, and original price series were compiled by, amongst others, E. Levasseur and G. Bienaymé.[7] Study of real wages was slow to get off the ground. One article by the French economist A. Aftalion in 1912 is a good example of these early French real-wage studies.[8] He was satisfied with the available (poor!) wage data and he considered his results *que comme très approximatifs* [only very approximate] (p. 548). Still, this article did contribute to real-wage research in one way: its starting point was the clearly defined setting-out of a problem. Aftalion tried to look at the consequences of business cycles on real wages (more precisely, the influence of rising prices on real wages). He was not so much concerned with empirical research; his main interest was theoretical.

The common characteristic of British, German and French research into real wages during this first stage was its pioneering empirical work: wages and prices series were compiled or improved and combined in order to pinpoint as accurately as possible the development of real wages. This

---

4. R. Kuczynski, *Arbeitslohn und Arbeitszeit in Europa und Amerika, 1870–1913*, Berlin, 1913.
5. C. von Tyszka, *Löhne und Lebenskosten in Westeuropa im 19. Jahrhundert (Frankreich, England, Spanien, Belgien)*, Munich-Leipzig, 1914.
6. M. Delaire, 'Les variations des salaires dans l'industrie du bâtiment à Paris depuis 1830', *La réforme sociale*, 1891; F. Simiand, *Les salaires des ouvriers des mines de charbon en France*, Paris, 1907. Also, see the information on wages by G. d'Avenel, 'Les riches depuis sept cents ans', *Revenus et bénéfices, appointements et honoraires*. Paris, 1909.
7. *Salaires et coût de l'existence à divers époques jusqu'en 1910*, Paris, 1911; G. Bienaymé, *Le coût de la vie à Paris à diverses époques*, Nancy, 1896–1900, 2 vols; E. Levasseur, 'Le coût de la vie. Influence du revenu sur le coût de la vie', *Revue de la société d'hygiène alimentaire*, 1908.
8. A. Aftalion, 'Le salaire réel et sa nouvelle orientation', *Revue d'économie politique*, 1912, pp. 541–52.

merely descriptive stage was the first but necessary step in the study of 'deflated' wages. New sources were used, the relevant methodology was tried out and improved, and statistical problems were dealt with. Modest theoretical concepts were also launched.

These very early studies carried a political ideological message as well, though generally not a very obvious one. Bowley and Wood were quietly enthusiastic about the economic liberalism that was assumed to be responsible for the rise in buying power, treating this as a logical result of the *laissez faire* economy. When anything occurred to cause a hitch in this increasing prosperity, they confessed themselves puzzled.[9] Aftalion and von Tyszka reacted in the same way. The latter suggested a new economic policy for the German Reich. He noticed that the British rise in real wages was caused by falling retail prices, whereas the increase of German real wages was caused by a pronounced rise in nominal wages. This, of course, put German industry at a disadvantage.

The large-scale introduction into real-wage research of theoretical concepts and specific problem areas occurred in close relation with the business cycle. During the early 1920s, many books and articles were devoted to the consequences of price inflation,[10] and in the late 1920s much was published relating to high wages and high purchasing power, both factors associated with American Fordism.[11] A. Gramsci looked at (high) wages and reproduction of the labour force within a Marxist framework.[12] Interest in empirical work somewhat declined.

The most important impact of the economy on the study of real wages occurred as a consequence of the 1930s' recession. J. M. Keynes's research is, of course, highly representative of this. His *General Theory* contained extensive coverage of wages, prices, purchasing power and consumption. These economic points of reference were used in conjunction with others (such as output, employment and investments) to provide the framework for a macro-economic model. Real wages themselves were given special attention in relation to output, savings, investment and — especially — employment.[13] The *General Theory* also contained a short passage which

9. G. Wood, 'Some Statistics Relating to Working Class Progress since 1860', *Journal of the Royal Statistical Society*, 1899, p. 662.
10. E.g. C. Gini, 'Sul livello dei salari reali nel dopoguerra in Italia', *Rivista di politica economica*, 1923; M. Soecknick, *Die Entwicklung der Reallöhne in der Nachkriegzeit dargestellt an typischen Thüringen Industrien*, Iena, 1927.
11. B. Austin & W. F. Lloyd, *The Secret of High Wages*, London, 1926; F. Bayle, *Les hauts salaires*, Paris, 1930.
12. A. Gramsci, 'Americanism and Fordism', *Selections from Prison Notebooks*. London, 1978, pp. 298–332.
13. M. Timlin, *Keynesian Economics*, Toronto, 1972, pp. 164–80.

suggested a direct link between the cyclical movements of nominal and real wages: 'the change in real wages associated with a change in money wages . . . is almost in the opposite direction' (p. 10). The debate arising as a consequence of this assessment involved Keynes, Pigou, Dunlop, Kalecki and others;[14] it is still going on.[15]

Keynes's theory on the relation of nominal to real wages, together with the economic conditions of the time, also inspired some historians (e.g. E. Gilboy) to look at economic laws and, as they did so, they hoped that politicians 'who control our destinies may see the light', as R. S. Tucker put it.[16]

It should be emphasised that Keynes viewed real wages in a larger theoretical framework which was very quickly to dominate economic policy and thought in the capitalist world. Since Keynes, the study of real wages has been inextricably bound up with employment, investment, gross national product and so on (see the contribution by P. Bairoch in this volume).[17] Following Keynes, state statistical offices have been based on a macro-economic approach and most attention has been devoted to global average series of prices, wages and purchasing power.

A theoretical contribution also emerged from an opposite ideological point of view when J. Kuczynski introduced Marxist concepts of wage labour, *Verelendung* and the labour reserve into the study of real wages.[18] This was the point of departure for his *magnum opus* on the living conditions of the working classes under capitalism in various countries.[19] There is probably no research in the field of wages, prices and real wages which has been quoted more than this, although quotation does not necessarily imply agreement.[20]

14. J. M. Keynes, 'Relative Movements of Real Wages and Output', *Economic Journal*, 1939, pp. 34–51.
15. S. Henry, 'Unemployment and Real Wages', *Oxford Economic Papers*, 1985, pp. 330–38; J. B. Schor, 'Changes in the Cyclical Pattern of Real Wages: Evidence from Nine Countries, 1955–1980', *Economic Journal*, 1985, pp. 452–68.
16. R. S. Tucker, 'Real Wages of Artisans in London, 1729–1935', *Journal of American Statistical Society*, 1937.
17. R. Grellet, 'Salaire monétaire et répartition', A. Barrere (ed.), *Keynes aujourd'hui*, Paris, 1985, p. 482; E. Preteceille & J.-P. Terrail, *Capitalism, Consumption and Needs*, Oxford, 1986, p. 12.
18. J. Kuczynski, *Die Entwicklung der Lage der Arbeiterschaft in Europa und Amerika, 1870–1933*, Basel, 1934; ibid., *Löhne und Konjunktur in Deutschland, 1887–1932*, Berlin, 1933.
19. J. Kuczynski, *Die Geschichte der Lage der Arbeiter unter dem Kapitalismus*, Berlin, 1960–1972, 40 vols.
20. E.g. T. Pierenkemper, 'The Standard of Living and Employment in Germany, 1850–1980: An Overview', *Journal of European Economic History*, 1987, p. 56; P. Thane, *The Foundations of the Welfare State*, London-New York, 1982, p. 169.

J. Kuczynski's theoretical contribution involved methodological and ideological aspects. With regard to the former, he proposed that real wages form the best measurement of the standard of living, if employment and the length of the working day are taken into account. He also suggested two distinct wage series — one for the 'labour aristocracy' (*Arbeiteraristokratie*) and one for the 'bulk of the workers' (*grosse Masse der Arbeiter*). Kuczynski also pointed to the danger of a limited short-term view. He introduced the *Relativlöhne* (relative wages) in order to compare workers' real wages with trends in development of other classes' standards of living. Finally, he estimated that a declining real wage pointed to a clear deterioration in living conditions, but that a rising real wage did not necessarily mean an improvement. He regarded the increase in English real wages during the 1900s and the 1910s, for example, as necessary for the reproduction of the power of working, because of the increasing effort required of labour and, therefore, the need for more, better and more expensive food.[21] In recent (non-Marxist) research, reference is often made to this view of the significance of real wage fluctuations.[22]

J. Kuczynski's approach was — and still is — discussed. His figures and conclusions were looked at with suspicion,[23] while he is cited as *the* pessimist in the debate on the standard of living.[24] Other 'pessimist' participants in this debate reproach him with his extremism, which 'has done some harm to the cause he wishes to propound'.[25] Marxists have looked at Kuczynski's work with scepticism because of his determinism[26] (see E. Mandel's interpretation of Marxist concepts of real wages in this volume). Nevertheless, Kuczynski has contributed to the study of real wages in the methodological, statistical and theoretical fields.

A similar position has been occupied by F. Simiand. He was one of the few individuals in France compiling French wages and prices series before 1914. As a positivist, he reacted against a romantic view of writing *l'histoire événementielle* (the history of events). This starting point was retained in his

21. See also K. W. Rothschild, 'Langfristige Reallohn- und Lebensstandardvergleich; allgemeine Problematik und österreichisches Beispiel', *Zeitschrift für Nationalökonomie*, 1956, pp. 423–60.
22. E.g. W. Zapf, 'Die Wohlfahrtsentwicklung in Deutschland seit der Mitte des 19. Jahrhunderts', W. Conze & M. Lepsius (eds), *Sozialgeschichte der Bundesrepublik Deutschland*, Stuttgart, 1983, p. 48.
23. E.g. M. Flinn, 'Trends in Real Wages, 1750–1850', *Economic History Review*, 1974, p. 406.
24. R. Hartwell, 'The Rising Standard of Living in England, 1800–1850', *Economic History Review*, 1961, p. 397.
25. E. Hobsbawm, 'The British Standard of Living, 1790–1850', *Economic History Review*, 1957, p. 61.
26. E. Mandel, *Der Spätkapitalismus*, Frankfurt, 1972, pp. 147–8.

influential publications of the 1930s.[27] He is considered to be one of those who influenced the renowned *esprit des Annales*, primarily because of his concept of time in history ('les divers temps: courts, moyens et séculaires') and because of his analysis of the business cycle. Simiand's contribution was located in the theoretical as well as the empirical-methodological field. With regard to the latter, his work on wages can be considered as making up lost ground for France in comparison with Germany or Great Britain. His contribution to the history of prices was of less importance. Simiand used existing data, turned these into weighted price index figures and linked these to the official series, thus obtaining an index figure from 1801 to 1930. His series of prices and especially of wages have been used up until very recently.[28]

Though Simiand had all the factors at his disposal with which to compute real wages, he expressly did not do so: 'S'attacher au salaire réel, c'est se condamner à ne pas apercevoir, et à ne pas comprendre, les relations majeures les plus explicatives du mouvement du salaire' [An attachment to the notion of real wages is to condemn oneself to not seeing, and not understanding, the main influences that do most to explain fluctuations in wages] (*Le salaire*, vol. 1, p. xxv). Indeed, his one and only concern was the fluctuations in wages. However, Simiand's research covered a much wider field than the study of wages alone: it has been said that through wages 'Il a cru découvrir les lois de l'évolution d'une société économique développée' [He thought he had discovered the laws governing the evolution of an economically advanced society].[29]

Clearly, research on real wages was given a strong theoretical impulse during the interwar years as a result of economic conditions. All the authors considered here incorporated the evolution of real wages into their specific, plainly ideological theories. Long-term developments were studied in order to derive economic laws which would have a bearing on economic policy. This concern is shown clearly by the opening sentence of R. S. Tucker's 1936 article: 'Probably no subject in the field of economic history is as important in its applications for present policy as the purchasing power of the working classes.' Such considerations somewhat pushed aside empirical research.

27. F. Simiand, *Le salaire, l'évolution sociale et la monnaie*, Paris, 1932, 2 vols; ibid., *Recherches anciennes et nouvelles sur le mouvement général des prix du XVIe au XIXe siècle*, Paris, 1933.
28. E.g. J. Singer-Kérel, *Le coût de la vie à Paris de 1840 à 1954*, Paris, 1954; J. Rougerie, 'Remarques sur l'histoire des salaires à Paris au XIXe siècle', *Mouvement social*, 1968, pp. 71–108.
29. J. Bouvier, 'François Simiand 1873–1935', A. Burguière (ed.), *Dictionnaire des sciences historiques*, Paris, 1986, p. 633.

While the years before 1914 were characterised by empirical research and the interwar years by theoretical studies, both approaches were combined after the Second World War. Within the framework of existing, original or altered theories new data and sophisticated statistics were put to work. The study of real wages was given a very strong impulse by the intense debate in British economic history over the standard of living during the industrial revolution in England.[30] After holding a central position for several years, real wages were later somewhat neglected but have come back strongly recently. This is linked to the publication of a number of econometric articles in which wages and prices are the focal point.

The 'new look' article written by P. Lindert and J. Williamson in 1983 can be considered a prime example.[31] Both researchers added new empirical evidence to existing wages data and, above all, to data on prices. Alongside this, they tried to establish the rate of unemployment by means of regression analysis. Their contribution was extremely fertile in the empirical-quantitative field and enriched the continuing debate, though they themselves did not take either an 'optimist' or 'pessimist' position. In introducing the 'new economic history' and a positivist-econometric basis, they adopted a neutral stance (above the ideological debate?). Lindert and Williamson suggested that, after their contribution, new research fields should be looked at (e.g. social inequality, or the eighteenth century).

However, this was not the final word on real wages! N. Crafts wrote that 'Lindert and Williamson's cost-of-living index is not acceptable',[32] and discussion ensued[33] (see the contribution by N. Crafts and J. Lucassen in this volume). Meanwhile, L. Schwarz criticised the selected rents and weightings, and E. Hunt and F. Botham commented on the representative-

30. For a survey of the state of the debate, see A. J. Taylor, *The Standard of Living in Britain in the Industrial Revolution*, London, 1975; P. O'Brien & S. Engerman, 'Changes in Income and Its Distribution during the Industrial Revolution', R. Floud & D. McCluskey (eds), *The Economic History of Britain Since 1700*, Cambridge, 1982, vol. 1, pp. 167–71; J. Rule, *The Labouring Classes in Early Industrial England 1750–1850*, London-New York, 1986, pp. 27–45. See also the contribution of N. F. R. Crafts in this volume.
31. P. Lindert & J. Williamson, 'English Workers' Living Standards during the Industrial Revolution: a New Look', *Economic History Review*, 1983, pp. 1–25.
32. N. Crafts, 'English Workers' Real Wages during the Industrial Revolution: Some Remaining Problems, *Journal of Economic History*, 1985, p. 139.
33. P. Lindert & J. Williamson, 'English Workers' Real Wages: Reply to Crafts', *Journal of Economic History*, 1985, p. 153; N. Crafts, 'British Economic Growth 1700–1850: Some Difficulties of Interpretation', *Explorations in Economic History*, 1987, p. 264; J. Williamson, 'Debating the British Industrial Revolution', *Explorations in Economic History*, 1987, p. 283. Also, see the article by J. Mokyr, 'Is There Still Life in the Pessimist Case? Consumption during the Industrial Revolution, 1790–1850', *Journal of Economic History*, 1988, pp. 69–92.

ness of the wage series.[34] The net result of Lindert and Williamson's 1983 article appears therefore to have provided extra stimulus for research into wages and prices. Some authors, however, have started to doubt seriously whether real wages are of any value at all in measuring the standard of living.[35]

German research into purchasing power has not been dominated by one debate. Originally, there was more interest in the period from 1871 to 1914, but more recent research has been oriented more towards the period of the Weimar Republic. Kuczynski's *Lage der Arbeiter unter dem Kapitalismus* has been criticised and his figures recalculated and reinterpreted. G. Bry did not change Kuczynski's price series, but limited himself to altering slightly and, above all, extending the wages series.[36] G. Bry himself very soon cast doubt on his own results when he realised the importance of using retail prices instead of wholesale prices. Probably the most original research was that led by A. Desai.[37] He used industrial accident insurance statistics alongside data from Kuczynski and Bry and was able to present yearly wages for several industries together with a revised global wage index figure. These series are to be preferred above other series and are still largely used today.[38] Desai also calculated a new cost of living index figure. He used retail prices (published by official statistics offices) and weighted these on the basis of new evidence on the spending patterns of working class families.

German writers on real wages seem to be satisfied with the methods used and the results obtained. K. Borchardt and W. Conze published both the series by Kuczynski and Desai, and argued their preference for the latter.[39] Recent authors have limited themselves to publishing the existing real wage series, commenting on the methodology, without suggesting what the best

34. L. D. Schwarz, 'The Standard of Living in the Long Run, 1700–1860', *Economic History Review*, 1985, pp. 24–41; E. Hunt & F. Botham, 'Wages in Britain during the Industrial Revolution', *Economic History Review*, 1987, pp. 380–99; R. Jackson, 'The Structure of Pay in Nineteenth-Century Britain', *Economic History Review*, 1987, pp. 561–70.
35. E.g. G. N. von Tunzelmann, 'The Standard of Living Debate and Optimal Economic Growth', J. Mokyr (ed.), *The Economics of the Industrial Revolution*, Totowa, 1985, p. 207.
36. G. Bry, *Wages in Germany*, Princeton, 1960.
37. A. Desai, *Real Wages in Germany, 1871–1913*, Oxford, 1968.
38. E.g. G. Hohorst, J. Kocka, G. Ritter, *Sozialgeschichtliches Arbeitsbuch*, Munich, 1975, p. 107; J. Mooser, *Arbeiterleben in Deutschland 1900–1970*, Frankfurt, 1984, pp. 73–6.
39. K. Borchardt, 'Wirtschaftliches Wachstum und Weschellagen 1800–1914', H. Aubin and W. Zorn (eds), *Handbuch der deutschen Wirtschafts- und Sozialgeschichte*, Stuttgart, 1976, pp. 225–6; W. Conze, 'Sozialgeschichte 1850–1918', ibid., p. 620.

series might be.[40] Investigation at present is directed towards the interwar years. It seems that a controversy has emerged with regard to the impact of the German (exaggeratedly high?) wage level on the 'sick' Weimar economy.[41] Other researchers concentrate on refining real wage series, focusing on sectors or regions. However, the first half of the nineteenth century is somewhat overlooked.

Recent French investigations into real wages devote a lot of attention to theory but, first, J. Singer-Kérel and, above all, J. Fourastié did an enormous amount of empirical work. Both were mainly interested in the history of prices. Fourastié wanted to study *real prices* in the very long term in order to look at the influence of mechanisation on output and consumption.[42] He compiled prices of very divergent goods and services and also included wages for wage-earners who were rarely considered (e.g. university teachers, office boys). Fourastié combined both series and presented real-wage series, launching some theoretical considerations in the process — amongst them a '*théorie du niveau de vie*' (theory of the standard of living).

While empirical research was important during the 1950s, it has been pushed aside by theoretical studies since the 1960s. J. Lhomme published a number of articles on real wages in which not a single new or revised wage or price series was used.[43] His sole concern was the '*enseignements théoriques*' and, finally, the role of the state in the evolution of purchasing power. A similar approach to real wages is to be found among the '*régulationnistes*', most of their interest in real wages being theoretical. The evolution of wages, prices and purchasing power is placed in a long-term framework and linked to the labour process, patterns of consumption, industrial relations, the role of the state, the monetary system and the international balance of power. Series of prices and nominal and real wages have a specific function within the '*régulation*' school. These factors (alongside others), lead to three types or models to be distinguished in the development of nineteenth- and twentieth-century society: a '*régulation à l'ancienne*' [traditional regulation] up until the 1850s, a '*régulation concurrentielle*' [competitive regulation] circa 1850–1914 and a '*régulation monopoliste ou admi-*

40. E. Wiegand, 'Zur Historischen Entwicklung der Löhne und Lebenshaltungskosten in Deutschland', *Historical Social Research*, 1981, pp. 18–41; T. Pierenkemper, 'The Standard of Living'; R. Goemmel, *Realeinkommen in Deutschland. Ein internationaler Vergleich (1810–1913)*, Nuremberg, 1979.
41. C.-L. Holtfrerich, 'Zu Höhe Löhne in der Weimarer Republik?', *Geschichte und Gesellschaft*, 1984, pp. 122–41.
42. J. Fourastié, *Le grand espoir du XXe siècle*, Paris, 1949; J. Fourastié & C. Fontaine, *Documents pour l'histoire et la théorie des prix*, Paris, 1958–60, 2 vols.
43. J. Lhomme, *Les enseignements théoriques à retenir d'une étude sur les salaires dans la longue période*, Geneva, 1967; J. Lhomme, 'Le pouvoir d'achat de l'ouvrier français au cours d'un siècle, 1840–1940', *Mouvement social*, 1968, pp. 41–70.

nistrée' [monopoly or administrative regulation] after 1920, but mostly after 1945[44] (see the contribution by I. Cassiers in this volume). The theoretical aspect, obviously, predominates since no new series or new methodologies are being presented.

It is worth noting that the national real-wage studies have developed alongside patterns which were launched by the pioneers in each country. British research focused on detailed, merely national but highly sophisticated statistics; German research had an eye for developments in other countries; French research was concerned with theorising. But above all it should be noted that researchers in each country had little knowledge of work being done elsewhere.

Making International Comparisons

Indeed, theories, methodologies, concepts or explanations launched in one country were but rarely heard of in another country. This is largely because, as stressed above, the international comparison of real wages forms a specific research field.

Any great interest in comparing national real wages primarily emerged among non-academics in the 1920s, when government services of all kinds started investigations into real wages in different countries. The British Ministry of Labour published a short article in 1923 giving the very first results of this new type of research.[45] The difficulties inherent in such a study led the International Labour Office to devote the Second International Conference of Labour Statisticians to short-run real wage comparisons. Similarly, the renowned International Institute of Statistics established a special committee to study international shifts in real wages (with, amongst other members, Bowley, Gini, Huber, Julin and Pribram).[46] Alongside these initiatives, much research was done on an individual basis. International organisations and national governments have remained interested in the international comparison of real wages up to the present.[47]

44. R. Boyer, 'Les salaires en longue période', *Economie et statistique*, 1978, pp. 27–57.
45. 'Comparative Real Wages in London and Certain Other Capital Cities Abroad', *Ministry of Labour Gazette*, July 1923.
46. F. Klezl, 'La comparaison internationale des salaires réels', *Revue internationale du travail*, 1925, pp. 500–18; M. Huber, 'La comparaison internationale des salaires réels', *Bulletin de l'institut internationale de statistique*, XXIII, 1928, pp. 693–718.
47. J. H. van Zanten, 'Some Observations on International Comparisons of Index Numbers of Cost of Living and Real Wages', *Revue de l'institut international de statistique*, 1933, pp. 20–39; F. Lehouiller, 'Salaires hebdomadaires réels dans divers pays de 1914 à 1939', *Bulletin de la statistique générale de la France*, 1944, pp. 207–47; W. Beckerman, *Comparaison internationale du revenu réel*, Paris, 1966.

What lies behind this widespread interest? Its main purpose has been practical: how to explain the differences in real wages between countries and how to eliminate them. Similarly, this kind of research is important for customs tariffs and international economic competition. Finally, it appears that real wages were of value 'to international trusts and companies as a basis for wage scales'.[48]

These practical motives have tended to elbow historical and theoretical research aside. Only J. Lehouiller (of the French statistical office) looked at the *development* of real wages, while the international scientific committee on price history started comparative research in 1931 into the very long-run development of prices (leading to the publishing of series by W. Beveridge, M. Elsas, N. Posthumus and others). Other contributions were merely snapshots of the differences in purchasing power in different countries at a given moment. This type of research during the interwar years had more importance from the point of view of methodology, in the search for ways of making meaningful comparisons of wages, prices and consumer patterns. The British Ministry of Labour's 1923 study compared 'the relative quantity of food purchasable with wages payable for 48 hours' work on 1st March, 1923' in thirteen European cities. Standard 'shopping baskets' and working hours were selected, two factors which in fact might be highly divergent. Later on, this method was discarded and the 'basic-need approach' came into use, in which the prices were recorded of a sample of goods and services (which could vary from one country to another but which was considered representative of the basic needs in each country).

The study of real wages in a historical and comparative perspective is more recent. E. H. Phelps Brown and M. Browne, and G. Bry and C. Boschan, did pioneering work on this in the 1960s.[49] However, they had few successors. It is only recently that some researchers have restarted comparative study of real wages[50] (see the contribution by V. Zamagni in this volume). There is therefore still a lot of work to be done. In the light of new series, problem areas and explanations that have been put forward in

48. J. Richardson, 'International Comparisons of Real Wages', *Journal of the Royal Statistical Society*, 1930, p. 398.
49. H. Phelps Brown & M. Browne, *A Century of Pay*, London, 1968; G. Bry & C. Boschan, 'Secular Trends and Recent Changes in Real Wages and Wage Differentials in Three Western Countries', *Second International Conference of Economic History*, Paris, 1965, pp. 175–201.
50. E.g. V. Zamagni, 'The Daily Wages of Italian Industrial Workers in the Giolittian Period (1898–1913), with an International Comparison for 1905', *Rivista di storia economica*, 1984, pp. 59–93; P. Scholliers, 'A Methodological Note on Real Wages During the Inter-war Years', *Historical Social Research*, 1987, pp. 40–50; J. Soderberg, 'Real Wage Trends in Urban Europe, 1730–1850: Stockholm in a Comparative Perspective', *Social History*, 1987, pp. 155–76.

recent years in the international, national and regional fields, it would seem appropriate to study comparative developments with new enthusiasm and a degree of criticism.

How Real Are Real Wages?

A number of fundamental questions concerning the study of real wages have obviously emerged from this survey. Perhaps the main question is: what exactly do trends in real wages (in various countries) tell us about standards of living, international competition, the class struggle or any other social, economic or political aspect? To answer this question we need to consider the methods used and the problems involved.

A fundamental point is the choice of the type of wage to be considered: Time wages are to be preferred to piecework rates; within time wages, a distinction must be made between the basic (hourly or daily) wage on the one hand and weekly, monthly and yearly wages on the other. The basic wage reflects the cost of labour and is referred to as 'rates of wages', *Tariflöhne* or *taux de salaire*. Divided by a deflator, this type of wage provides merely an economic indicator. A social indicator is provided by using actual earnings (*Arbeitsverdienste, salaire effectif*), in which working time (per week, per year), possible bonuses and premiums, overtime and (partial) unemployment are included. Yearly wages are to be preferred. The choice of the type of wage is therefore linked to the purpose of the research, according to whether it has an economic or social starting-point or some combination of the two. G. Bry, for instance, clearly distinguished the economic and the social intentions of his study when he noted that 'hourly real wages roughly doubled . . . whereas weekly earnings increased by about 50 per cent' (p. 4). P. Combe, too, considers the *coût de production* (hourly wage) and the *coût d'entretien* (weekly wage).[51] The importance of the wage series selected is obvious: When making international comparisons, it goes without saying that the merging of wage series of different character is totally unacceptable! This often means that the possibility for comparison is rather limited, or that the researcher has to go through the time-consuming process of reconstructing comparable series.

A second important point is that wage series provide information only with regard to market-oriented wage labour, namely the buying and selling of the power of working. If the interest is primarily in economic development (e.g. the movement in the cost of production), this does not constitute a problem. But if the development of the standard of living is to be

51. P. Combe, *Niveau de vie et progrès technique en France depuis 1860*, Paris, 1955, p. 120.

investigated, it should be kept in mind that wages are not the only source of income[52] (see the contribution by L. Schwarz, P. Van den Eeckhout, F. Daelemans and R. Wall in this volume). Other income (besides wages) includes monetary and non-monetary income, such as garden produce, poultry or gifts, forms of income entirely external to the market economy. At the same time it is necessary to consider *payments in kind*, which, though non-monetary, are clearly part of the workings of the labour market and still exist today. As far as (non-wage) monetary income is concerned, examples frequently encountered include keeping a shop or alehouse, or letting rooms. In addition to such sources of income, social security systems have emerged which at first were only marginal, but have gradually become important providers of additional income. A distinction has therefore been made between *direct* and *indirect* wages (see the comments by J. Vuchelen in this volume). Some authors even mention three 'wages': the individual, the social and the common wage. The first one is of course the direct wage, the second is the income provided in different forms by the social security system (sick benefit, unemployment pay, pensions and so on) and the third wage is that provided for by company social services and by the state (education, nurseries, etc.).[53] However, most established wages series reflect only the direct, individual wage, ignoring the rest. International comparisons become even more complicated since it can be expected that the non–monetary income and/or the social wage differ from one country to another.

Additional incomes accrue to either the wage earner himself (e.g. unemployment benefits) or to members of his family (e.g. child allowance). However, the development of the living standard is almost always measured in terms of the wage of an adult male. Wages of children and women are seldom incorporated into real-wage studies, so that total family income is totally ignored. It seems clear that new insights might be obtained by combining the separate wage data into one family income. Indeed, recent research has shown that money incomes of women and children are largely determined by the income level of the male bread-winner. A low income of the latter obliges the rest of the family to look for relatively well-paid work (mostly in factories), thus leading to a narrowing of global income distribution within the working class[54] (see the comments by R. Wall, M.

52. Noted already by S. J. Chapman, *Work and wages*, London, 1904, vol. 1, p. 18.
53. P. Bauchet, 'Evolution des salaires réels et structures économiques', *Revue économique*, 1952, pp. 299–300.
54. J. Modell, 'Patterns of Consumption, Acculturation and Family Income Strategies in Late 19th-Century America', T. K. Hareven & A. Vinovski (eds), *Family and Population in 19th-century America*, New York, 1978, pp. 206–40; P. van den Eeckhout & P. Scholliers, 'Geld in 't laatje. Arbeid en inkomen van gentse arbeidersgezinnen circa 1900', *Arbeid in Veelvoud* (Huldeboek J. Craeybeckx en E. Scholliers), Brussels, 1988, pp. 192–213.

Daunton, R. Leboutte and P. Van den Eeckhout in this volume). Again, things grow more complicated when international comparisons are made: composition of the family and participation of women and children in the working process differ within the international context.

To conclude this section on wages, it can be said that wages series obviously have a highly specific content, and certainly are not always internationally comparable. When these series are used to compare real wages, their peculiar features naturally remain. Real-wage series therefore have a precise and limited significance.

This 'warning' with regard to the precise but limited meaning of wages series remains valid when we turn our attention to prices. When a wage is being divided by the price of just one consumer item, the resulting quotient has a specific, rather narrow significance which may still be of interest (see the contributions by P. Bairoch, D. Morsa and E. Ebeling in this volume). However, as a general rule price fluctuations are recorded of a 'shopping basket' of goods and services representing a given consumer pattern. This involves a considerable amount of time-consuming research, tiresome ledger work, statistical problems and repeated controls (see the contributions by C. Schroeven, P. Solar and N. Crafts in this volume).

The first problem is the type of prices to be used. Since the earliest calculations of real wages, the need to use retail, rather than wholesale, prices has been obvious. A large range of sources has been used (price lists, official statistics, accounts from all kinds of institutions) but these do not record exactly the same types of prices. For instance, there is a marked difference between the trend of prices provided by the *mercuriales* and by charitable bodies.[55] Despite the fact that retail prices are to be preferred, many researchers have been obliged by the lack of any other data to use wholesale prices (e.g. Lindert and Williamson). This probably causes no great harm when development over the very long term is considered, but should be rigorously eliminated in the short-term view.

The cost of living index should reflect the price of a range of goods and services corresponding to a known spending pattern. Generally, results of budget enquiries are used to get information on such patterns, as well as the accounts of institutions and consumption data. The main question concerns the representiveness of these sources: to what extent are they an accurate reflection of spending by unskilled or skilled workers, by artisans, by civil servants, by non-wage-earners and by farmworkers? To what extent can an *average* spending pattern possibly be a faithful reflection of social-historical reality? (See the contributions by C. Schroeven, P. Solar and J. L. Van

---

55. E. Scholliers, 'De gentse textielarbeiders in de 19e en 20e eeuw: een reactie', *Tijdschrift voor Geschiedenis*, 1980, pp. 262–3.

Zanden in this volume).

This problem is linked to shifts in the pattern of family spending through time: how can these changes be incorporated in the index figure? This question leads on to the more general one of the formulae for computing price index figures. The very first cost of living indices (Wood, von Tyszka, Kuczynski) were fairly simple and often used unweighted formulae. It was only after the Second World War that the formulae by Paasche and Laspeyres were more commonly used. J. Singer-Kérel tried to solve the problem of suitable adjustment weightings by constructing a sophisticated (and criticised) chain index figure.[56] D. Loschky showed that the choice of formulae does influence the results to an important extent, though other researchers suggested that neither the formulae nor the weightings were of decisive importance.[57] The latter case involved mainly short-term developments and, therefore, rather limited shifts in spending.

Most European statistics offices started calculating cost of living indices after the First World War. Students of real wages almost always followed these index figures blindly. Some researchers, however, have warned against the deceptive reliability of official price index figures.[58] Research into the Belgian official cost of living index during the interwar years has concluded that this index was constantly manipulated in one way or another in order to even out sudden fluctuations and to avoid overstepping thresholds that would lead to index-linked wage increases.[59] Such findings must lead to caution in the use of official index figures.

Cost of living indices, therefore, have a well-defined significance too. They are satisfactory when they comply with a number of conditions as regards their composition, adjustment weighting, calculation and so on. A very important question remains the comparability of different national consumption habits: how to incorporate these in the international comparison of the evolution of prices and purchasing power? Are national (and thus, specific) price index figures acceptable, or should one consider some kind of standardised basket of goods and services? (This problem is tackled in this volume by V. Zamagni, R. Leboutte, M. Daunton and D. Van der Veen.)

56. J. Singer-Kérel, Le coût de la vie, p. 68; J. Fourastié, 'Le coût de la vie à Paris de 1840 à 1954', Revue d'économie politique, 1962, pp. 64–72.
57. D. Loschky, 'Seven Centuries of Real Income Per Wage Earner Reconsidered', Economica, 1980, pp. 459–65; J. Poelmans, 'Calcul d'un indice des prix pour les "cadres"', Cahiers économiques de Bruxelles, 1973, pp. 189–213.
58. N. Branson & N. Heinemann, Britain in the Nineteen-thirties, St Albans, 1973, p. 154; A. Sauvy, Histoire économique de la France entre les deux guerres, vol. 2, p. 353; J. Mueller, Nivellierung und Differenzierung der Arbeitseinkommen in Deutschland seit 1925, Berlin, 1955, pp. 110–11.
59. P. Scholliers, Loonindexering en sociale vrede, Brussels, 1985, pp. 134–40.

Many of the methodological problems, divergent explanations and ideological points raised are bound up with different attitudes to real wages. Yet
real wages have a clear-cut and, in point of fact, limited significance. It is
well known that nominal wages series exclude a number of variables such as
non-monetary income, unemployment and welfare payments; it is well
known, too, that price series might be based on an insufficient number of
goods and services, on interpolations or on wholesale prices. In other
words, it is clear what is being measured and what is not; no more than this
(no less than this either!) should be expected from the results of calculations
of real wages. Real wages give an indication of the purchasing power of a
given wage and are therefore bound up with other complex social factors
and forces. These considerations should warn us against attaching too much
importance to the significance of real wages on their own!

Some Final Remarks

The study of real wages has emerged in conjuction with the attempt to
assess and control economic, social and political developments.[60] This
aspect of research on real wages has never in fact disappeared, and practical
motivations aiming at influencing and shaping state policy have continued
to exist. This element was obvious as long ago as the interwar years, when
the movement of wages, prices and purchasing power became one of the
main interests — perhaps *the* main interest — of official statistical offices,
and when the first international comparisons were attempted. Later on,
theoretical starting points emerged which aimed at an analysis and explanation of the development of industrial capitalism (see the contributions by
E. Mandel, J. Vuchelen and I. Cassiers in this volume).

Each country contributed in specific ways to the study of real wages.
French researchers were primarily concerned with theorising within a broad
framework, whereas the German researchers strove for accurate description
within specific problematics (for instance, the *Alltagsgeschichte*); British
researchers dealt with real wages, largely contributing to heuristic and
empirical investigation. International institutions tried to compare the
results of national research, proposing new methodologies.

The main problem with regard to real wages has been and still is their real
significance. It seems certain that the division of the nominal wage by the
cost of living must tell us something about economic and social factors, but
it is not clear what. This brief survey has indicated that the problems
involved are not easy to solve. As repeatedly stated, the real-wage problematic becomes more complex when international comparisons are made. The

60. Already stressed by S. J. Chapman, *Work and wages*, p. vi.

papers and the comments in this volume largely stress the different kinds of problems, dealing with methodology, source material, *Fragestellung*, interpretation, etc. The conclusions in this volume will tackle some of the proposed solutions.

Above all, doubts seem to be in order with regard to the contribution of real wages to the standard of living debate. Not a single author fails to warn against attributing too great degree of accuracy or too great a significance to a fluctuation of few index points. Scepticism with regard to its precise significance is far from allayed when one of the staunchest defenders of the use of real wages as a measure of living standards (J. Kuczynski) estimates that a rise in real wages does not necessarily entail an improvement in the standard of living.[61] These repeated warnings seem to have convinced some researchers that real wages cannot solve the problems involved in assessing standards of living, no matter what new theories or econometric techniques might be used.[62] This might be right. However, the contribution of wages, prices and real wages to the study of the standard of living has not only a descriptive interest, but also — and perhaps primarily — an explanatory importance for economic, social and political history (with regard to shifts in consumer patterns, diet, investment strategies, migration, strikes and so on). So continuing research into prices, wages and purchasing power is still of decisive importance for the study of economic and social development. One must simply be aware of the precise significance of what one is calculating. But isn't this obvious for all econometric study?

61. J. Kuczynski, *Die Entwicklung der Lage*, p. 11.
62. J. Mokyr & N. Savin, 'Some Econometric Problems in the Standard of Living Controversy', *Journal of European Economic History*, 1978, p. 518.

L. D. SCHWARZ

2. The Formation of the Wage: Some Problems*

Once, there would have been little difficulty in writing this paper. All over Europe the formation of the waged labour force, industrialisation and urbanisation were all supposed to have arrived together. Before industrialisation — the meaning of which was assumed to be self-evident — most of the population was rural; wages were only a part of their remuneration, quite possibly only a small part. Of the urban remainder, much was artisan or self-employed. Those who did earn wages worked in small establishments in any case, so if there was a waged labour force it was not particularly large, and it lacked the coherence of a proletariat.

Now this has all become very much more difficult to accept in its original form. 'Industrialisation' has been decomposed into a relatively gradual process: 'the survival of pre-industrial forms of activity' is diagnosed as very widespread and persistent; the transmutation of many 'artisans' into 'small employers' was widespread in many trades. France did not undergo a 'classic' industrial revolution with 'take-off', large-scale factories and enormous concentrations of factory workers, but still it managed to industrialise; in Germany, the Rhineland and Upper Silesia may have had their concentrations of factories, but much of the country did not: many parts of England went a different way from the paradigm. Historians now make their reputations by lovingly describing the intricacies of this transition,

---

* This paper has benefited from criticisms by Prof. J. R. Harris, Dr. A. J. Randall, the Economic History seminars at Oxford and the Institute of Historical Research in London and the comments at the Colloquium published in this volume, especially those of Dr F. Daelemans. But the greatest tribute must go to the exceptionally penetrating, not to say scathing, criticisms of Dr P. van den Eeckhout, who will doubtless disagree with much of what follows. It was written before I had the opportunity to read the very interesting paper by D. Morsa, 'Salaire et salariat dans les économies préindustrielles (xvi–xviii siècle): quelques considérations critiques', *Revue belge de philologie et d'histoire*, LXV, 1987, pp. 751-84, much of which I agree with and which it is hoped will not escape the attention of Anglo-Saxon readers.

whether reasserting it in a revised form[1] or qualifying it.[2]

Secondly, the assumption that by some point in the nineteenth century non-monetary forms of remuneration were irrelevant has likewise a limited validity. We are being assured that Victorian England had a substantial peasantry, that 'a considerable part of exchange in south-east England at least, took place through non-commercial reciprocal relations without recourse to cash'.[3] Even substantial farmers might be found paying their men in kind. In 1843, farm workers on both sides of the border of eastern Scotland — an area by no means backward in its agriculture — were having between eighty and ninety-five per cent of their wages paid in kind, and 'the only money items in the wage were generally fixed and identifiable commutations of traditional allowances in kind'.[4] The local workers 'ate better but spent less on clothes, small luxuries and general town wares than other ploughmen'.[5]

We cannot even be sure that the 'modern factory-employed proletariat' depended *entirely* on wages. There existed a range of perquisites about which little is known, but which were probably as important in many factories as they were in agriculture. One may guess that the better-paid workmen probably had greater access to these perquisites, but even that is only a guess. There might be free coal for miners or wood allowances for carpenters; there was a wide range of ways in which the respectable poor appropriated for themselves some of the means of production according to a sense of priorities that the bourgeoisie preferred to attribute to the criminal classes.[6] Little is known of workplace appropriation and — given the intractability of the sources — little is likely to be known. We know little enough about workplace appropriation at the present time.

Furthermore, for those factory workers who *did* have some spare time, there were perfectly acceptable earnings to be made, not breaking any law,

1. For instance, D. Levine for England. See his 'Production, Reproduction and the Proletarian Family in England, 1550–1851', in D. Levine (ed.), *Proletarianization and Family History*, 1984, pp. 87–127.
2. For instance, W. Fischer for Germany: see the various papers in Part iv of his *Wirtschaft und Gesellschaft im Zeitalter der Industrialisierung*, Göttingen, 1972.
3. M. Reed, 'Nineteenth-Century Rural England: A Case for "Peasant Studies"?', *Journal of Peasant Studies*, xiv, 1986, pp. 78–99; see also M. Reed, 'The Peasantry of Nineteenth-Century England: A Neglected Class', *History Workshop*, xviii, 1984.
4. C. Smout and I. Levitt, *The State of the Scottish Working Class in 1843*, Edinburgh, 1979, p. 73. But this was only a small part of East Scotland, and was probably a rather exceptional situation.
5. Ibid., p. 74.
6. J. Davis: unpublished paper presented to Conference on 'Crime, Perquisites and the Customary Economy', University of Birmingham, 1986.

but simply taking up time. Detailed work would doubtless uncover examples everywhere of the sort that George Alter has illustrated in the industrialised parts of Belgium, such as Verviers, in 1853, where it was said that 'every worker had a pastime, producing a poor supplementary income, making bird cages, making furniture at home at night, becoming a baker, a shoemaker, etc.' Many of them ran a cabaret or a small pub of their own, which they failed to record in the census,[7] running them for a few hours in the evenings. It was often the better-paid workers who did this; the Verviers chief of police himself was reprimanded by the city council for conducting police business out of the cabaret that his wife ran in their home.[8] The income from this sort of activity may not have been very important in 1853 — regional comparisons can hardly be disavowed because of it — but it must have made a little difference then, and probably very much more difference in an earlier age, before the emergence of specialised factory labour. Nevertheless, it *is* true that it is possible to examine the regional variations of wages in England between 1850 and 1914 as Hunt has done, and to do so in a meaningful way — with barely a look at these things — deliberately ignoring the income from allotment, gleaning, poaching, perquisites, etc.[9] Hunt has, however, recently been pushing regional comparisons back into the later eighteenth century, on the assumption that his methodology for the later nineteenth century is fundamentally justified when used for the earlier period.[10]

This suggests a role for the history of 'the formation of the wage'. What does the history of the wage tell us of the nature of work, of proletarianisation, of the nature of mutual obligations, etc? Does the wage itself reflect these changes as Phelps Brown and Browne would have it — unchanging for long periods of time before the mid nineteenth century, then rising with the upswings and failing to fall much with the downswings?[11] Alternatively, can we see the money wage as relatively stable for most of the nineteenth century, with the greater part of any major increase in living standards coming through changes in agricultural prices, as had traditionally been the case?

This paper discusses some aspects of what might be called the social history of the wage. I would not pretend to have the answers for most of the

7. G. Alter, 'Work and Income in the Family Economy: Belgium, 1853 and 1891', *Journal of Interdisciplinary History*, xv, 1984–5, p. 269.
8. Ibid., p. 271.
9. E. H. Hunt, *Regional Variations in Wages in England, 1850–1914*, Oxford, 1973.
10. E. H. Hunt, 'Industrialization and Regional Inequality: Wages in Britain, 1760–1914', *Journal of Economic History*, xlvi, 1986, pp. 935–66.
11. E. Phelps Brown and M. Browne, *A Century of Pay*, London, 1968, pp. 74–5, 151–7.

questions, but it is important that the questions are put. In what follows the stress will be mostly upon the pre-industrial period. First, there is some discussion about the different ways in which economic historians on the one hand, and social historians on the other hand, have seen the wage. Secondly, there are some fairly specific questions about wages and wage rates, thirdly, some discussion of the extent of waged labour in the pre-industrial period and fourthly, a consideration of the nature of the subsistence wage.

The fundamental question to be asked of statistics of wages is 'what do they mean'? In pre-industrial societies, do they mean anything at all? Or more precisely, can they be used to indicate anything more than *very* general trends indeed?

It is easy to say that they mean very little. The money wage rates pursue their paths across the page; usually these paths are flat, they appear impervious to price movements in the short run and not particularly responsive in the medium run. 'In many places', said Adam Smith, 'the money price of labour remains uniformly the same sometimes for half a century together', whatever the price of provisions. 'These vary every-where from year to year, frequently from month to month.'[12] Admittedly it is possible to connect the rate of population growth with long-term shifts in real wages, as Wrigley and Schofield have done. When population showed a long-term tendency to rise faster than a certain rate, real wage rates tended to fall; when population grew slowly or not at all, real wages increased. But since Wrigley and Schofield use twenty-five-year moving averages for real wages and find the demographic indices lagging twenty to twenty-five years behind these, we are certainly looking at a very long-term trend indeed.[13] In fact, the producers of a wage rates index for building craftsmen in southern England that commences in the thirteenth century and continues into the twentieth century contrast 'the frequency of change after 1848 with the years before, when the inertia of wage rates was rarely overborne save in time of war.'[14] And of all the wars, it was only the Napoleonic War that had a particularly noticeable effect.

They continue that the reason for the change after the mid nineteenth century was straightforward enough: workers seized favourable opportunities during the upward phase of the trade cycle, while they could offer at least some resistance to wage cuts during the downswing. Each cycle

12. A. Smith, *Wealth of Nations*, ed. Cannan, bk 1, ch. 8, i. 83.
13. E. A. Wrigley and R. Schofield, *The Population History of England, 1541–1871*, 1981, p. 434.
14. Phelps Brown and Browne, *A Century of Pay*, p. 75.

therefore operated on balance to raise money wages.[15] But this was only from the mid nineteenth century.

Is this negative view of the importance of wages before the mid nineteenth century going too far? Most historians of eighteenth-century England would say that it is excessive. We have to be cautious of what we can learn from wage rates — we are always advised never to look at isolated years — but the trends over a number of years are meaningful. But *what* are they meaningful of?

There is a certain degree of tension — not contradiction, but tension — between the rather slight importance that social historians ascribe to the money wage in pre-industrial England, not to say Europe, and the much greater importance that economic historians give to it. To social historians, before the eighteenth or nineteenth century the money wage was not of supreme importance. Dependants, with only — or mainly — their labour power to sell are important, money-wage earners less so. Pre-industrial wage earners were marginal persons in society; wages were but one element in the family income, and perhaps not a very important element. In the towns there were more wage earners than in the country, but a great number of the lower orders of the towns were apprentices or servants — and therefore boarded and fed by their employer — or they were self-employed artisans, or they fell into that sink of underemployed casual labour now known as the service sector — part-time servants, porters, carriers, dockers, hawkers, peddlars, criminals, prostitutes, washerwomen, etc. An unspecified proportion of those who remained worked in gangs, hiring themselves out for a lump sum for each job, as did stevedores and dockers. Quite a number of people may have earned wages for a part of the year, very many had only their labour power to sell, but not all that many would have been full-time wage earners, whatever they called themselves in a tax assessment, where wage earners were the least-taxed group.

Against this, there is the employer's worry about his costs, the mercantilists' obsession with the wage level of their country compared with its neighbours, the moralists' insistence that higher wages invariably led to an increase in immoral leisure activities, and the economic historian's stress on the level of wages and the extent of home demand.

The two approaches are not, of course, necessarily contradictory. A certain part of the economy had its costs largely influenced by the prevailing level of wages. Nevertheless, it is the difference between these two points of view that makes the answers to certain questions rather delphic. For example, if we believe in the 'wage as wage' in the market economy of England during the eighteenth and earlier nineteenth centuries, then we

15. *Ibid.*, pp. 73, 75, 151–2.

have some things to explain. Not only do we have to explain the ratchet after 1815 (but that may not be too difficult as ratchets appear to be so universal), but also we have to explain why money wages in some towns sometimes failed to rise much during the 1790s, and hardly ever tried to keep up with prices.[16] In eighteenth-century London, for instance, we have to explain the odd timing of wage increases in the building trades in the midst of a building depression and the cheap bread and gin and the allegedly high leisure and alcohol preference of the earlier 1730s.[17] We cannot be sure that the value of the alcohol traditionally distributed free to building workers was valued with much care. For instance, in 1760, after 38 years of stability, the price of beer in London went up, but neither the amount of beer distributed nor the wages paid to building workers appears to have fallen in compensation.[18]

More generally, we have the problem that the macro-economic evidence — admittedly weak — points to virtual stagnation in average per capita wages between 1750 and 1790 (0.3 per cent growth per annum) while there is *some* evidence that the middling groups in society increased their proportion in society — which would suggest declining real wages in many parts of the country for much of the population.[19] This is difficult to reconcile with the increase in demand customarily associated with the onset of industrialisation. After all, one cannot have mass demand rising and real wages falling unless *either* wage rates are not very important *or* there is a shift towards the middle-income earners, whose profits derive (at least in part) from the return on capital. If this was the case, it needs to be proved.

On the other hand, we cannot discount the wage entirely: there are far too many examples of it functioning as such. Money wage rates tended to reduce themselves in accordance with distance from London, yet in the long run there was a narrowing differential between London and the industrialising regions.[20] Wages in building, which was not subject to international competition, were rather stable, but wages in other industries appear to

---

16. For instance, in Greenwich Hospital: see J. R. McCulloch, *A Dictionary of Commerce and Commercial Navigation*, 1840, pp. 952–3. This was used by R. S. Tucker, 'Real Wages of Artisans in London, 1729–1935', *Journal of the American Statistical Society*, xxxi, 1936, pp. 73–84, who wrote of real wages falling to 'Asiatic Standards'.
17. E. W. Gilboy, *Wages in Eighteenth-Century England*, Cambridge, Mass., 1934, p. 254.
18. P. Mathias, *The Brewing Industry in England*, Cambridge, 1959, pp. 111–13.
19. See the references in L. D. Schwarz, 'The Standard of Living in the Long Run: London 1700–1860', *Economic History Review*, 38, 1985, pp. 24–41.
20. E. W. Gilboy, 'Demand as a Factor in the Industrial Revolution', *The Industrial Revolution*, R. M. Hartwell (ed.); Gilboy, *Wages*; Hunt, 'Industrialization and Regional Inequality'.

have been less stable.[21] Furthermore, there existed in eighteenth-century London a common idea of what was a fair day's pay and a fair day's work. What is more, contemporaries, and not only economists, took the wage rate seriously as well:

> During the Ferment raised last Winter [1751], all over the Nation, by the Proposal of a general Naturalization, few of either Side of the Question descended to the Examination of Particulars. All our Arguments . . . turned to the Increase of Numbers, the lowering of Wages, and other Advantages to the Nation. . . . In this Case the lower Class was most immoderately divided, on the subject of lowering Wages. This was a Consequence on all hands presumed to follow. . . .[22]

A reconciliation of these two points of view on the importance of the wage depends, of course, on the nature and extent of non-monetary remuneration, a question that lies at the heart of the proto-industrialisation debate. It will be examined later, in the context of 'perquisites' in eighteenth-century England. However, the tension is reflected even in relatively limited analyses which assume that a wage existed and that some people were earning it.

(1) *Differentials.* Between artisan and labourer there appears to have been about a differential of about 50 to 60 per cent in eighteenth-century England;[23] however, the differential was nearer 100 per cent in Germany.[24] It is unclear what significance should be attached to such differences, or to the fact that a labourer in London was usually earning between 60 and 67 per cent of a bricklayer's or a carpenter's wage rate between 1700 and 1860, while in Göttingen he was earning half in the 1770s and two-thirds in the 1820s — not a decade when the supply of unskilled labour in Northern Germany is supposed to have been unduly restricted.[25]

(2) *Women* — often supposed to obtain about half the male wage rate. How

21. K. H. Burley, 'An Essex Clothier of the Eighteenth Century', *Economic History Review*, 2nd ser. xi, 1958–9, pp. 293–4. Between 1747 and 1759 this particular clothier gave extensive discounts from the standard rate for his spinners, but did not give discounts to his weavers.

22. Richard Parrot (?), *Reflections on Various Subjects Relating to Arts and Commerce . . .*, 1752, pp. 52–3.

23. Gilboy, *Wages*, pp. 254–87.

24. Admittedly this is based on a relatively unsystematic examination of the wage data in M. J. Elsas, *Umriss einer Geschichte der Preise und Löhne in Deutschland*, Leiden, 1936–49 (hereafter Elsas, *Umriss*) and H. J. Gerhard (ed.), *Löhne in vor- und frühindustriellen Deutschland*, Göttingen, 1984 (hereafter Gerhard, *Löhne*).

25. Gerhard, *Löhne*, pp. 238–63, 295–342.

far is this a reflection of the weak situation of women on the labour market?
How far is it a reflection of cultural norms? How do cultural norms,
restricted job opportunities and low wages for women interact?

(3) *Differentials between towns and regions.* Was there a 'market-clearing
wage', and if so, how large was the market that it cleared? We know there
was a great deal of migration in eighteenth- and nineteenth-century Europe
within countries.[26] How far can different wage rates be said to reflect labour
preferences, as Lindert and Williamson have sought to do in quantifying
urban disamenities during the industrial revolution?[27] Newspaper advertise-
ments for labour are an important and little-explored source.

(4) *Frequency of payment* — an issue that has recently been examined by
Sonenscher for the Parisian building trades in the 1780s. During their strike
of 1785, the latter emphasised that not only were they fighting against a
wage cut, but they also wanted more frequent pay days. They were
traditionally paid at the end of each month; the nature of their work
involved daily meals at the inn, which required credit, thereby tying them
to particular inns and giving the innkeeper an excuse to raise prices.
Weekly, instead of monthly, pay might increase the cost of credit for the
master, but would reduce it for themselves. Compared with their colleagues in Lyons, who claimed that they might have to wait for up to six
months before being paid, the Parisian building workers were fortunate.[28]
But six months was efficiency itself compared with the pay schedules of the
nearly bankrupt monarchies of the seventeenth century.

(5) How does 'wage drift' operate? What about overtime? Were these things
monetized, and to what extent was a favoured worker favoured with extra
credit or food or lodging?

(6) How far are historians justified in discussing a 'median' or 'modal' wage
rate? That there was a considerable spread between the earnings of the most
and the least skilled workers is not open to question; what is, however,
open to question is the assumption that there is a certain wage rate (for
instance, that of a bricklayer or a carpenter) which approximates to the
earnings of many workers of a comparable degree of skill, and that the
researcher's task is to produce the trend of this wage rate. This has been the
tradition in English research on wage history,[29] but it has not been the

26. See, for instance, O. H. Hufton, *The Poor of Eighteenth-Century France*, Oxford,
    1974, pp. 69–106.
27. J. G. Williamson, 'Urban Disamenities, Dark Satanic Mills and the British
    Standard of Living Debate,' *Journal of Economic History*, xii, 1981, pp. 75–83.
28. M. Sonenscher, 'Journeymen, the Courts and the French Trades, 1781–1791',
    Past and Present, 114, Feb. 1987.

custom of the historians of German and Belgian wage rates, who are prepared to publish the full range of wages — which can be quite wide — in a town. Three fairly recent English Ph. D. theses likewise draw attention to the very wide range of wage rates within relatively small areas.[30]

(7) Are we even correct in our perception of the raw data itself? How flat is the trajectory followed by money wage rates? Most of the available data is institutional, and institutions may well have been much less flexible in adapting their pay, pleading security of employment, while permitting a wage drift that would not show in the data. Are we accurate in our view of the ratchet? Money wages did fall from time to time; however, when prices fell extensively — like in England after 1815 — there were continual complaints of the 'hollowing out' of the official wage rate: it remained on the books — that is to say, it remained the officially recommended wage — but in fact it was paid to fewer and fewer workmen, while deductions were greater. The London bricklayers complained a great deal about this; the London tailors were pushed increasingly onto piecework. More women were employed where possible — and of course women never earned the 'full' wage.[31]

(8) To what extent was it that those workers who had a certain amount of control — or at least influence — over the labour market were paid by time?

The more interesting general questions resolve themselves into two related groups. First is the connection between the creation of a labour force suitable for an industrial or industrialising society (whatever that might be) and the development of remuneration by a money wage and only a money wage. Second is the question of the nature of subsistence wages, wages that appear to be below subsistence, the general problem of the levels of wages attained in a society with unlimited (or almost unlimited) supplies of labour, and the question of 'exchange entitlement'.

29. A tradition begun by A. L. Bowley, *Wages in the United Kingdom During the Nineteenth Century*, London, 1900. For Germany, see Elsas, *Umriss* and Gerhard, *Löhne*; for Belgium C. Verlinden and others (eds), *Documents pour l'histoire des prix et des salaires en Flandre et en Brabant* (hereafter Verlinden, *Documents*) esp. vol. ii, Brussels, 1965.
30. T. L. Richardson, 'The Standard of Living Controversy, 1790–1840, with Special Reference to Agricultural Labourers in Seven English Counties', University of Hull Ph. D. thesis, 1977; B. Eccleston, 'A Survey of Wage Rates in Five Midland Counties, 1750–1834', Leicester Univ. Ph. D. thesis, 1976; F. W. Botham, 'Working-class Living Standards in North Staffordshire, 1750–1914', London University Ph. D. thesis, 1982.
31. To be discussed in my forthcoming book, *London in the Age of Industrialisation*.

On the first question, the connection between the development of a labour force, the extent of pre-industrial waged labour, and the growth of the money wage, we are rather ignorant. From a certain conceptual point of view, what matters is that people have only their labour power to sell, and the process of how they come to arrive in such a condition, the form for which they sell their labour power, is a secondary consideration. Nevertheless, the change to industrial capitalism did progress alongside a change towards more widespread remuneration in cash. The market economy depended to a large extent on payment in cash (or equivalent tokens, bonds, etc.); when considering 'the growth of the wage' we are considering a form of remuneration that is not so typical of earlier ages and different types of society.

The common view, stated earlier, would be that in an earlier age, money wages would not have been centrally important. Most of the workforce was rural. Money wages were not likely to have been of central importance in a world where the entire household made a crucial contribution to survival, and where 'an economy of makeshifts'[32] operated, pulling revenues from wherever they could be found — an allotment, gleaning, 'traditional' entitlements, domestic industry, day labour, begging, charity, etc. Gradually this changed, and we find ourselves with a 'real waged labour force', whose money wages are their major sources of income which can be compared across the country and internationally.

In England, the transition would *appear* to be seen clearly in the different approaches of Adam Smith and David Ricardo to the issue. Smith wrote quite clearly about the economics of domestic manufacture, 'When a person derives his subsistence from one employment, which does not occupy the greater part of his time; in the intervals of his leisure he is often willing to work at another for less wages than would otherwise suit the nature of the employment.'[33]

However, he regarded this as a temporary phenomenon — it is significant that the example he gave was of Highland crofters: 'In opulent countries the market is generally so extensive, that any one trade is sufficient to employ the whole labour and stock of those who occupy it. Instances of people's living by one employment, and at the same time, deriving some little advantage from another, occur chiefly in poor countries'.[34] By the time that Ricardo was writing his *Principles* opulence had spread so widely that he did not consider it necessary to stress this point.[35]

Needless to say, the transition was more complex than this, and the

32. The phrase is that of Hufton, *Poor of Eighteenth-century France*, chs. 3 and 4.
33. A. Smith, *Wealth of Nations*, ed. Cannan, i. 130.
34. *Ibid.*, i. 130.
35. Chapter 5 of his *Principles*.

search for the connection between the growth of the waged labour force and the disappearance of the handicrafts will be a familiar labour to historians. In England the disappearance of the handicrafts was a slower process than was once thought, while many new crafts were created. Those acquainted with the difficulties of interpreting the statistics of the Prussian trades and the debate on the survival of the *Mittelstand* in twentieth-century Germany will know that if industrialisation brings about the destruction of the handicrafts it does so in a manner that is often slow and always complex. The boundary does not move inexorably in the same direction all the time. Certain trades saw a remarkable growth of waged labour while others did not — and some may have been so skilled as to have been virtually independent inside the factory. It is notoriously difficult to know which trades to examine, when to examine them and — more fundamentally — what the concept of an 'independent master' meant at different times.[36]

As important, for the present discussion, is that we do not know how many 'pure' wage-earners there were in pre-industrial Europe and how important they were. The normal response of historians would be to suggest that any significantly large and concentrated groups would have been urban, and that these groups were not very large. Many wage earners in continental Europe were only earning wages for a season, coming into town from their fields to help with building work. Others, especially young women, came into town to go into service. Most of the male immigrants would have joined the chronically underemployed and seasonal service sector, where most of them would have been engaged in various forms of transport, or carrying, to be paid at piece rates. Not very many would have depended on a regular money wage for their support all the year round. Even fewer women would have done so. However, there was still a wage-earning group in the towns, a group that was employed for daily wages or — perhaps more commonly — had their piece rates fixed to a notion of a comparable daily wage. Woodward has argued that in early seventeenth-century England wage-earners were very much at the bottom of the urban social pyramid and very much a minority within the plebeian population.[37] Others would reduce this group even more, arguing that even after we have deducted servants, apprentices, professional people, shop-keepers and full-time criminals from the workforce we are left with a great deal of subcontracting — thus a hierarchy of employers and a great deal of petty trading by hawkers, pedlars, etc. Nicholas Barbon, the master builder of later seventeenth-century London, subcontracted to smaller builders, and

36. For a large literature on this, see for instance, Fischer (note 2 above).
37. D. Woodward, 'Wage Rates and Living Standards in Pre-Industrial England', *Past and Present*, 91, 1981, pp. 28–45.

so forth.[38] Subcontracting worked down the social scale — the artisan brought along his apprentice, perhaps also his wife and children, and is supposed to have tendered his services as an independent man in the labour market. Furthermore, many single people lived in their employer's house, women as domestic servants, men as servants or apprentices or perhaps sometimes even as journeymen, possibly only setting up independent households when they married and hoped to have enough skills to work on their own, or in a gang. In addition, the labour market was even more baroque than it is now. It was the expansion of demand that meant that there was enough work for a class of 'labourers'.

The alternative view is that in seventeenth-century England *'life-long wage labourers may well have been a majority of the population'*.[39] This statement may well be rather misleading, as it appears to include all dependants — apprentices, servants, etc. — under the heading of 'wage labourers'. But it would surely not be very difficult to find other societies in seventeenth-century western and central Europe where a very large proportion of the population was in some form of economic dependance, with only its labour power to sell, so the figures produced are not in themselves proof that seventeenth-century England had an exceptionally high proportion of its population engaged in *wage* labour. Everitt, more cautiously, suggested that perhaps a third of the population lived from wages[40] — but the farm workmen studied by Everitt were actually smallholders who occasionally worked for wages — a situation not so different from that in France. More significant is Lindert and Williamson's estimates of eighteenth-century population structure which, crude though they are, nevertheless suggest that about half the adult males in England and Wales were in the pool from which full-time wage labour *could* be drawn — the building trades, mining, skilled and menial services (which excluded the professions), 'labourers' and 'manufacturers' (weavers, spinners, other textile trades, shoemakers, blacksmiths and other manufacturers).[41] This figure can be reduced by any proportion that one likes in order to allow for employers, not to mention errors, but it remains indicative of a large dependant sector, potentially wage-earners. Whether they earned a regular money wage is another matter: London at

38. J. Summerson, *Georgian London*, London, 1962, p. 45.
39. Christoper Hill, 'Pottage for Freeborn Englishmen: Attitudes to Wage Labour in the 16th and 17th Centuries', in C. H. Feinstein (ed.), *Socialism, Capitalism and Economic Growth: Essays Presented to Maurice Dobb*, Cambridge, 1967, p. 347; see also C. B. Macpherson, *The Political Theory of Possessive Individualism*, Oxford, 1962, appendix.
40. A. Everitt, 'Farm Labourers', in *The Agrarian History of England and Wales*, iv, ed. J. Thirsk, Cambridge, 1967, pp. 396–400.
41. P. H. Lindert, 'English Occupations, 1670–1811', *Journal of Economic History*, xi, 1980, pp. 683–712.

the end of the eighteenth century had relatively few masters and a large dependant population. For some of the latter — such as young women — working for a money wage was very rarely a viable way of life: domestic service, living in the employer's house, with some additional money at regular intervals, was far more likely. Young males, with some support, would have an apprenticeship, others might become manservants. Living on one's own, away from one's employer and dependent on a money wage, was for adolescent males a state of misfortune; for adolescent females it was usually a calamity; for adult males, out of their apprenticeship, it was — hopefully — a stage through which they passed en route to becoming a master, although few might arrive at their destination. And as a result of these divergent processes — demonstrated by young men who could not serve an apprenticeship, journeymen who could not become masters, women who could not work in somebody else's household, and a multitude of other factors — there were, it would seem, more money wage-earners by the later eighteenth century than there had been two centuries earlier.

This leads to another set of questions, concerning the nature of the wage, the role of non-monetary remuneration and the problems of a subsistence wage.

The subsistence wage is perhaps not a topic that has been extensively researched for this period. As was wisely pointed out at the beginning of the nineteenth century, 'God has decreed that the men who carry on the most useful crafts should be born in abundant numbers'.[42] There are quite prolonged periods of time in European history — such as the 1590s — when it is impossible to see how most of these abundant numbers earned a living wage. Historians sometimes suggest that it was possibly quite a good idea to become a beggar at this point of time — it required little capital and the pay was likely to be better.[43]

Economists' traditional answer has been that a wage at or above subsistence level will not necessarily be paid when there is surplus labour on the family farm. Adam Smith has already been quoted to that effect. The example he gave was of Scottish crofters: 'When such occupiers were more numerous than they are at present, they are said to have been willing to give their spare time for a very small recompence to any body, and to have wrought for less wages than other labourers'.[44]

42. F. Galliani, 1803, quoted by P. Kriedte, H. Medick, J. Schlumbohm, *Industrialisation before Industrialisation*, Cambridge, 1981, p. 81.
43. L. A. Clarkson, Introduction to K. D. Brown, *The English Labour Movement, 1700–1951*, Dublin, 1982.
44. A. Smith, *Wealth of Nations*, ed. Cannan, i. 130.

Historians have not found it difficult to agree — facing seasonal unemployment one might well work for a wage that was below subsistence. Such a wage was one source of income for the family, and better than nothing. Nevertheless, sometimes people did depend on their wages, and in this case — when there was no alternative source of income — the classical economists took it for granted that a psychological minimum subsistence wage would be paid.[45] Common sense alone, with no mathematics, would suggest some reasons why wages would be above subsistence. Labour would have no reason to work efficiently for a wage that was below subsistence. Employers knew very well that they would have difficulty in attracting such a labour force and, once having attracted it, they would have difficulty in disciplining and motivating it. Even their personal safety might be jeopardised. Essentially, issues of control are involved. It is easier to control and motivate a labour force that is not starving to death and needing to be replaced regularly. Not all the governments of eighteenth-century Europe, with their workhouses and prisons, could change that, and in any case the attempts by authorities to hold down the level of wages was only likely to be successful if the labour force's leisure preference was extremely inelastic — something which, despite the outcry of moralists was usually not the case.[46] This was well enough known in eighteenth-century England, where there was a continual concern with the best methods of increasing output per man[47] and a growing doubt whether the pressures of want alone were enough to attract the quality of labour desired. All this was without the benefit of Leibenstein's demonstration of 1957 that in a world where landowners employed landless labour, and higher wages resulted in more labour per man, it would pay landowners to set a higher wage than the market-clearing wage, leaving some unemployment.[48]

Furthermore, there is relatively little demand for completely unskilled labour. Some degree of skill is usually involved, even in carrying or being a bricklayer's labourer, and such skill would command a premium. Nor would an employer wish labour to be continually weak through undernourishment.

Nevertheless, study after study points out that it was impractical to expect the poor to subsist as wage-earners. If they were employed for some

45. D. P. O'Brien, *The Classical Economists*, Oxford, 1975, pp. 116–17.
46. A. W. Coats, 'Changing Attitudes to Labour in the Mid-Eighteenth Century', *Economic History Review*, xi, 1958; P. Mathias, 'Leisure and Wages in Theory and Practice', in P. Mathias, *The Transformation of England*, London, 1979, pp. 148–67.
47. See the references in note 46 above — for instance Defoe or Tucker.
48. H. Leibenstein, 'The Theory of Underemployment in Backward Economies', *Journal of Political Economy*, lxv, 1957, pp. 91–103.

300 days in the year — or even more — they might just manage, but that was a virtual impossibility. Supporting their family was of course even more difficult. Gregory King — notoriously — did not know how half the kingdom survived;[49] Continental observers had reason to be even more baffled. Historians reconcile things by suggesting that if the wage was not earned by the individual, it would somehow be earned by his family and that the lowest-paid members of the adult workforce would have had a farm or a husband to support them. In any case, the poor were under-nourished and did not grow very tall.[50] However, small or not, the poor must have had something to keep them going in the 1590s, and one is also entitled to a certain amount of scepticism of the extent in the fall of real wages that is reported from all over Europe in the decades after 1750, unless it can be shown that hours of work increased, or alternative occupations — such as rural industry — came into existence. Self-exploitation may have increased, or the organisation of work may have improved, with more output for not much more physical effort.

This produces some temptation for the historian to make use of W. A. Lewis's interpretation of the classical economists, put forward some thirty years ago, where the fact that there is not enough capital to provide employment for everyone is a vital distinction between the classical model and neo-classical analysis. There has to be a noncapitalist sector, in which people earn or consume more than their marginal product. Income is shared out, rather than distributed according to any contribution to output. The self-employed family, whether peasant or urban, is the archetype. In a very poor economy there must be a large part of the economy operating through such income-sharing arrangements.[51]

The weakness of the argument is of course the failure to draw sufficiently close links between the different sections of the economy, to assume that the 'backward' parts of the economy operate in isolation, having little function other than providing an endless supply of labour to the 'advanced' sector. So Amartya Sen, in doubting that the marginal return on labour on the family farm is ever zero, and therefore that the existence of surplus labour is not a sufficient condition for unlimited supplies of labour — i. e. a constant real wage — has argued that 'the simultaneous existence of surplus labour and positive wages is not a genuine problem at all, except in the special

49. See his estimate for 1688, reprinted in various places, e. g. P. Mathias, *The First Industrial Nation*, London, 1969, p. 24.
50. R. Floud, 'Poverty and Physical Stature', *Social Science History*, vi, 1982, pp. 422–52; 'Wirtschaftliche und soziale Einflüsse auf die Körpergrösse von Europäern seit 1750', *Jahrbuch für Wirtschaftsgeschichte*, 1985, ii, pp. 93ff.
51. W. A. Lewis, 'Economic Development with Unlimited Supplies of Labour', *The Manchester School*, 1954.

model of surplus labour where zero marginal disutility of effort is assumed'.[52] If Sen is right then his argument can be applied to considering those reforms of charity and of poor relief that are especially noted by their hostility to beggars and by the obligation of work — all because, according to some historians and not a few contemporaries, the price-wage relationship was so bad that begging was preferable to working for a wage.[53] The argument would presumably be applicable only if there were such zero disutility in the surrounding agriculture: if correct it would modify some cherished notions. The need would be to prove that this agriculture did not consist largely of family farms, and that there was a large rural proletariat.

Another of Sen's concepts — that of 'exchange entitlement' — may be more useful, at least in western and central Europe. The question is how one obtains consumer goods, whether by payment in kind, by perquisites, or by advances of money, food, etc. Exactly how and when and why were non-monetary rewards monetised? How much of the apparent urban-rural wage gap is explained by this? How much of the presumed narrowing differential in the wages of different regions is caused by this monetisation? Perhaps we are too ready to make a distinction between, on the one hand, payment (partly) in kind, with the perquisites and truck that was so typical of the 'ancien régime économique' and, on the other hand, the 'modern' monetary wage.

Entitlement came in many forms. Basically there were two: exchange entitlement and political entitlement. A third supreme entitlement was discovered during the sixteenth century and was called the Kingdom of Heaven, but that is not our area of concern here. On earth, suitable labour service — known as apprenticeship — was supposed to entitle a man to full civic rights as a member of a guild — a right that meant rather little in England in the eighteenth century though it meant more in France and more still in certain German cities. In England, the entitlements of a steady worker with a reputation for industriousness were more prosaic. If the eighteenth-century plebs were not to be assured daily that their labour was a proof that the Kingdom of Heaven was theirs, they could at least be reasonably sure that it improved their chances of obtaining poor relief and made it less likely that they would end up in the workhouse. And, if they came before the courts convicted on one of the myriad of capital statutes that made the English criminal code so unique, it might even lead the judge to excuse the death penalty.[54] After 1795, agricultural labourers living in the

52. A. Sen. 'Peasants and Dualism With or Without Surplus Labour', *Journal of Political Economy*, 74, 1966, pp. 425–50.
53. See note 43.
54. D. Hey, 'Property, Authority and the Criminal Law', in E. P. Thompson, D. Hay, P. Linebaugh (eds), *Albion's Fatal Tree*, London, 1975.

south of England often had to work in order to obtain poor relief.

For the employer, the entitlements of wages were rather harder to bear. They frequently involved beer, and could involve much more. Entitlement went across the social scale. The ancien régimes *were* regimes of entitlement. Entitlement pervaded everything. Office holders, notoriously, had the right to conduct certain exploitations that later ages would view with horror. The higher government posts were 'natural' routes for self-enrichment. We know less about the lower office-holders in England, but it is hard to believe that the political appointment carefully made by the government to run a naval dockyard and ensure that its dependants voted correctly in elections did not stretch his entitlements. The limits to how far he could stretch them were of course important and determined by a multitude of diverse factors, but the view of the office as providing an entitlement for the amassing of wealth and support for dependants was universal.

A large and immediate entitlement for a man with a job was credit. This might be from his employer, as Sonenscher has shown for eighteenth-century Paris,[55] or it might be from a retailer or a publican. The immediate bearers of the cost of this entitlement were of course the poor, who had to pay the higher prices always demanded by chandlers. In the longer term, the costs were presumably born by the wholesalers unable to retrieve their credit from the bankrupt chandlers.

What should not be done is to view these entitlements as 'moral'. The term 'moral economy' is dangerous. The exchange entitlements may not have been made in cash, but that is not to say that they were not influenced — perhaps dominated — by movements in the monetary economy. An employer paid beer, a shopkeeper gave credit. Apprentices provided a form of labour that was in theory supposed to be outside the market system and was certainly paid as though it was; apprentices might be 'given' to a favoured workman as of right and were always liable to be used as cheap labour. They were increasingly boarded out — as were farm servants — a tendency that accelerated rapidly during periods of inflation, such as the Revolutionary and Napoleonic Wars.[56]

One sees the 'wage as entitlement' rather obviously when the money wage fails to increase at the same rate as prices during the 1790s. Whether

55. M. Sonenscher, 'Work and Wages in Paris in the Eighteenth Century', in P. Hudson, M. Berg, M. Sonenscher, *Manufacture in Town and Country before the Factory*, Cambridge, 1983, pp. 147–72.
56. K. D. M. Snell, *Annals of the Labouring Poor: Social Change and Agrarian England*, Cambridge, 1985, pp. 67–103.

the towns examined are in England, Belgium[57] or Germany[58] one finds that
in virtually every town there were workers whose money wage rates did
not increase during the 1790s. There were also large groups of workers
whose money wages did increase; however, the increase might not appear
until two years after prices had increased. In Göttingen and Augsburg the
increase was in 1797, two years after the famine year of 1795 — and not all
workers obtained wage increases.[59] Unskilled labourers at the Göttingen
corn exchange did not see their wage increase throughout the entire period;
neither did roofmakers, nor unskilled building labour. In England, wage
rates in London increased substantially from 1795, but wage rates at
Greenwich Hospital, near London, did not increase.[60] The pay of those
employed there must have been made up in some way, a way presumably
cheaper to their employers than higher money wage rates. Possibly it was in
a manner similar to the cooks in one of the hospitals in Frankfurt-am-Main
whose wages were unchanged between 1773 and 1820 — but who, it
emerges, had free board and lodging in the hospital, and so in fact probably
had improving living standards. In Ansbach, apprentices did not see significant changes in their wage rates between 1770 and 1800,[61] but apprentices
didn't receive a proper wage anyway, so it didn't matter that it wasn't raised
during the 1790s. Masters were liable to regard the wage as only one —
possibly not very large — element in the total remuneration that was forced
on them. Other things — credit, beer, food and fuel, for example — cost
money, but it might be cheaper for an employer to acquire those things than
to have to go into the cash economy. Naturally all those items were in
intimate dependence on the cash economy, but beer and food, for instance,
might be obtained more cheaply by an employer than by the men whom he
employed. What was emphatically not involved was 'money illusion'.

   Furthermore, when one finds that some independent artisans in Germany
(Meister) did not see much increase in their daily wage during the 1790s,[62]
then one must remember that they could make up for this in other ways,
especially if they held stocks of material during periods of rising prices.
When workers in large institutions were not being paid more, one can
assume that the failure to give them wage increases was being made up
elsewhere. Those who ran the corn exchange in Göttingen knew better than
anyone else that a labourer could not survive by the later 1790s on the wages

57. Verlinden, *Documents* ii. 450–1.
58. Elsas, *Umriss* i. 733–6 (Augsburg), ii. 589–93, 598–600 (Leipzig), 606–14
    (Speyer); Gerhard, *Löhne*, passim.
59. Gerhard, *Löhne*, pp. 33, 76 for Ansbach; Elsas, *Umriss* i. 733–6 for Augsburg.
60. See note 16.
61. Gerhard, *Löhne*, pp. 43–6.
62. Ibid., pp. 191–3. For instance, Göttingen bricklayers.

that he had obtained in 1780, but they did not increase it.[63] Yet they could hardly have been worrying about a ratchet effect, since there should, in theory, have been no problems in cutting their wages later. The operation of the ratchet can be taken too much for granted. In England, plenty of evidence exists that money wage rates did not fall in accordance with prices after 1815, but what does appear to have happened quite often was the 'undermining' of the wage. The wage that was publicly quoted was not necessarily paid to a majority of workers. It is unlikely that the process was sufficiently widespread to undermine gains in real wages achieved by the price fall of the post-war years, but it is certainly a factor of which historians should be aware, and it may be as difficult to observe in action as the hidden means by which labour received more entitlements during the preceding years of inflation.[64]

'Exchange entitlements' have an important part to play in the analysis of pay. Obviously one would not wish to argue that they alone account for the difference between 'wage rates' and 'earnings'. Many factors contributed to this difference, among which unemployment and underemployment were particularly important, and they are well known to all students of living standards. But an analysis of wages in terms of exchange entitlements shifts the perspective from a solitary preoccupation with the money wage towards the total package of rewards that were obtained by the sale of labour. The progress from customary entitlement to 'perquisites' to 'crime' — and the creation of a money wage is a crucial experience of the labour force during industrialisation.

---

63. Ibid., pp. 357–60.
64. See Schwarz, 'Standard of Living in the Long Run'.

P. VAN DEN EECKHOUT

2.1 Wage Formation: Some More Problems

L. Schwarz's paper makes a provocative inventory of the problems inherent in the use, significance and evolution of wages in the pre-industrial period. It raises a lot of questions and gives a critical survey of the answers that these have received. Reading his text, students of wages, prices and purchasing power in the pre-industrial period will get a pretty good idea of the methodological problems encountered in this kind of research.

Given the character of the article, it is remarkable that the author pays little or no attention to the definition and delimitation of his subject matter, i.e. wages. More conceptual clearness would have increased the relevance of this critical inventory. An article bearing the title 'The Formation of the Wage: Some Problems' cannot ignore the question of the necessary conditions that determine the existence of a wage and a wage-dependent population. Stressing the many forms of remuneration and the complexity of the pre-industrial labour market does not preclude one from trying to define what is wage labour and what is not. Although the author hardly raises this question explicitly, he does answer it implicitly. This implicit answer to an unformulated question is, however, ambiguous; although the author points to the many complex forms of wage in the pre-industrial period, he also systematically associates the concept of 'wage' with that of 'money wage'. He speaks of a 'real-waged labour force' when talking about that part of the population 'whose money wages are their major sources of income'. In other words, it is implicitly assumed that the form taken by the remuneration of the selling of labour power is decisive in defining waged labour. Those who sell their labour power without being wholly or largely paid in money would not then be part of the wage-dependent population. The ambiguity arises from the fact that elsewhere the author remarks that economic dependence is crucial and that the remunerative form is of secondary importance. Three pages further on, economic dependence seems to have lost its decisive importance again, since here the author argues against historians who define wage dependants as those who have only their labour power to sell. He minimalises the number of wage-earners in seventeenth-century England with the argument that the use of 'broad' criteria (including servants and apprentices who received board and lodging from their employers in the category of wage-earners) would reveal a large wage-dependent population in the rest of Europe too. Apart from the fact that this is a questionable argument with which to exclude categories like servants and apprentices from the group of wage-earners, it reveals an approach which is at least contradictory. The same ambiguity is reflected in the author's statement that 'dependants, with only — or mainly — their labour power to sell are important, money-wage earners less so'. It is unclear whether he considers these dependants to be wage-earners even though they did not earn money-wages. A few lines further he states 'in the towns there were more wage-earners than in the country, but a great number of the lower orders of the towns were apprentices or servants'. This remark gives the impression that the author does not include these dependent categories in the wage-earning population. Other examples could be added. It would appear that the author is unable to decide which criteria are decisive in defining what wages and wage-earners are.

Despite the author's ambiguity in defining the concept of wage-labour, it is clear that by 'wage-labourers' he implies those who sell their labour power in exchange for money-wages. I cannot agree with that. For what is a wage? A wage allows the wage-labourer to purchase the necessary means of subsistence in order to reproduce his labour power. Money is the silver or gold or copper or paper form of the necessary means of subsistence, into which it is constantly transformed. Money functions as a means of circulation, as a transient form of exchange-value.[1] Whether one is paid in exchange value, i.e. in money that will be converted into use-values, or directly in use-values, changes nothing in the fundamental nature of the transaction. It does not in any way alter the fact that the receiving party has sold labour power in exchange and has therefore performed wage-labour.

I do not, however, wish to minimalise the importance of the transition to a money economy. The monetary wage is in fact far more than a simple substitute for the non-monetary wage, since it has the added advantage to the employer of wiping out every trace of the division of the working day into necessary labour and surplus labour, into paid labour and unpaid labour. The money-wage conceals the uncompensated labour of the wage-labourer.[2] In this way, the monetary form of the wage has played a crucial role in the development of capitalism.

Apart from his ambiguous use of the concept of what constitutes a wage,

1. K. Marx, *Capital*, vol. 1, introduced by E. Mandel, Harmondsworth, 1976, p. 1033.
2. Ibid., p. 680. P. Linebaugh, 'Labour History without the Labour Process: A Note on John Gast and His Times', *Social History*, 1982, p. 325.

it is also unclear whether the author is inclined to exclude from the category of wage-earners those members of the population who are wage-dependent for only part of their lives or part of the year. That the population of pre-industrial societies was obliged to exploit alternating income sources in order to survive is of course not a justification for excluding them from the wage-dependent population altogether. I admit that the available primary sources do not facilitate the weighing of the relative importance of the different income sources involved, but the omission of these 'problem' categories in order to quantify a hypothetical group of 'pure' wage earners is not a solution either. A large part, for instance, of the population of seventeenth- and eighteenth-century England probably belonged to these 'problem' categories, since economies based on self-reliance and on wage-dependence existed side-by-side and were interrelated.[3] Craftsmen, for example, often supplemented their craft earnings by farming both for subsistence and for the market while cottagers, country labourers and smallholders obtained wages on nearby farms, were employed in cottage industries and produced some of their own provisions from their use of common land or their own cottage gardens. The fact that people tried to obtain viable sustenance from combining a wide range of activities places severe limits on the measurability of pre-industrial social reality.

The fact that the author is inclined to accept as wage-labour that part of the population earning only or mostly money-wages does not mean that he is blind to the concept that even for these 'pure' wage-earners the money-wage had only a limited importance. The author remarks that the money-wage seems impervious to price movements in the short run and not particularly responsive in the medium run. The inertia of nominal wages arouses his suspicion and he is sceptical of the pronounced fall in real wages in certain periods. For instance, at the end of the sixteenth and eighteenth centuries, he considers non-monetary remunerations (such as perquisites and entitlements) to be important, but often unknown variables that would probably reveal an entirely different picture of the evolution of the purchasing power. Data on non-monetary remuneration might well indeed result in substantial corrections to the level evolution of nominal wages. It surprises me, however, that the author hardly mentions another, perhaps more important, variable, about which in many cases equally little is known, namely the frequency of work and unemployment. I shall illustrate this with some Belgian and Dutch evidence.

At a conference on the frequency of employment E. Scholliers stressed that, for the pre-industrial period, it is very difficult to collect exact and

---

3. R. W. Malcolmson, *Life and Labour in England 1700–1780*, London, 1981, pp. 11–58, 136–46.

reliable data on work frequency, length of the working day and the number of working days in a year.[4] In fixing the number of working days in a year, most authors have to rely on estimations. The number of holidays is not always known, and it is sometimes unclear whether the prescribed (religious) holidays were consistently respected. Furthermore, there were regional differences in this respect which we are not always able to quantify. Depending on the author or the period considered, people might have worked from 245 to 275, sometimes even 290 to 305 or 310 days.[5] The conditional is doubly important since these estimations take no account of fluctuations in the business cycle or seasonal unemployment. We may not forget that these theoretical estimations can be used properly only if we have information on time-based wages and that such wages were exceptional in the pre-industrial period, when piecework was the rule.[6] Task orientation was prevalent as long as there was no intricate subdivision of the labour process. Time-wages were common only in the building trade, agricultural labour and domestic service.

If opinions diverge on the number of working days in a year, it is even more difficult to take the influence of the business cycle into account. When it is taken into account, however, the evolution of wages might appear less level than at first thought. Some developments in real wages might well prove to be less improbable.

Faced with the drop in real wages around 1590, the author says that 'the

4. E. Scholliers, 'Werktijden en arbeidsomstandigheden in de pre-industriële periode', *Durée du travail et diminution du temps de travail*, Brussels, 1983, p. 11. See also the chapter 'Uncertainty, Irregularity, Hours and Wages' in J. Rule, *The Experience of Labour in Eighteenth-century Industry*, London, 1981, pp. 49–73 and the chapter 'The Wage and its Form' in J. Rule, *The Labouring Classes in Early Industrial England, 1750–1850*, London, 1986, pp. 107–29.

5. E. Scholliers, *Loonarbeid en honger. De levensstandaard in de XVe en XVIe eeuwen te Antwerpen*, Antwerp, 1960, pp. 84–7. L. Noordegraaf, *Daglonen in Alkmaar 1500–1850*, n.p., 1980, pp. 33–40. L. Noordegraaf, *Daglonen in Holland 1450–1600*, Amsterdam, 1984, pp. 20–2. L. Noordegraaf, *Hollands welvaren? Levensstandaard in Holland 1450–1650*, Bergen, 1985, pp. 56–61. See also the discussion concerning Noordegraaf's estimates with Jan De Vries, Herman Van der Wee and Noordegraaf himself in *Bijdragen en mededelingen betreffende de geschiedenis der Nederlanden*, 1987, p. 232, 254. D. Morsa, 'Salaire et salariat dans les économies préindustrielles (XVIe–XVIIIe siècle): quelques considérations critiques', *Revue belge de philologie et d'histoire*, 1987, p. 760.

6. E. Scholliers, 'Remuneratiemodaliteiten bij loontrekkenden', *Archives et bibliothèques de Belgique*, 1973, pp. 41–2. D. Morsa, 'Salaire et salariat', p. 757. E. P. Thompson, 'Time, Work discipline and Industrial Capitalism', *Past and Present*, Dec. 1967, pp. 60–1, 70.

poor must have had something to keep them going'. Indeed, but the situation was perhaps less disastrous then the comparison of nominal wages and prices leads us to believe. L. Noordegraaf, who studied the evolution of purchasing power in Holland, noticed that at the end of the 1580s and the beginning of the 1590s, purchasing power took some heavy knocks. When, however, he took the evolution of the business cycle into account, he noticed that unemployment had fallen rapidly and that, as a result, the situation was perhaps less dramatic than we might have thought.[7] E. Scholliers, in turn, noticed that in a period of economic boom and expansion — for instance in the first half of the sixteenth century, when there was a high frequency of work combined with relatively low wages — the evolution of purchasing power showed fewer extremes than might be expected from a simple comparison of wages and prices.[8] The converse has also been established. Taking the evolution of unemployment into account gives us a far less favourable picture of purchasing power in Antwerp in the second half of the sixteenth century.[9] Noordegraaf stresses that a favourable economic situation did not necessarily lead to higher nominal wages but to an increase of the number of days worked instead. An economic slump did not necessarily result in wage reductions but in a decrease in the number of days worked. These examples give some idea of the realities hidden behind the level evolution of nominal wages.[10]

An increase in the number of working days is of course not necessarily a sign of prosperity. It is also possible for these to increase as a result of a decline in real wages. E. Scholliers noticed that working time increased in the course of the Ancien Régime and more particularly in the eighteenth century, when the working day was lengthened.[11] Noordegraaf established that carpenters' apprentices worked 230 to 250 days a year before 1750 and 275 to 300 days a year in the second half of the eighteenth century. In the same period he noticed a fall in real wages.[12] Possibly, people were trying to cope with a deteriorating living standard by increasing their work effort. The fall in real wages after 1750 was perhaps less extensive than the evolution of nominal wages and prices might lead us to suppose. These few examples show that entitlements and perquisites are certainly not the only

7. L. Noordegraaf, *Hollands welvaren?*, pp. 143, 175.
8. E. Scholliers, 'Werktijden en arbeidsomstandigheden', p. 11.
9. H. Van der Wee, *The Growth of the Antwerp Market and the European Economy (Fourteenth–Sixteenth Centuries)*, vol. I, The Hague, 1963, pp. 540–4. L. Noordegraaf, *Hollands welvaren?*, p. 155.
10. Ibid., pp. 90–1. Jan De Vries does not agree with Noordegraaf; see the discussion already mentioned, pp. 233–6.
11. E. Scholliers, 'Werktijden en arbeidsomstandigheden', pp. 12–14.
12. L. Noordegraaf, *Daglonen in Alkmaar*, pp. 35–6.

variables that have to be taken into account when discussing the problems of the evolution of nominal and real wages.

The last problem I would like to take up here is that of the subsistence wage. The author states that 'labour would have no reason to work for a wage that was below subsistence'. As not everybody understands the concept of 'subsistence wage' in the same way, I suppose he is referring to the idea that a wage must enable the working class to reproduce its labour power and, presumably, at the same time to the fact that this reproduction encompasses both the physiological and the historical-moral needs of the working class.[13] It goes without saying that these vary in both time and space.

Making general statements such as 'labour would have no reason to work for a wage that was below subsistence' is begging the question. The willingness, or otherwise, to work for a wage that was lower than that required for the reproduction of labour power will have depended on various considerations. First, it will have depended on whether the wage was the only source of income and whether the person earning the wage was the only breadwinner. This sounds rather self-evident, though the author seems less than convinced. He refers to historians who try to 'reconcile things' by suggesting that the wages were not earned by individuals. I am surprised by his scepticism, since more than one study has been published showing that income-pooling was a reality and that the earnings of a family were provided not only by different family members but also in different economic sectors.[14]

It is precisely the phenomenon of income-pooling that made it possible in certain periods for people in cottage industries to work at piece-rates that will not have enabled them to reproduce their labour-power. Let me specify here that I consider the cottage producer working in a putting-out system where the putter-out owns the raw materials and the means of production to be a wage-labourer. Cottage-industry producers were able to work for such low wages because these were not their only source of income. Their incentive to do so was that this work gave them access to the market. To the author's remark that 'something must have kept them going', I would reply that he underestimates the part played by self-exploitation. The 'something' that kept them going consisted of increased work effort; more people, including wives and children, worked more and longer. This increased labour would go beyond what would be considered profitable under a

13. K. Marx, *Capital*, pp. 66–7.
14. See, for example, the bibliography in P. Kriedte, H. Medick, J. Schlumbohm, *Industrialization before Industrialization*, Cambridge, 1981 and D. Levine, *Reproducing Families. The Political Economy of English Population History*, Cambridge, 1987.

generalised system of wage labour and capital relations, since the decisive criterion was the preservation of the family's subsistence. The effort of women and children contributed a necessary share to the family wage without which the subsistence gap could never have been bridged, but this share was not proportional to the increased labour effort.[15]

The phenomenon of working for a wage that was below subsistence was not limited to the proto-industrial world. Budgets with respect to working-class families in Ghent at the end of the nineteenth century show that flax labourers' wages were too low to keep them and their families. In some 60 per cent of the cases, however, work by the women provided an additional income. Wives and children contributed 35 per cent of the family income. This enabled the family to survive despite the low wages of the head of the household.[16] In the English cotton towns of the nineteenth century it was customary for wages to be set for men on the assumption that they were part of a family wage economy and that several members of the family would be working. Husband's wages alone would have reduced many families into poverty.[17]

It appears that the willingness to work for low wages was related less to the objective level of the individual wage than to the complementary function of this wage in the total family income. I therefore conclude that general statements about the willingness to work for a wage that was largely or marginally below that required for the reproduction of labour power are fairly meaningless when the complementarity of the different sources of the family income is ignored.

Another factor to influence the willingness to work for less than subsistence wages is coercion. I will not go into this here. Although Schwarz does mention it, he gives the impression of underestimating the relation between social policy in general and the regulation of the labour market in particular.[18]

My last comment takes up the author's statement that it is difficult (or impossible; he uses the word 'failure') to point to sufficiently close links between the different sections of the economy. Can we assume that the 'backward' parts of the economy operate in isolation, having little function

15. H. Medick, 'The Proto-industrial Family Economy', P. Kriedte et al., *Industrialization before Industrialization*, pp. 38–73, and J. Schlumbohm, 'Relations of Production—Productive Forces — Crises in Proto-Industrialization', ibid., pp. 94–125.
16. P. van den Eeckhout, P. Scholliers, 'Geld in 't laatje. Arbeid en inkomen van Gentse arbeiderfamilies circa 1900', *Arbeid in veelvoud*, Brussels, 1988, pp. 197–219.
17. D. Levine, *Reproducing Families*, pp. 176–8.
18. See, for example, C. Lis, H. Soly, *Poverty and Capitalism in Pre-industrial Europe*, Hassocks, 1979.

other than providing an endless supply of labour to the 'advanced' sector? It is a fact that certain parts of Europe were used as labour reservoirs in this way. J. Lucassen found, in his study on migrant labour in Europe and especially on labour attracted to the eastern part of the North Sea coast (1600–1900), that the areas that attracted labour revealed a number of characteristics belonging typically to the capitalist mode of production.[19] Employers there were able to offer remuneration that was sufficiently attractive for labourers elsewhere to be willing to leave their homes for the season. Migrant labour was recruited from 'backward' areas where there was surplus labour on family farms. Income from migratory labour helped in this way to preserve the small farms which the migrants left behind in the care of their families. Areas where surplus labour was utilised in cottage industries tended not to provide any appreciable number of migrant workers. As well as the 'North Sea system' studied, there were other comparable self-contained circulations of labour in Europe. After the decline of its cottage industry, Flanders too became a reservoir of labour (migrant labour and emigration) for Walloon and French industry. Analogous links can be established, for example, between the Mezzogiorno and the North of Italy and between Ireland and England.

19. J. Lucassen, *Naar de kusten van de Noordzee. Trekarbeid in Europees perspectief, 1600–1900*, Gouda, 1984, pp. 243–8.

F. DAELEMANS

2.2 Wages of Servants of the 'Cense-du-Sart' in Ernage (Brabant), 1783–1849

L. Schwarz's paper gives a negative and even a pessimistic picture of the study of real wages. In this comment, I want to be more optimistic and I will try to prove that wages can be used in economic and social history, providing more than limited information and validity. I will try to illustrate that the waged labour force was not that small in the countryside. I shall concentrate on the remuneration of agricultural labourers and, more particularly, on farm servants. Concerning the latter, Schwarz noted that 'wages were only a part of their total remuneration, quite possibly only a small part'. To prove this, he provides some examples with regard to south-east England and both sides of the border of eastern Scotland for the second half of the nineteenth century. I do not think that these case studies can be generalised for the whole of Western Europe. The situation of agriculture was quite different: e.g. there were enclosures in England, but none on the continent.

To prove my point, I shall use two account books of a farm, owned by the family Everarts de Velp, situated in the Walloon part of Brabant, Belgium. Day by day, the farmer recorded the wages of his servants. Thus, these books not only provide copies of the individual contracts, but also a picture of the daily life on the farm. The books were also used to note the sale of crops, and contain some remedies for illness of horses.

Firstly, allow me to give some general information about the farm, called 'Cense-du-Sart'. The family Everarts de Velp became the owner of the farm in April 1782, through a marriage of Pierre-Joseph with Catherine Legrain, the niece of Jacques Legrain, abbot and count of Gembloux, who was an important man in the region. The farm belonged to the abbey of Gembloux. The 'Cense' was one of the most extensive farms of the area, with 150 hectares of very good land. On 16 June 1787, the farm was forfeit and the widow of Pierre-Joseph became the owner. In November 1802, she died and was succeeded by her eldest son, Maximilien-Pierre-Joseph, then only 19 years old. Still, he managed to turn the farm into a success. He worked with a staff of five full-time *domestiques*, one swine-herd, one

48

Table 2.1 Wages of *Domestiques* and Maids of the Cense-du-Sart at Ernage, 1783–1840

	Domestiques				Maids		
1	2	3	4	1	2	3
1783 23 ecus = 100%	74	61	–	47	43	47
1820 30 ecus = 100%	60	53	47	42	42	–
1830 30 ecus = 100%	67	67	47	48	42	–
1840 33 ecus = 100%	84	66	54	60	54	48

shepherd, one to four maids and temporarily a nurse. The names and Christian names, the birthplaces, and the dates of the start and end of contracts are known for all of these people. However, I am not sure whether they were living-in servants or not. I believe they were, since only one third of them lived in the nearby village of Ernage, whereas the others came from the surrounding villages.

Turning now to the wages: Table 2.1 provides a comparison amongst all the categories of labourers, both male and female. The remuneration of each category underwent approximately the same development: wages increased between 1820 and 1840. The first *domestique* had 43 per cent more in 1840 than he earned at the end of the eighteenth century. The first maid and the second *domestique* had 56 per cent more, and the third *domestique* received 69 per cent more. So, clearly money wages were not stable at all between the end of the *ancien régime* and the middle of the nineteenth century. It is therefore hard to believe that an increasing living standard, if any, was only obtained by changes in agricultural prices.

Table 2.1 also shows that the lowest wage rose faster than the high wages, and thus the span between the highest and the lowest pay became smaller in the middle of the nineteenth century. But the second-best-paid labourer never earned more than four-fifths of the first *domestique*. Only from 1840 did maids obtain a little more than half the remuneration of the best-paid servant. From that moment on, her pay equalled the wage of the fourth *domestique*.

I will no longer consider the remuneration and the standard of living of the servants; I would instead prefer to concentrate on the way these wages were paid: in kind or in coins? Schwarz wrote that 'Even substantial farmers might be paying their men in kind . . . . Farm workers were having between 80 and 95 per cent of their wages paid in kind'. This was clearly not the case on the Cense-du-Sart. This becomes obvious when considering both the contracts and the account books. All sums were always indicated in coins in the contracts, but only *exceptionally* did some servants receive a surplus in kind. Just a few examples: In 1790, Marie-Louise Forley from Ernage was paid a sum of 20 florins a year and two shirts. In 1840, the first and the second *domestique* received 92 and 77 florins a year and one wagon of coals for their work. In all other contracts, all sums were indicated in coins, i.e. in more than 90 per cent of the cases!

As for the account books, various considerations can be made. Firstly, in considering the frequency of the payments, it appeared that there was no fixed pay-day. Some of the servants (22 per cent) were paid at the end of their contract on 2 November, but one servant asked for no less than 23 payments (small advances) during the year. However, most of the servants were paid four to seven times a year on different days. Most servants asked for small advances of their wages during the first half of the year, but rarely from August to December, an exception being November when the contracts came to an end.

Was it possible to save any money at the end of a year's work? This might have been the case, since only 8 per cent of the labourers asked for a small advance of their pay of the coming year. The farmer did allow such small advances, and it is not clear whether this was an exception or whether this can be seen as a paternalistic attitude. The advances were always small sums paid in different coins (florins, crowns, ecus, etc., after 1830 also in francs). I have to stress that even twenty years after the independence of Belgium, the Everarts family still made their accounts in florins and guilders.

In some cases, the farmer noted what the servants wanted to do or to buy with their wages: a pair of shoes, handkerchiefs, some cotton and so on (all bought by the farmer's brother-in-law), or wood, corn or a heifer (bought on the farm). The farmer always noted the quantity and the price of the purchased goods. In rare cases, the wages or a part of the wage was paid to the parents of the servants. Thus, the mother of a Jacques Delvaux received one sixth of her son's wages, and the father of a Charles Bidoule got the entire wage of his son's work.

To summarise, more than 80 per cent of the payments were made in coins at the Cense-du-Sart between 1783 and 1849. When payments in kind were made, this occurred at the request of the employed. For instance, a Joseph Flemal asked for payments in kind, and in 1840 he obtained nine out of fifteen payments in kind (corn, butter), meaning a total of 44 per cent of his yearly wages.

I hope to have shown that the situation in south-east England and eastern Scotland cannot be generalised with regard to the European continent. In Brabant, land labourers and servants were paid in money. Moreover, their wages did follow the general trend of increase. However, more research is of course required. It is obvious that we shall need more accounts. Still, the scarce information that does exist points in the direction outlined above, which allows me to stress that the situation on the Cense-du-Sart was not an exception.

P. BAIROCH

3. Wages as an Indicator of Gross National Product

Introduction[1]

It is obvious that wages are an important component of the national income of any country. What I want to show is that the level and evolution of wages are a very good indicator of the level and evolution of national income (either in real or in nominal terms) of societies before the period when income transfers became significant. And since this phase began only in the early part of the twentieth century, it means that this indicator is useful for a very large part of the history of developed and non-developed countries.

This research is part of what is called short-cut, indicator or indirect methods of calculating national income or other similar aggregates. The pioneer in the early 1950s of this type of approach was Bennett.[2] Although a wide array of indicators are used by various authors, as far as I know only I have proposed and tested the use of this wage indicator, which I have good reason to believe is comprehensive.

Taking into account the availability of data in nineteenth-century and pre-nineteenth-century societies, I came to the conclusion that it was possible to use a certain multiple of the average wage of unqualified urban labourers as a good indicator of nominal per capita GNP. And in order to evaluate the real per capita GNP the previous indicator should be expressed as purchasing power in terms of the dominant cereals.

In this short paper I shall present the following three elements: (1) wages and nominal GNP,[3] (2) wages and real per capita GNP and (3) some limitations and an agenda for research.

1. I want to thank my colleague Gary Goertz for having corrected my English and translated parts of this paper from the French.
2. M. K. Bennett, 'International Disparities in Consumption Levels,' *American Economic Review*, XLI, no. 3, September 1951, pp. 632–49. For a general survey of this approach, see P. Bairoch, 'Les méthodes indirectes de calcul du revenu national et les méthodes de comparaison internationales du revenu national dans une perspective historique', *Scritti in onore di Giuseppe de Meo*, vol. I, Rome, 1978, pp. 39–52.
3. GNP or gross national product is only one of the various concepts of national

51

1. Wages and Nominal GNP

Before showing the results of my calculations, which were first presented ten years ago, it is necessary to define more precisely the kind of urban wage used as reference. By average urban unqualified male wage, I mean a salary which must satisfy the following six conditions:

(1) It must include total remuneration including, if necessary, the monetary equivalent of payment in kind.

(2) It must be an *adult unqualified* worker's wage, i.e. requiring no or minimal training.

(3) It must be the wage in a non-marginal section that does not require exceptional physical effort such as 'terrassier' (road labourer), in which case it is necessary to reduce the wage by about 10 per cent.

(4) It should be the actual wage earned and not wage rates.

(5) It must be urban wages; if rural wages are used, these must be corrected to take into account differences between these.

(6) It must also be the average wage (not the least important) for the category of worker involved. This implies taking into account higher wages in capital cities (or other large cities) than in small urban areas.

I have decided to take as reference the daily wage. This is motivated by two considerations. The first and most important is that, in general,

accounting (national income, gross domestic product, etc.). The one used here is GNP at market prices. On the basis of existing data for the nineteenth-century developed countries, I calculated the following ratios allowing one to move from one concept to another.

To move from gross national product (A) at market prices to gross national product at factory prices (B), I propose to reduce A by 6 per cent or to increase B by 7 per cent to get A. To move from B to net national product (C), I propose to reduce B by 5 per cent or to increase C by 6 per cent to get B. To move from C to net domestic product at factory prices, it is unrealistic to propose a coefficient since the difference consists of the net revenue from foreign sources. In any case, for large societies these represent only 2 to 3 per cent of the gross national product at factory prices.

From the coefficients presented above one can reduce A by 10 per cent to get C or increase C by 12 per cent to get A. For more details see P. Bairoch, 'Estimations du revenu national dans les sociétés occidentales durant les périodes pré-industrielles et le XIXe siècle: propositions d'approches indirectes', *Revue économique*, XXVIII, no. 2, March 1977, Paris, pp. 197–208, esp. 202–3.

Table 3.1 Historical Series on the Ratio Linking the Daily Wage of an Average Urban Unqualified Male and the Gross National Product per Capita (at Current Market Prices)

Country, Units and Periods	Daily Wage	Gross National Product per Capita	Ratio
Germany (mark)			
1871–1875	2.26	450	199
1881–1885	2.13	423	199
1891–1895	2.65	518	195
1899–1903	3.11	627	202
1911–1913	4.10	851	208
France (franc)			
1781–1790	1.15	243	210
1803–1812	1.68	309	184
1815–1824	1.73	334	194
1825–1834	1.80	372	207
1835–1844	2.00	419	210
1845–1854	2.30	465	202
1855–1864	2.70	595	220
1875–1884	3.40	691	203
1885–1894	3.60	696	193
1895–1904	4.00	753	188
1905–1913	4.60	982	213
Great Britain (pound)			
1830–1832	0.125	23.9	191
1839–1840	0.131	25.5	195
1848–1850	0.136	25.5	188
1859–1861	0.148	29.5	199
1866–1871	0.158	34.6	219
1877–1880	0.180	37.1	206
1883–1886	0.178	36.5	205
1892–1894	0.183	40.2	220
1898–1902	0.215	47.4	220
1913–1914	0.248	57.0	230
Norway (krone)			
1865	1.58	282	178
1870	1.57	311	198
1875	2.31	427	185
1880	2.21	374	169
1885	1.91	346	181
1890	2.11	388	184
1895	2.26	392	174
1900	2.59	497	193
1905	2.57	477	186
1910	3.28	600	183

Table 3.1 continued

Country, Units and Periods	Daily Wage	Gross National Product per Capita	Ratio
Sweden (krone)			
1861–1865	1.13	203	180
1871–1875	1.37	287	209
1881–1885	1.50	301	201
1891–1895	1.85	332	179
1901–1905	2.42	460	190
1911–1913	3.23	668	207

Source: Author's calculations

regional and sectoral differences are smaller when using daily wages than when using hourly wages, because sectors and regions with lower wage rates have generally longer working days. The second consideration is related to the availability of data and the need to reduce the margin of error resulting from their conversion. The conversion of weekly wages into daily wages has a lower risk of error than their transformation into hourly wages. For example, in the middle of the nineteenth century the variation of the length of the working time expressed in days is about 6.0–6.5 while the same expressed in hours is 60–100 resulting in a difference of 10 per cent in the former and 70 per cent in the latter.

The main reason (other than that which comes from the comparisons below) for the choice of the wages of an urban *unqualified* worker as the key element in estimating GNP is that this factor is, as a general rule, the most stable sectorally, i.e. the differences in wages across sectors are smaller than those of qualified workers. Also, it appears historically that the relation between GNP/capita and an unqualified worker's wage is as good as the one between GNP/capita and a qualified industrial worker's wage. For the three cases where data are available for these three variables, two cases had a higher correlation for the wages of an unqualified worker and in the third case, the difference was negligible (qualified worker's wage being slightly superior).

Two procedures are used to determine the validity of this relationship between the daily salary of an unqualified urban worker and GNP. The first is to develop time-series data (before 1913) for European countries for which both these elements can be ascertained reliably. This was possible for Germany, France, Great Britain, Norway and Sweden. The second approach is to complement these series by partial calculations for other countries.

Table 3.1 gives the results of these calculations for the time-series data. I was surprised myself by their convergence, both temporally as well as cross-nationally. As the table indicates, the range of these ratios is very small — the variance of the average value is 4.7 per cent. This average value is 197, that is, when it is multiplied by the average daily wage of an unqualified worker, it equals the estimated GNP/capita (at market prices). This average varies little historically, as well as cross-nationally. For example, the largest variance is a small 4.9 per cent for Great Britain. The variance of all these nations together is only 7.1 per cent, with a standard error of 2 per cent.

In addition, the correlation coefficient for these two variables is very high and quite significant. These correlation coefficients are (followed by their Z-statistic):

Germany	0.999	(5.37)
France	0.990	(7.49)
Great Britain	0.995	(7.92)
Norway	0.984	(6.38)
Sweden	0.991	(3.82)
All above mentioned countries	0.983	(14.86)

Furthermore, the variation of this ratio over time shows no particular tendency, indicating that this ratio is perhaps independent of the level of economic development (at least for the historic period used here). I also did some calculations with less precise data (especially for GNP data), which yield the following result for England: around 1688 the ratio is 160 and for 1770–96 it is 260.

Recently, I was able to have an additional test of this indicator's validity, since Toutain has just published his revised series for France.[4] With these new figures, the correlation coefficient is slightly better (0.992 as opposed to 0.990) and more significant.

2. Wages and Real GNP

After analysing the kinds of information available for traditional economies, as well as those of the nineteenth century, and their usefulness as economic indicators, I have chosen for production per capita the quantity of cereals in terms of the salary (daily) of a male urban worker. This has the practical

4. J.-C. Toutain, 'Le produit intérieur brut de la France de 1789 à 1982', *Economies et sociétés série, Cahier de l'ISMEA, Histoire quantitative de l'économie française*, no. 15, Paris, 1987, pp. 99–237.

Table 3.2 Correlation between the Ratio of the Daily Wage of an Average Urban Unqualified Male Expressed in Kg of Wheat and the Gross National Product per Capita (in 1960 US Dollars and Prices)

Country	Number of Observa- tions	Correlation Coeffi- cient	Formula of the Regression[a]	$\dfrac{Z}{\sigma_z}$
Germany	5	0.978	Y = 26.5x + 175	3.18
France	9	0.985	Y = 30.4x + 65	5.98
Great Britain	10	0.955	Y = 20.7x + 312	4.99
Norway	4	0.979	Y = 26.2x + 74	2.27
Sweden	6	0.990	Y = 26.4x + 56	4.58
Above countries combined ...	34	0.921	Y = 26.9x + 136	8.88
Concerns GNP per capita below $500	16	0.775	Y = 22.3x + 145	3.72
Concerns GNP per capita between $500 and $1000 ...	17	0.793	Y = 17.2x + 333	4.04
Concerns data before 1905 (all observations)	25	0.876	Y = 29.1x + 107	6.37
Concerns data before 1905 (one observation per country)	8	0.933	Y = 14.2x + 460	3.76
Concerns data before 1905 (one observation per country for each of the three periods)	3 × 5	0.953	Y = 29.8x + 54	2.67

(a) Y = gross national product per capita in 1960 US dollars and prices
    x = daily wage of an average urban unqualified male expressed in kg of wheat

Source: Calculated from the figures of Table 3.3

advantage of needing only one additional datum, as opposed to those needed to calculate GNP in current prices. At the present state of research we are limited to wheat; probably a weighted average of cereals would be better.

As noted above, I consider these data as provisional for two reasons. The first is that not enough information has been gathered to establish comparable prices. As we will see, in all cases I used wholesale prices, but at different points in the distribution network (e.g. production prices or urban market prices). The second, more fundamental, reason is that usable data on real salary levels are not always available. If this is true for contemporary data, it is even more so for nineteenth-century data.

As for the preceding indicator, I have been surprised by the high correlation between the real GNP/capita and the salary of a working man expressed in wheat (see Table 3.2). For every country the correlation is greater than 0.95 (the probability of this occurring by chance is less than

0.05). The correlation for all countries together is a high 0.921.

A very high correlation (0.933) is also obtained when taking purely cross-sectional data (one observation per country per time period). Thus, in all possible cases, time-series (by nation), cross-sectional time series (all nations over time) and pure cross-sectional data (all nations one time period), the correlations are high. Since in this case the number of observations is thirty-four, this implies that the correlation is very significant.

As would be expected, the correlation between salary expressed in cereals and real GNP per capita is lower than its correlation with GNP per capita in current values. This may be due to the fact that the real GNP per capita data are more unstable as well as the fact that the price data for wheat are, as we noted before, not strictly comparable. Practically, it is possible to modify these prices slightly, taking into account the purchasing power of wheat relative to other goods. In some cases (e.g. USA and Canada, exporters of cereals), it is a reduction (say 10 per cent). Or, for importers that protect their agriculture (e.g. Switzerland), it is an increase (say 5 per cent).

Finally, it appears reasonable to propose for the nineteenth century and early twentieth century the formula:

$$y = 29 + 107x$$
y = GNP per capita in 1960 US dollars
x = daily wage of a working man expressed in kilos of wheat

For traditional societies with a real GNP per capita of less than 500 (in 1960 US prices and dollars) the formula is:

$$y = 22.3 + 145x$$

I also tried to apply this method in order to estimate the range of per capita GNP in traditional societies before the industrial revolution. This was done using six other approaches in addition to the present indicator.[5] The results were coherent enough to indicate that the use of this indicator is also valid on the city level and for the very long-term evolution of real salaries. As far as cities are concerned it was tested for thirteen cities for the period 1550–1700. For long-term series of wages, it proved consistent not only for European traditional societies but also for other cases. This gives additional interest to the object of the present volume. One of my students has used it for the case of nineteenth-century Egypt and there too the result agreed

5. See P. Bairoch, 'Ecarts internationaux des niveaux de vie avant le révolution industrielle', *Annales ESC,* 34, no. 1, Jan–Feb. 1979, pp. 145–71, esp. 158–62.

Table 3.3 Historical Series on the Comparison of the Ratio of the Daily Wage of an Average Urban Unqualified Male Expressed in Kg of Wheat and the Gross National Product per Capita (in 1960 US Dollars and Prices)

Country, Units and Periods	Daily Wage	Price of a kg. of bread	Ratio	Gross National Product per Capita (US $ and prices)
Germany (mark)				
1871/1875	2.26	0.240	9.4	430
1881/1885	2.13	0.195	11.0	470
1891/1895	2.65	0.174	15.2	565
1899/1903	3.11	0.164	18.9	645
1911/1913	4.10	0.209	19.5	730
France (franc)				
1815/1824	1.73	0.280	6.2	240
1825/1834	1.80	0.255	7.1	265
1835/1844	2.00	0.256	7.8	300
1845/1854	2.30	0.268	8.6	335
1855/1864	2.70	0.294	9.2	365
1875/1884	3.40	0.274	12.4	465
1885/1894	3.60	0.229	15.7	515
1895/1904	4.00	0.210	19.1	605
1905/1913	4.60	0.244	18.8	680
Great Britain (pound)				
1830/1832	0.125	0.0145	8.6	410
1839/1840	0.131	0.0141	9.3	450
1848/1850	0.136	0.0119	11.4	515
1859/1861	0.148	0.0116	12.7	615
1866/1871	0.158	0.0126	12.5	675
1877/1880	0.180	0.0109	16.5	700
1883/1886	0.178	0.0085	20.8	780
1892/1894	0.183	0.0067	27.3	860
1898/1902	0.215	0.0065	33.1	925
1913/1914	0.248	0.0076	32.6	1,025
Norway (krone)				
1875 and 1880	2.26	0.151	15.0	455
1885 and 1890	2.01	0.126	15.9	510
1895 and 1900	2.43	0.125	19.4	565
1905 and 1910	2.93	0.135	21.7	650
Sweden (krone)				
1861/1865	1.13	0.162	7.0	230
1871/1875	1.37	0.198	6.9	260
1881/1885	1.50	0.162	9.2	310
1891/1895	1.85	0.134	13.8	385
1901/1905	2.42	0.143	16.9	490
1911/1913	3.42	0.159	21.5	645

Table 3.3 continued

Country, Units and Periods	Daily Wage	Price of a kg. of bread	Ratio	Gross National Product per Capita (US $ and prices)
United States (dollar)				
1925/1929	4.29	0.052	82.7	1,720
Switzerland (franc)				
1924	9.86	0.400	24.7	1,060
Canada (dollar)				
1926/1929	3.53	0.050	71.0	1,315

Source: Author's calculations.

with other indicators that could be assembled on income levels.[6] Finally, we also tested the revised figures of France and it gave a little less positive correlation (0.983 against 0.985).

3. Some Limitations and an Agenda for Research

There is no doubt that the indicator described here has limitations, not even taking into account that any single indicator cannot be sufficient. The first limitation is because there were (and still are) differences in the relative level of income between cities and countryside. So, normally a correction should be included for exceptional cases. It is, however, also true that the standard of living of the countryside has an influence on the type of wage we have chosen.

The use of the dominant cereal (or even a group of cereals) to deflate the wages in order to obtain the indicator of real income implies implicitly that the price relation of cereals to other goods and even other food products is relatively constant. This is generally the rule, but there are exceptions, e.g. in desert regions, mountainous regions, etc. And since this paper is written in Switzerland, let us note that in general the relation between the price of cereals and of meat is different in all the mountainous regions than it is in flat countries. (Meat is cheaper or, if one prefers, cereals are more expensive in mountainous regions.) The best solution in this case is to deflate by a basket of goods, even a limited one (cereals and meat).

So this specific indicator can be improved, but it is also important to explore the other possible indicators that can be assembled for the type of

6. J. Batou, *L'entreprise de Mehemet-Ali ou le développement possible d'une nation arabe moderne au XIXe s.*, Geneva, 1978.

societies for which no real estimates of GNP can be made. The recent research of Fogel[7] showing a clear relation between body size and income is one example, but an example that can be implemented in too few cases. More operational are the demographic data on life expectancy. But I still feel, in view of the importance that wages play in the economy, that it is around this element that the most fruitful research could be done.

7. R. W. Fogel (ed.), 'Long Term Changes in Nutrition and the Standard of Living', *Ninth Congress of the International Economic History Association*, Bern, 1986.

D. EBELING

3.1 Some Remarks on the Relationship Between Overall Economic Output and Real Wages in the Pre-Industrial Period

Wage labour is unquestionably a form of value creation that did not originate with modern factory industry. Historical statistics show continual wage series since the late middle ages. At least since the work of the International Committee initiated by William Beveridge in the 1930s, wage history has formed a firm part of economic history alongside price history. Empirical evidence is only available for a few economic sectors in which wage employment and product price formation have left records. Yet work by scholars such as Labrousse and Abel have accorded the relationship between nominal wages and consumer prices a determining influence on the overall economic process from the late middle ages onwards.[1] Amongst more recent studies that assign a central role to wage indices, Paul Bairoch's work certainly belongs to those that go the farthest.[2] His objective is a diachronic and geographical comparison. The 'location' of a country or an economic region should be made measurable and thus comparable. In view of the insufficient data on overall output, these are replaced by real-wage data for the pre-industrial period. This substitution is derived fom the empirical findings that Bairoch has made regarding the various national economies of the nineteenth century, according to which the index series show high correlations for gross national product and real wages.

The problem inherent in the preparation of a real-wage index is avoided using a corn equivalent. Gustav Schmoller considered such corn wages to be an adequate indicator of living standards at the close of the nineteenth

---

1. C. E. Labrousse, *Esquisse du mouvement des prix et des revenus en France au XVIIe siècle*, Paris, 1933 and W. Abel, *Agrarkrisen und Agrarkonjunkturen*, Hamburg/ Berlin, 1978.
2. P. Bairoch, 'Estimations du revenu national dans les sociétés occidentales pré-industrielles et au dix-neuvième siècle', *Revue économique*, 18, 1977, pp. 177–208; idem, 'Ecarts internationaux des niveaux de vie avant la révolution industrielle', *Annales ESC*, 34, 1979, pp. 145–71.

century.[3] Indeed, it is the norm for the economic history of the pre-modern period, which lacks the material for a comprehensive basket of goods. The use of corn equivalent is justified in terms of Bairoch's objective because the largest part of value creation took place in the agricultural sector. The methodological problems that nevertheless remain are put aside in the following remarks in favour of a discussion of several basic questions.

Werner Sombart, who was in no way an enemy of empirical research, refused to make use of the 'rich store of studies on wage history' available at this time, 'because the individual wages said nothing other than the platitude: that under particular circumstances at a particular place and in a particular trade this or that wage was paid'.[4] In the pre-industrial period the wage was, in his view, a form of maintenance and not a wage paid for work done, which consequently meant that it did not reflect the value of labour on the employment market but what its owner required to live. In Knut Borchardt's view, too, the pre-industrial labour market was 'still tied in many ways to traditional orders and regulations as well as to social protective mechanisms'.[5]

In the agricultural sector, the use of free wage labour was the exception. The manorial system in Eastern Europe used farm labour with the help of feudal law. The freer tenant farming and rent economy in Western Europe was based on the family farm that could be supported by hired labour. However, only a small part of the work performed by farm labourers was paid in wages. The most important requirements for life, such as accommodation and food, were provided by taking the workers into the family. In a similar way, handicraft production was based on family enterprise supported by journeymen and apprentices who lived in the family. This state of affairs is reflected in historical statistics. Wage series refer throughout to the construction sector, for the character of this trade had very early on made the journeyman into a wage worker who, as a rule, led an independent existence. Non-money benefits were seldom granted. The unrepresentativeness of wages even in this sector may be illustrated by an example:[6] In Cologne, the nominal wages for bricklayer journeymen and unskilled workmen were only raised once during the whole of the eighteenth century, despite the fact that there was not usually a surplus of labour, and the construction trade was buoyant. At the same time, the rise in corn prices in the second half of the century pushed real wages down sharply. The wage

3. G. Schmoller, *Grundriss der allgemeinen Volkswirtschaftslehre*, II, Leipzig, 1904, p. 292f.
4. W. Sombart, *Der moderne Kapitalismus*, II.II, Munich/Leipzig, 1916, p. 829f.
5. K. Borchardt, *Grundriss der deutschen Wirtschaftsgeschichte*, Göttingen, 1978, p. 35.
6. D. Ebeling, *Bürgertum und Pöbel. Wirtschaft und Gesellschaft Kölns im 18. Jahrhundert*, Cologne/Vienna, 1987, pp. 165–78.

taxes levied by the town council gave the affected workers little room for manoeuvre in putting forward their wage demands. A 'just' balance between the interests of the producers and the consumers still applied as the basis of municipal policy, and instead of raising nominal wages the town helped wage earners by intervening in the corn market to offset a loss of purchasing power.

There were doubtlessly other ways of restoring the balance between supply and demand of labour. By working more slowly, by lengthening breaks, and by unauthorised reductions of working time, the workers withheld a part of their labour which they then tried to sell by carrying out small jobs in their spare time. As far as their standard of living is concerned, the decisive factor was therefore — apart from the corn price — not primarily a measurement of their performance at work but more or less the complete utilisation of their labour. Without doubt, there were other sectors of the economy in Western Europe which were based to a high extent upon wage work. The English and Dutch agricultural sectors, which were organised largely on capitalistic lines, used external labour. Large-scale public projects such as the Dutch canal construction could only be undertaken with the help of wage labour. In shipping, and in businesses involved in the sales trade, wage work prevailed. In the textile trade, which was the leading sector in the pre-industrial artisanal economy (and leaving aside manufacturing organisational forms that were only of marginal significance), sales and purchasing systems dominated as organisational forms which left the producer with formal independence.

The accounts of public institutions in Cologne show not only strong seasonal variations but also considerable variations in the employment structure in the building trade over the years. This development does not correspond with the cycle of agricultural prices. This points to a further problem that stands in the way of taking nominal and real wages of municipal wage workers as an indicator of overall economic output. One, perhaps the most, decisive determinant of the success of modern factory industry in Europe was the rapidly rising productivity of the agricultural sector. The model developed by Abel and Labrousse of the periodic booms and slumps in the economy of pre-industrial Europe shows that the repeated failure of commercial expansion due to the lack of productivity from the agricultural sector was decisive for overall economic performance. Only a particular form of international division of labour, such as the Netherlands' marked reliance on Baltic corn, was able to overcome this barrier.

The wage of the town worker did not in any way develop synchronously with overall economic performance. Phases of expansion in the pre-industrial economy were always associated with an increase in population, which went not only into an expansion of the artisanal sector, but also into the expansion of agriculture. Under conditions of stagnating agricultural productivity, the per capita output of the agricultural sector fell from a certain point. An increase in prices was the inevitable result. The urban worker was hit by this development in two ways. First, real wages declined at constant nominal wages. Second, the opportunity to utilise their labour was reduced. The inelastic demand for food products had an unfavourable effect on the sales opportunities of the industrial sector when agricultural prices were rising. Abel has called this the Janus-face of pre-industrial development.

Only the advent of a mechanised agricultural economy based on scientific methods and capitalist profit orientation made a decisive shift possible in favour of the industrial sector. Agricultural and industrial productivity were then able to develop in tandem. The Janus-face of the business cycle disappeared. If one disregards the struggle between wage labour and capital, the preconditions for participation of industrial wage labour in overall economic output were thus created.

These conditions might have come into effect in some European regions long before factory industrialisation. But one must warn against the idea that the development of the agricultural and industrial economy ran in opposite directions. Here reference is made again to the example of Cologne: Numerous public institutions were to be found amongst the clients of the construction trade whose income was derived to a great extent from leases and rents from their agricultural property. This income flowed to some extent into urban industry via contracts, purchasing and wages. To a certain extent, urban industry therefore participated in increasing agricultural prices. The charitable operations of many of these organisations, such as monasteries and hospitals run by religious orders, also drew on this income. They contributed to making a part of the able-bodied population independent of wage work, which enabled them to stay away from the labour market. Despite the weakened position of urban industry, the nominal wage level could be maintained. Incidentally, Jan de Vries has stressed this effect as an explanation of the fact that the wage level in the Netherlands remained high in the eighteenth century.[7]

Finally, one should point to a third problem. With the development of transport, the location of production and consumption drifted apart from the end of the middle ages. Closed economic regions, in which the performance of the economy could be entirely expressed in terms of the purchasing power of the wage received by labour, tended to be the exception. The

7. J. de Vries, 'An Inquiry into the Behaviour of Wages in the Dutch Republic and the Southern Netherlands from 1580 to 1800', M. Aymard (ed.), *Dutch Capitalism and the World Capitalism*, Cambridge, 1982, p. 51.

Dutch case is only an extreme example. The normal pattern of the eighteenth century was that presented by the example of the Cologne area. On the left-hand bank of the Rhine a fertile agricultural industry developed, laid out in Thuenen's semicircle, which satisfied Cologne's demand. This situation changed in the course of the seventeenth and eighteenth centuries. In the *Mittelgebirgs* region on the right-hand side of the Rhine, the textile and metal processing industries developed vigorously. Cologne's industry in part stagnated, and in part decayed, having a constant number of consumers. The growing population on the right-hand side of the Rhine absorbed a growing share of agricultural products of the left-hand side of the Rhine, and drew food from distant markets. The people supporting the prospering industry on the right-hand side of the Rhine were in a better position to cope with rising prices than consumers in Cologne. The original unity of production and consumption, which had been illustrated in Cologne by Thuenen's region, was destroyed. The demands of a second region of consumption drove prices up and depressed real wages in Cologne. It is therefore of little use as an indicator for the performance of the economy of the *ancien régime*. Bairoch's proposals to determine economic regions is geared towards modern economic units, and is not well-suited to pre-industrial society.

3.2 The Place of the Unskilled Male Worker in the Economy of a Nation: A Comment*

The remuneration of the unskilled male worker of the town bears an almost fixed relationship to the total wealth of the nation as measured by its gross national product. Such is the claim advanced by Paul Bairoch on the basis of an examination of wage and GNP differentials between countries and their evolution over the nineteenth century. Grant for the moment that there is such a correlation and that it is close. Even in these circumstances it is far from clear why such a relationship exists: whether it is endogenous to the method of calculating the GNP or, alternatively, whether it is exogenous, the movements of both the wage and the GNP being influenced by independent (and currently unknown) factors, or even simply the product of coincidence.

Historians interested in the size of pre-industrial economies, without the opportunity to compare data or wages with an estimated GNP, may be tempted to take the relationship on trust. In his paper Paul Bairoch asserts that the methodology has been successfully tested in pre-industrial societies with six other 'approaches' yielding similar results, but no detail of these trials is provided, and success at city level is no guarantee of success with national aggregates. Furthermore, although there is reassurance to be gained from having the methodology confirmed both for the nineteenth century and earlier, there is no substantive interest in being able to estimate what can be measured in all probability with a greater degree of accuracy by other means. Only through the application of the methodology to economies whose size cannot be otherwise measured would the methodology come into its own.

However, there would be no point in attempting this in the absence of

* I would like to thank Tony Wrigley and Osamu Saito for their advice in connection with the calculation of the gross national product. My debt to David Thomson of Massey University, New Zealand, and Keith Snell of the University of Leicester is also evident. The responsibility for the views expressed in the paper, however, is my own.

any theory to explain how it is that through much of the nineteenth century in diverse parts of Europe the ratio of the unskilled urban male wage to the GNP appears to be relatively stable. The relative stability of this ratio is all that it is safe to claim since it is not clear what importance should be attached to small variations. Moreover, even the seemingly impressive correlation in the movement of the wage and the GNP over time may be seriously flawed. With both series following a rising trend[1] a good correlation is to be expected, whereas a less impressive correlation might be suggested if the two series were de-trended — that is if a measure of the annual variation was provided that was independent of the trend. Yet whether the ratio is stable or varies, interpretation seems likely to remain problematic.

Consider the case of Britain between the 1830s and 1860s, when for three successive periods (out of four) there was a rise in the ratio. The implication would appear to be that the wages of unskilled urban males had declined relative to the earnings of the rest of society, but as the GNP is measured relative to their daily wage rather than to the wages they earned over the year, it is possible that the decline was apparent rather than real, with a greater number of days being worked to compensate for what was a relatively lower return for their daily labour. If, on the other hand, such variations in the ratio are dismissed as unimportant, the problem is how to explain the stability of a ratio, so many of the constituents of which could be expected to have changed in a century of economic transformation. For example, a stable ratio would imply not only a fixed relationship between national income and GNP, but also that the wages of the unskilled in the towns remained a more or less constant share of the national income. In theory this is not impossible in that contrary trends in the contributions of the wages of the unskilled, the returns of the self-employed and profits might be offsetting, but given the pace of capital accumulation in the nineteenth century it is not likely. Nor does it seem probable that the demand for unskilled male labour in the towns, as measured by the relative reward for this sort of work, would remain constant as these towns became major industrial centres.

Both the reliability and representativeness of the underlying wage data should also not go unchallenged. It is the rare document that records the actual wage as opposed to a wage rate. To find a time series for different countries that successfully selects an actual wage for a representative group of unskilled urban workers, follows it as long as it remains representative and replaces it as necessary, seems to demand a perfection in economic data

1. Paul Bairoch, 'Wages as an Indicator of Gross National Product', Table 3.1, columns 1 and 2.

that is the dream of every historian and the reality of none. However, were all these doubts to be resolved then the discovery of the fixed relationship between the unskilled urban male wage and the GNP would become a finding of considerable importance. It would suggest that societies of various types, the pre-industrial city and the nineteenth-century industrial, needed to secure a fixed reward to unskilled labour.

Yet Paul Bairoch is concerned not just with national economies but with the workers' own budgets, which he attempts to measure by setting the average male wage against the gross price of a kilo of wheat. Unfortunately, this is perhaps not the best indicator as he himself realises, for the price of wheat (particularly the wholesale price) does not necessarily indicate what the worker had to pay for bread, or permit an accurate estimate of his expenses on other goods vital for his survival. Nor, of course, was the wage of the worker his only resource. To a greater or lesser extent depending on the nature of the local economy, his wife and children might contribute a significant proportion of the family budget. In the working-class district of St George in the East in East London in 1848, selected by the Statistical Society of London as indicating what they suggested was the average experience, women and children contributed 23 per cent of the budgets of labourers.[2] Some fifty years earlier in the West Country parish of Corfe Castle, the families of wage earners were contributing 30 per cent of the budget and this despite the low earnings of women.[3]

Along with other members of the wage-earning population the unskilled workers of concern to Paul Bairoch would also have relied (when necessary) on support in money and kind from the community, through the medium of the Church or a state-run poor-law system, or from friends, wealthy neighbours and employers. Paul Bairoch in fact was inclined to dismiss the transfer of income between rich and poor through the medium of the community as of no significance before the early twentieth century. Admittedly it is difficult to quantity this assistance which, by its very nature, was spasmodic and concentrated both seasonally and at particular points in the individual's life cycle, notably in old age, widowhood and when families were burdened with many children under working age.[4] In this

2. 'Report of the Investigation into the State of the Poorer Classes in St George in the East', *Quarterly Journal of the Statistical Society of London*, 1848, pp. 200–1, reprinted in Richard Wall (ed.), *Slum Conditions in London and Dublin*, Farnborough, 1974.
3. My own calculations on the local census of Corfe Castle of 1790, of which there is a copy in the Library of the Cambridge Group. Payments by the Poor Law authorities are excluded. The wage-earning population were all those whose weekly earnings were specified and includes some of the poorer craftsmen and fishermen as well as claycutters and labourers.
4. The nature of the poverty life cycle, and the extent of its recognition by the

paper the aim will simply be to present two admittedly crude estimates, both based on English evidence, of the contributions that could be made to the budgets of the wage-earning population that supplemented their earnings. First, there is Gregory King's celebrated calculation of the income and expenditure of each strata of English society in 1688 which implies a fairly modest 7 per cent contribution from sources other than earnings to the budgets of sailors and soldiers, 14 per cent to the budgets of the cottagers and the poor, but only two per cent to the budget of labourers. Even vagrants supposedly earned half their income.[5] Unfortunately, the basis for King's calculations in this instance, as in so many others, is unclear, and the data scarcely exist to permit a verification of his results. The second estimate is my own calculation of the extent of the support provided to the families of the parochially dependent poor by the English Poor Law authorities, as a proportion of the earnings of the wage-earning population over the life cycle. Much of the evidence assembled concerns the early nineteenth-century. For example, David Thompson has concluded that it would not have been unusual in the first four decades of the New Poor Law (1830s to 1870s)[6] for elderly paupers to have received from the Poor Law authorities at least two-thirds of the adult equivalent manual wage, and Keith Snell has argued that Poor Law support for widows with children was equally generous in the period between 1800 and 1834.[7]

However, calculating what share such payments represented of all income acquired over the life cycle is not so easy. Regular payments were likely only when earnings consistently failed to balance outgoings or ceased altogether in extreme old age, and not all the elderly or lone parents would receive relief.[8] Payments were also made to specific individuals, illegitimate

---

authorities in various European countries charged with responsibility for the poor, formed one of the themes of a 'C' session at the International Economic History Conference in Berne in 1986 organised by myself and Osamu Saito of Hitosubashi University. A revised set of the papers under our joint editorship is to be published by the Cambridge University Press as *The Economic and Social Aspects of the Family Life Cycle: Europe and Japan Traditional and Modern* (scheduled for publication in 1990).

5. Gregory King, 'Natural and Political Observations and Conclusions upon the State and Condition of England 1696', pp. 48–9, reprinted in Peter Laslett (ed.), *The Earliest Classics*, Farnborough, 1973. Inclusive of the vagrants, 6.7 per cent of the income of the group came from sources other than earnings.

6. David Thomson, 'The Decline of Social Welfare: Falling State Support for the Elderly since Early Victorian Times', *Ageing and Society*, 4(4), 1984, p. 453.

7. Keith Snell and J. Millar, 'Lone Parent Families and the Welfare State: Past and Present', *Continuity and Change*, 2(3), 1987, pp. 405–8.

8. For example, in the Norfolk parish of Cawston in 1601, not quite four out of ten of those listed as poor above the age of sixty were in receipt of weekly relief

children and orphans, for example, as well to families and it is unlikely that the income of each individual pauper was increased to two-thirds of the adult equivalent wage. If we assume, however, that mothers bringing up children on their own would usually receive just 54 per cent of the adult equivalent wage[9], and that such households represented the same proportion of households whose heads (when employed) would work for wages as of households in general (about 8.7 per cent),[10] then on this count alone the Poor Law authorities provided close to 5 per cent of the resources of the wage-earning population. Similar assumptions applied to elderly householders married or living on their own, but based on an estimated contribution of two-thirds of the adult equivalent wage as suggested by David Thompson, instead of 54 per cent, would account for a further 4.6 per cent of the resources[11]. Taken together, these calculations would imply

---

from the Poor Law. See Tim Wales, 'Poverty, Poor Relief and the Life Cycle: Some Evidence from Seventeenth-Century Norfolk', Richard M. Smith, *Land, Kinship and Life Cycle*, Cambridge, 1984, p. 371. Newman Brown also found that only around four in every ten widows regularly received poor relief in the Hertfordshire parish of Aldenham in the late seventeenth century, but the proportion receiving relief of those who might have been deemed 'poor' but were not in receipt of regular relief at the time would no doubt have been higher: W. Newman Brown, 'The Receipt of Poor Relief and Family Situation: Aldenham, Hertfordshire 1630–90', in Smith, *Land, Kinship and Life Cycle*, p. 412.

9. In order not to overstate the contribution of the Poor Law authorities I have relied on the lowest of the various estimates of support from the Poor Law suggested by Keith Snell (43 per cent in Worcester, 58 per cent in Yorkshire and 61 per cent in the Essex parish of Terling), which average out at 54 per cent of the adult equivalent wage. Of course, not all such women would necessarily have received this level of support, for example, those residing elsewhere than in the parish of settlement (Keith Snell, personal communication). On the other hand, other women might conceivably have been treated more generously.

10. Snell and Millar, 'Lone Parent Families', p. 392. Families of lone mothers represented 8.7 per cent of all single-family households with children in communities that were enumerated within the period 1752–1851. The mothers formed a considerably larger group (16 per cent) in communities enumerated before 1700.

11. Only rarely were ages specified in enumerations of English communities before 1821. Ten of the most detailed enumerations have been used for the purposes of this calculation (Ealing 1599, Chilvers Coton 1684, Lichfield 1692, Stoke 1701, Wetherby 1776, Wembworthy 1779, Corfe Castle 1790 and Ardleigh 1796) and these indicated that about 7 per cent of all households were headed by elderly married couples or elderly people living alone. Elderly lone parents are excluded from this particular count to avoid any possible double count (as lone parents and as elderly), as are elderly persons living with other persons since the costs of their support may have been somewhat less than the two-thirds of the adult equivalent wage.

that the wage-earning population received a greater degree of support from this one source alone than Gregory King supposed would arrive from all sources other than earnings.

In estimating the contribution of the Poor Law authorities the intention has been to under- rather than over-estimate its significance. For example, it would have been possible to have assumed that the Poor Law authorities were sufficiently generous as to ensure that the income of those unable to support themselves from their earnings reached 80 per cent rather than 54 per cent of the adult equivalent wage,[12] and to allow for a modest contribution to the income of other groups, for instance to married men burdened with a particularly large family.[13] Our suggestion above, therefore, of a contribution from the Poor Law authorities of over 9 per cent of the budgets of the wage-earning population may be unduly modest.

However, it must be recognised that all these estimates are at the best only approximate. Snell and Millar are inclined to the view that the Poor Law authorities in some cases did not reduce the level of support they provided lone parents to take account of what women and children might earn. In their higher estimates of Poor Law support (80 per cent of the male manual wage), they also included an allowance for rent and payments in kind as a supplement to what the families received in cash.[14] Yet there was not always evidence to show that such support was being provided to families who received monetary benefits, and the likelihood remains open that in some cases payments in kind did not supplement payments in cash but represented an alternative form of assistance.

By way of a final comment we can consider the situation of the poor in the parish of Corfe Castle at the end of the eighteenth century. The local census of 1790 is the most detailed of all those conducted before the nineteenth century. Not only are the occupations of the inhabitants — family members as well as family heads — specified, but so are the probable weekly earnings of the poorer part of the population.[15] A note was also made if an individual or family received poor relief, although unfortunately without specifying the sums involved. Altogether some 372 males and 410 females were dependent, directly or indirectly, on wages or poor-relief payments for their subsistence. If we consider these two groups (wage-

12. Snell and Millar, 'Lone Parent Families', pp. 407–8; Wales, 'Poverty, Poor Relief and Life Cycle', p. 357; Thomson, 'The Decline of Social Welfare'.
13. For example, Snell and Millar suggest a contribution to the income of such families from the Poor Law authorities in the Essex village of Terling in the early nineteenth century of between 9 and 16 per cent: Snell and Millar, 'Lone Parent Families', p. 411.
14. Ibid., pp. 407–8.
15. Cf. above, note 3.

earners and paupers) as constituting a labouring class, it emerges that 13 per cent of the males and 22 percent of the females within this labouring-class population were in receipt of poor relief in this parish in 1790. As was pointed out above, however, it is unlikely if all these would have received such generous support as envisaged by David Thomson and Keith Snell. We will therefore confine our estimates to the heads of family, defining 'family' as all married couples, lone parents, bachelors and spinsters who headed their own households or resided in lodgings. Of these labouring-class 'families' some 17 per cent were in receipt of poor-relief payments, representing (on an assumed contribution from the Poor Law authorities of a minimum 54 per cent and maximum 80 per cent of the adult equivalent wage) a contribution to the budget of the labouring-class population of between 9 and 14 per cent. The lower of these estimates seems the more probable as with four out of ten of the 'families' in receipt of poor relief described as lodging in other households, on occasion in the households of persons who were themselves partly dependent on the Poor Law for their subsistence, a considerable saving seems likely on the 20 per cent of the male wage estimated by Keith Snell as necessary to cover the payment of rent.[16]

Nevertheless, even with all these qualifications our estimate of the contribution of the Poor Law authorities to the budgets of the wage-earning population in this one late eighteenth-century population is surprisingly close to our initial estimate, which involved the additional assumptions about the proportion of dependents (lone parents and elderly) in the labouring-class population. Admittedly, both estimates suggest a some-what greater contribution from the Poor Law than, according to the calculations of Gregory King, originated from all sources other than earnings but the situation in the late seventeenth century may have been markedly different from that of the late eighteenth. It is known that the forms of support (institutional care, out-relief), the types of dependency causing vast concern to the authorities (children, families, the elderly) and the generosity of the relief could all vary over time. David Thomson, for example, has argued that there was a hardening of attitudes towards the elderly poor in the later decades of the nineteenth century, while Tim Wales has documented for Norfolk an increasingly generous relief of the poor during the course of the seventeenth century, supplanting informal alms-giving as the major source of relief.[17] Such changes were much more than a simple reaction to demographic change, although undoubtedly this was critical in determining both the proportion and the visibility of particular

16. Snell and Millar, 'Lone Parent Families', p. 407.
17. Thomson, 'The Decline of Social Welfare', p. 453; Wales, 'Poverty, Poor Relief and the Life Cycle', p. 357.

categories of dependent: the elderly, when population was stagnating as in the later seventeenth century; the young, when population was expanding as in the later eighteenth century. What was also required was the political will on the part of the privileged to meet the needs of the disadvantaged, something which was probably easier to achieve when both belonged to the same local community than when (in the course of the nineteenth century) the creation of the Poor Law Unions, and increased intervention by central government to stipulate when and how relief could be provided, further distanced the providers of relief from the receivers.[18]

To return, however, to Bairoch: his dismissal of transfers of income between rich and poor as being of no significance before the early twentieth century clearly does less than justice to the scale of relief provided by the English Poor Law. An average contribution of 9 per cent of the budget of the labouring-class population may not seem great, but such support came at critical moments of the life cycle — in sickness, during periods of unemployment, and above all in widowhood and in old age — and may have been the more highly valued for that reason. Our crude estimates of the degree of support from the Poor Law over the life cycle of the wage-earner need to be refined by investigations of the readiness of Poor Law authorities in parishes with differing economies and attitudes to the 'problem' of poverty to respond to likely crisis points in the individual life cycle. It is a tedious if not an impossible task to see how Poor Law payments varied in particular circumstances by matching poor relief payments to entries in the parish register,[19] but an assessment of how many needed but did not get relief is likely to pose a much greater problem. At present the best evidence is provided by the calculation by Tim Wales that just 40 per cent of the elderly poor were in receipt of regular relief in Cawston, Norfolk, in 1601.[20] Yet even though we lack detailed knowledge of how individual wage-earners balanced receipts and expenditure over the course of their life cycle (an ignorance that seems likely to continue) it is at least clear that the wage-earners in pre-industrial England were not solely dependent on their earnings for their subsistence, and any study of their standard of living has to take this into account.

18. Snell and Millar, 'Lone Parent Families', p. 413.
19. Certain local censuses though reflecting the situation only of one point in time can also yield useful information. My own workings on the census of Corfe Castle of 1790 indicate that 35 per cent of labouring-class family heads over the age of 50 received relief but only 7 per cent of those under 50.
20. Cf. above, note 8.

N. F. R. CRAFTS

4. Real Wages, Inequality and Economic Growth in Britain, 1750–1850: A Review of Recent Research

Introduction

The 1980s have seen a substantial research effort on trends in real wages and income inequality during the British Industrial Revolution. Such has been the volume of literature that even such masterly surveys of the standard of living debate as those of Flinn[1] and Taylor[2] are now seriously out of date. The purpose of this paper is to enable the reader to form judgments on recent developments in this controversy, and it can be seen as a supplement to the surveys of the 1970s and my own earlier review of the evidence.[3]

Revisions to earlier views of trends in real wages have come mainly from the construction of new cost of living indices. It must be recognised, however, that we are still some way from obtaining a fully satisfactory cost of living index for the years 1750–1850. The use (and misuse) of cost of living indices remains fundamental to the standard of living debate, and the current state of knowledge is reviewed in the next section of the paper. That section also restates the 'consensus' view of real wages for all blue-collar workers reached in the interchange between Lindert and Williamson[4] and Crafts,[5] which argues that — broadly speaking — real wages grew roughly in line with real national income per head, which is a much more optimistic

1. M. W. Flinn, 'Trends in Real Wages, 1750–1850', *Economic History Review*, 27, 1974, 395–413.
2. A. J. Taylor, 'Editor's Introduction', A. J. Taylor (ed.), *The Standard of Living in the Industrial Revolution*, London, 1975, pp. xi–lv.
3. N. F. R. Crafts, *British Economic Growth during the Industrial Revolution*, Oxford, 1985a, chapter 5.
4. P. H. Lindert and J. G. Williamson, 'English Workers' Living Standards during the Industrial Revolution: A New Look', *Economic History Review*, 36, 1983, 1–25, and idem, 'English Workers' Real Wages: Reply to Crafts', *Journal of Economic History*, 45, 1985, 145–53.
5. N. F. R. Crafts, 'English Workers' Real Wages during the Industrial Revolution: Some Remaining Problems', *Journal of Economic History*, 45, 1985b, 139–44.

result than that obtained using the well-known Phelps Brown and Hopkins series.[6]

Recent contributions by Schwarz[7] and Botham and Hunt[8] are considered in the following section. Both these papers seek to disassociate themselves to some extent from the recent 'consensus' and both stress regional variations in real-wage growth. I shall argue that, although it is valuable to be reminded of regional diversity, which is ignored in Lindert and Williamson[9] though not in Crafts,[10] these two recent articles in fact make relatively little difference to what was already known, and that in both cases the evidence is discussed in a somewhat misleading way.

Although firmly in the optimists' camp on overall real wage growth, Williamson[11] has suggested that the Industrial Revolution saw large increases in inequality on the lines of a Kuznets Curve, with the ratio of skilled to unskilled workers' pay rising as a result in particular of imbalances in productivity growth between industry and agriculture. These claims have subsequently been subjected to severe criticism.[12] The last section inquires what remains of Williamson's claims.

Cost of Living Indices for the British Industrial Revolution Period

The chief problems in constructing cost of living indices for this period are, of course, well known. They include the poor quality of available budget studies in terms of their lack of detail on purchases other than food, and their inadequacy as a source of information on weightings to reflect differences in regional tastes, income levels or family sizes. Most available budgets are for poor workers and representative examples are reproduced in the Appendix 4.1. Also problematic is the scarceness of data on important

6. E. H. Phelps Brown and S. V. Hopkins, 'Seven Centuries of the Prices of Consumables Compared with Builders' Wage Rates', *Economica*, 23, 1956, 296–314.
7. L. D. Schwarz, 'The Standard of Living in the Long Run: London, 1700–1860', *Economic History Review*, 38, 1985, 24–41.
8. F. W. Botham and E. H. Hunt, 'Wages in Britain during the Industrial Revolution', *Economic History Review*, 40, 1987, 380–99.
9. Lindert and Williamson, 'Living Standards', pp. 1–25.
10. Crafts, *British Economic Growth*, chapter 5.
11. J. G. Williamson, *Did British Capitalism Breed Inequality?*, London, 1985.
12. See, for example, N. F. R. Crafts, 'British Economic Growth, 1700–1850: Some Difficulties of Interpretation', *Explorations in Economic History*, 24, 1987a, 245–68; idem, 'Cliometrics, 1971–1986: A Survey', *Journal of Applied Econometrics*, 2, 1987b, 171–92; R. V. Jackson, The Structure of Pay in Nineteenth Century Britain', *Economic History Review*, 40, 1987, 561–70; and C. H. Feinstein, 'The Rise and Fall of the Williamson Curve', *Journal of Economic History*, 48, 1988.

prices, most notably for rents, manufactured goods including clothing and all services.

The price indices used in the standard of living debate until recently have been distinctly unsuitable for the calculation of the real wages of blue-collar workers. Although Phelps Brown and Hopkins's index continues to be widely used, it should be recognised that it contains several unfortunate features: most obviously, its weighting appears to be very different from that suggested by the budget studies which are much better reflected in the weights chosen by Lindert and Williamson for their 'best guess' index.[13] The Phelps Brown and Hopkins index takes no account of rent; its cereals do not include bread or flour; drink is very largely represented by beer.[14] No one should use this index without first considering adjustment to deal with these points, which is certainly feasible for the period 1750–1850.

Lindert and Williamson's cost of living index was objectionable chiefly because of its treatment of the price of clothing, in particular for the years after 1819 where the export price of cottons unadjusted for quality was used. Lindert and Williamson later accepted that this was inappropriate and produced a reasonably satisfactory clothing-price index based on a quality adjusted cotton price and including woollens after 1819.[15] This is probably the best index available at the moment, although it is crude and subject still to obvious problems such as the complete absence of cotton goods prior to 1819. Crafts also drew attention to the unsatisfactory reliance of Lindert and Williamson on rents for one particular location, but his alternative attempt to use tax data is probably even less acceptable.[16] It should also be noted from Crafts that alterations to weightings within the food category may be regarded as desirable by some investigators and could affect estimated price changes by an amount of the order of 10 per cent over 1810–50. Until further research refines our knowledge, Lindert and Williamson's cost of living index probably should be thought of as a 'best guess' for all blue-collar workers for 1780–1850. For the years 1750–1780, my earlier discussion has already indicated that Lindert and Williamson were unwise in their 1983 paper to accept the Phelps Brown and Hopkins index and splice it to their own. For the present a better alternative seems to be to include the available information on rent and reweight Phelps Brown and Hopkins in accordance with Lindert-Williamson for a 'best guess' at 1750–1780.

Tables 4.1 and 4.2 indicate the quantitative implications of the preceding discussion. It is apparent from Table 4.1 that Lindert and Williamson's

13. Lindert and Williamson, 'Living Standards', pp. 1–25.
14. E. H. Phelps Brown and S. V. Hopkins, *A Perspective of Wages and Prices*, London, 1981, pp. 28–44.
15. Lindert and Williamson, 'Real Wages', pp. 145–53.
16. Crafts, 'Some Remaining Problems', pp. 139–44.

Table 4.1 Clothing Price Indices, 1780–1850

	Lindert and Williamson, 1983	Crafts, 1985	Lindert and Williamson, 1985
1780	299.8	202.3	204.5
1790	313.9	182.6	213.4
1800	348.3	179.2	240.6
1810	374.2	219.7	256.2
1820	394.0	175.7	209.8
1830	213.1	121.9	137.8
1840	147.2	111.4	128.3
1850	100	100	100

Source: Crafts (1985b, Table 2) and Lindert and Williamson (1985, Table 1); figures are five-year averages centred on the date quoted, except for Lindert and Williamson's estimates for 1780 (both series) and 1780, 1790 and 1800 new series.

Table 4.2 Cost of Living Indices, 1750–1850

	Phelps Brown and Hopkins	Lindert and Williamson, 1983	Lindert and Williamson, 1985	Crafts 1985
1780	76.2	118.8	108.4	111.2
1790	86.1	120.7	110.0	107.7
1800	135.4	175.8	165.7	162.5
1810	162.9	208.2	195.1	195.9
1820	130.6	168.1	148.5	139.6
1830	118.1	140.7	132.0	126.9
1840	121.7	135.1	133.4	127.0
1850	100	100	100	100

Sources: Phelps Brown and Hopkins (1956); Lindert and Williamson 'best guess' (1983, Table 4); Lindert and Williamson (1985, Table 1); Crafts (1985b, Table 3, col. (5)). Figures are five-year averages for the date shown wherever possible.

Weighting: Phelps Brown and Hopkins weights vary but are approximately 20 per cent for cereals and potatoes, 25 per cent meat, 12.5 per cent butter and cheese, 22.5 per cent drinks, 7.5 per cent fuel and light and 12.5 per cent textiles. Lindert and Williamson and Crafts weights are 12.6 per cent bread, 31.2 per cent flour, 9.4 per cent bacon, 1.2 per cent beef, 0.6 per cent mutton, 1.8 per cent tea, 2.6 per cent sugar, 4.4 per cent butter, 16.6 per cent rent, 2.2 per cent candles, 4.4 per cent fuel, 13 per cent clothing.

revision of clothing prices is indeed a large change. From Table 4.2 it is clear that the differences between Crafts and Lindert/Williamson were by 1985 very small relative to those between these authors and Phelps Brown and Hopkins. The difference in weighting between these indices is also revealed in Table 4.2.

An improvement to the Phelps Brown and Hopkins index to incorporate

Table 4.3 A Revised Phelps Brown and Hopkins Index and a 'Best Guess' Cost of Living Index for 1750–1850

	Phelps Brown and Hopkins	'Best Guess'
1750	68.9	88.1
1760	74.0	94.6
1770	86.6	110.7
1780	84.8	108.4
1790	94.2	110.0
1800	140.8	165.7
1810	170.0	195.1
1820	133.3	148.5
1830	120.1	132.0
1840	122.8	133.4
1850	100	100

Sources: The revised Phelps Brown and Hopkins index uses weightings of 43.8 per cent for cereals and potatoes, 11.2 per cent for meat, 4.4 per cent for butter and cheese, 4.4 per cent for drinks, 6.6 per cent for fuel and light, 13 per cent for textiles and 16.6 per cent for rent and the prices reported in Phelps Brown and Hopkins (1981, pp. 55–7) plus a series for rent in Staffordshire based on Lindert and Williamson's data for 1780–1850 spliced to Botham and Hunt (1987, p. 388) at 1780.
　'Best Guess' is Lindert and Williamson's 1985 index extended back to 1750 using the revised Phelps Brown and Hopkins index reported in this table.

available (admittedly imperfect) information about rent and to reweight in the light of available budget studies is shown in Table 4.3. This reworking of Phelps Brown and Hopkins is also used in Table 4.3 to extend back to 1750 Lindert and Williamson's 'best guess' of 1985 to provide a new 'best guess' index for the whole period 1750–1850. In no way can this be regarded as definitive for the reasons reviewed earlier, but this index of the cost of living is probably at least as good as any other available for all blue-collar workers in this period and without doubt superior to Phelps Brown and Hopkins.[17]

As Table 4.4 shows, the outcome of the interchange between Crafts and Lindert and Williamson is to provide a 'consensus' view of real-wage growth for all blue-collar workers for 1780–1850, which is that it was virtually equal to overall personal consumption growth and modest prior to 1820. The revisions made by Lindert and Williamson in their 1985 paper are shown to be much larger than they admitted at the time. The Phelps Brown and Hopkins view of real wages diverges significantly from overall personal consumption growth in each period (but only relates to workers in the south of England).

Although Table 4.4 offers a 'best guess' estimate for all blue-collar

17. Phelps Brown and Hopkins, 'Seven Centuries', pp. 296–314.

Table 4.4 Growth of Real Wages and Real Personal Consumption per Head (Per cent per year)

	Phelps Brown and Hopkins Real Wages	Lindert and Williamson, 1983 Real Wages	Crafts, 1985 Real Wages	'Best Guess' Real Wages	Real Personal Consumption per Head
1760–1800	−0.57	−0.15	na	−0.17	0.25
1780–1820	−0.03	0.28	0.71	0.56	0.47
1820–1850	0.92	1.92	0.94	1.27	1.24
1780–1850	0.38	1.00	0.80	0.88	0.80

Sources: Phelps Brown and Hopkins (1956), Lindert and Williamson 'all blue-collar' (1983, Table 5) using 1755–1800 for the first period, Crafts (1985b, Table 4). 'Best Guess' is again for Lindert and Williamson's 'all blue-collar' group of workers and uses the 'Best Guess' Cost of Living Index of Table 3 above. Real personal consumption is from Crafts (1985a, Table 5.2).

real-wage growth in the years 1750–1850, it must be emphasised both that there was substantial variation in the experience of subsets of this group and that future research may well alter these conclusions through the provision of improved data. Indeed, although I have presented point estimates, it should be clear from my earlier discussion that the margins for error of any particular year's real wage figure are at least plus or minus 10 per cent.

A Review of Two Recent Papers on Real Wages in the Industrial Revolution

To supplement Gilboy's earlier work, Schwarz (1985) provides new data on money wages for London builders' craftsmen and labourers based on builders' bills in the Middlesex Sessions Papers for 1787–1820.[18] This represents a useful improvement on the data used by Phelps Brown and Hopkins for the further investigation of living standards in the period prior to 1820 on which Lindert and Williamson advised pessimists to concentrate.[19] Schwarz's calculations of real wages are based on the original Phelps Brown and Hopkins cost of living index and also, for the period after 1780, the 1983 Lindert and Williamson index. He finds an 'enormous fall in real wage rates during the second half of the eighteenth century: over three-quarters of this fall takes place before 1790' and concludes that 'While the "industrial revolution" can hardly be ignored, the question of its direct (and even indirect) impact on living standards in London — and perhaps on much of

18. Schwarz, 'The Standard of Living', pp. 24–41.
19. Lindert and Williamson, 'Living Standards', p. 24.

Table 4.5 Real Wages of Southern Building Craftsmen, 1750–1850

	Schwarz 1985	Schwarz Money Wages deflated using 'Best Guess'	Phelps Brown and Hopkins	Phelps Brown and Hopkins deflated using 'Best Guess'
1750	101.8	68.1	83.3	55.6
1760	91.9	63.4	74.9	51.8
1770	79.0	54.2	64.5	44.3
1780	78.6	55.4	77.3	54.6
1790	69.7	54.5	68.3	53.8
1800	60.0	47.5	56.2	44.4
1810	66.9	55.7	57.6	48.1
1820	79.3	67.3	76.4	66.0
1830	84.6	75.8	82.8	74.2
1840	82.2	75.0	80.3	73.5
1850	100	100	100	100

Sources: Phelps Brown and Hopkins (1956), Schwarz (1985) based on Phelps Brown and Hopkins's cost of living index and 'Best Guess' calculations using the Cost of Living Index from Table 4.3.

the rest of England — requires both caution and scepticism'.[20]

In fact, Schwarz's findings are fairly similar to those of Phelps Brown and Hopkins, if their cost of living index is used, and can be regarded as broadly confirming their view of the development of money wages in the South of England. For the reasons discussed in the previous section, Schwarz was unwise to rely on the cost of living indices which he adopted. Use of the 'best guess' cost of living index of Table 4.3 reduces somewhat the extent of decline, but would still leave Schwarz's London craftsman in 1820 with a real-wage rate marginally below that of 1750 following notable falls between 1750 and 1770 and 1790–1800. Schwarz's work at most makes a slightly more pessimistic case for southern real wages in the years 1750–1820 than was already accepted from the work of Phelps Brown and Gilboy and subsumed in Lindert and Williamson's aggregate figures. Calculations using Schwarz's data and comparisons with Phelps Brown and Hopkins are shown in Table 4.5.

Botham and Hunt present the results of a detailed investigation of real wages in north Staffordshire. They find skilled workers in the building trades experiencing real-wage increases of 10–14 per cent between the early 1750s and the early 1790s, while potters' real wages rose by 49 per cent in the same period. Botham and Hunt's work is a useful addition to the data on real wages in the eighteenth century and is based on a new cost of living index based on local prices with weights of 40 per cent for cereals, 20 per

20. Schwarz, 'The Standard of Living', pp. 28 and 36.

Table 4.6 Real Wages of Northern Building Craftsmen, 1750–1790 (1850 = 100)

	Botham and Hunt	Botham and Hunt Money Wages Deflated using 'Best Guess'	Gilboy Money Wages Deflated using 'Best Guess'
1750	43.2	34.2	37.8
1760	36.9	30.4	35.2
1770	30.7	27.2	36.9
1780	47.6	34.8	41.0
1790	42.2	42.2	42.2

Sources: Botham (1987, Tables 5 and 7), Gilboy (1934, pp. 285–7) and spliced at 1790 to an estimate based on Bowley (1900, p. 310) deflated using 'best guess' price index of Table 4.3.

cent for animal products (including butter and cheese), 10 per cent for drinks, 10 per cent for lights, fuel and soap and 10 per cent for rent (for which a local series was obtained but no clothing for which prices were unavailable). Botham and Hunt suggest that 'by generalising London's experience to most of the country Schwarz has greviously underestimated the significance of the industrial revolution in the north and in the midlands and presented a view of eighteenth-century English wage history which is decidedly "wencentric"'.[21] They also see their results as inconsistent with the recent research that has produced lower estimates of economic growth during the Industrial Revolution and claim that 'its implication is that far more, and far better, evidence is required before the industrial revolution can be written out of student textbooks',[22] and that 'revisionism has been overdone: there is far more substance in Gilboy's work on wages and in the traditional belief in an eighteenth-century "industrial revolution" than Schwarz, Lindert, Williamson, Crafts, Fores et al. have allowed'.[23]

In fact Botham and Hunt's figures for money wages of building workers are not very different from Gilboy's data for similar workers elsewhere in the north of England in this period — though if anything her data (which were subsumed in Lindert and Williamson's aggregate) are somewhat less optimistic.[24] Botham and Hunt's cost of living index appears reasonable in the circumstances but a more optimistic result would be obtained by using the 'best guess' index of Table 4.3. These results are summarised in Table 4.6.

While Botham and Hunt's calculations of real wage growth in north Staffordshire are a useful, if modest, contribution to our knowledge about

21. Botham and Hunt, 'Wages in Britain', p. 398.
22. Ibid., p. 381.
23. Ibid., p. 398.
24. E. W. Gilboy, *Wages in Eighteenth Century England*, Cambridge, Mass., 1934.

Table 4.7 Regional Variations in Real Wage Growth (Per cent per year)

	'South' Schwarz Deflated using 'Best Guess'	'Favoured North' Botham and Hunt	Aggregate	'South' Phelps Brown and Hopkins deflated using 'Best Guess'	'Favoured North' Gilboy delfated using 'Best Guess'	Aggregate
1760–1780	–0.6	1.3	0.0	0.3	0.8	0.4
1780–1820	0.5	0.8	0.6	0.5	1.2	0.7
1820–1850	1.3	1.4	1.3	1.4	1.4	1.4

Sources: Derived using estimates of earlier tables plus the following assumptions:
1) that northern building craftsmen's money wages were 98 per cent of the 1850 level in 1820 which seems reasonable based on Wood (1899) and
2) that the 'favoured North' has a weight of 0.25 and 'South' of 0.75 in arriving at the aggregate which seems reasonable based on the discussion of regional variations in wages in Hunt (1986).

eighteenth-century living standards, their somewhat hysterical denunciation of recent work on overall economic growth is neither acceptable nor implied by their results.

My estimates of growth of overall real national product showed about 0.7 per cent per year in 1700–80, 1.3 per cent per year in 1780–1800 and 2.0 per cent per year in 1801–31 compared with the previous generally accepted Deane and Cole figures of 0.7 per cent, 2.1 per cent and 3.1 per cent per year respectively.[25] I stressed the unevenness of industrial-output growth between sectors and associated with this discrepancies in technological progress and localised gains for workers from productivity growth.[26] Indeed, uneven industrial advance is implicit in a situation of dramatic growth in a few activities coupled with modest acceleration in overall economic growth. Botham and Hunt's results are perfectly consistent with this picture and can be combined with Schwarz's data on money wages in a fashion basically yielding estimates much the same as those in Table 4.4.

Table 4.7 demonstrates this proposition. When combined using weights of 0.75 and 0.25 for 'the South' as represented by London building craftsmen and the 'favoured North' as represented by north Staffordshire building craftsmen (wages for what is widely accepted as a 'bellwether group'), growth in real wages is estimated at 0.0 per cent per year for 1760–80, 0.6 per cent for 1780–1820 and 1.3 per cent per year for 1820–50 for the national

25. Crafts, *British Economic Growth*, p. 45.
26. Ibid., pp. 105–7.

aggregate. This is not very different from what would have been obtained using Phelps Brown and Hopkins and Gilboy (as also shown in the table) with the 'best guess' price index and generally in line with overall consumption patterns as shown by recent estimates of macro-economic growth.

Finally, in the light of Table 4.7 it may be interesting to consider changes in the trend rate of growth of industrial output on the basis of the best currently available series, Hoffman's index revised to eliminate the errors noted by Harley.[27] Like the real-wage series this also exhibits steady advance from 1760 to a high plateau in 1820 to 1850 (see Figure 4.1). Moreover, this estimate of the trend was obtained using Kalman-filter techniques which eliminate the need to impose periodisation artificially on the data. There really seems no reason to allow Botham and Hunt to reinstate the idea of marked discontinuities of the kind favoured by Rostow and his followers into our view of British industrialisation.

Where the work of Schwarz and Botham and Hunt is valuable is not so much in radically altering the picture obtained in the 'recent consensus' but rather in underlining the need to keep regional diversity in mind, a point I am happy to agree with and have indeed stressed in my debate with Williamson.[28]

Williamson on Inequality during the Industrial Revolution.

Williamson's claims of a surge in inequality during the Industrial Revolution — in particular between 1815 and 1871 — are based on analyses of pay ratios, i.e. ratios of the wages of skilled to those of unskilled workers, and examination of income distributions drawn from tax data and corrected 'social tables' based on the work of Gregory King, Joseph Massie, Patrick Colquhoun and Dudley Baxter. His findings contrast with those of Soltow, who claimed that 'long-run inequality did not change in the eighteenth and nineteenth centuries',[29] and of Phelps Brown: 'In Great Britain . . . down to 1914, differentials were largely ruled by custom . . . A conspicuous instance of the stability of differentials has been traced to the building trade: from about 1410 until 1914 one and the same differential between the craftsman and the labourer persisted in the South of England'.[30]

27. C. K. Harley, 'British Industrialisation before 1841: Evidence of Slower Growth during the Industrial Revolution', *Journal of Economic History*, 42, 1982, 267–89.
28. Crafts, 'Some Difficulties of Interpretation', p. 265.
29. L. Soltow, 'Long Run Changes in British Income Inequality', *Economic History Review*, 21, 1968, p. 22.
30. E. H. Phelps Brown, *The Inequality of Pay*, Oxford, 1977, p. 6.

Figure 4.1 Trend Growth in Industrial Production

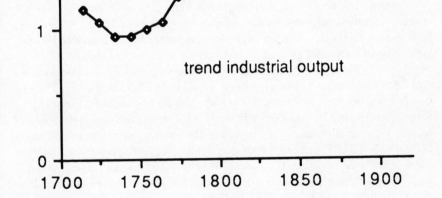

trend industrial output

Source: Crafts et al. (1987)

Williamson's evidence from rising ratios is based mainly on his use of information on salaries paid to civil servants to supplement the traditional data provided by Bowley-Wood. This would in principle lead to a more complete coverage of earnings and certainly there is a danger that views such as those of Phelps Brown have been based on too narrow a data set. Unfortunately, however, as both Feinstein and Jackson have documented at length, the evidence Williamson obtained on civil servants is fatally flawed. Jackson suggests dropping the data on doctors and lawyers where it is clear that changes over time in the composition of the sample drawn produce

Table 4.8 Pay Ratios in Britain, 1815–1911

	Williamson	Jackson	Feinstein
1815	2.56	2.26	1.74
1819	2.80	2.44	1.77
1827	3.00	2.65	1.85
1835	3.56	2.90	1.87
1851	3.64	2.73	1.92
1871	3.44	2.80	1.90
1911	2.64	2.25	1.86

Source: Based on Williamson (1985, pp. 31, 48), Jackson (1987, p. 567) and Feinstein (1988).

massive swings in nominal earnings,[31] while Feinstein argues that this problem also applies to the series for clerks, engineers and high-wage civil servants whose behaviour he shows to be inconsistent with other (admittedly incomplete) information. The impact of these suggestions on the pay-ratio calculation is reported in Table 4.8.

Feinstein also concludes that tax-assessment data does not support the surge in inequality claimed by Williamson but does not address the question of the social tables. Income tax evidence as reported by Williamson does not reflect rising inequality (as measured by the inverse of the Pareto coefficient) after 1815,[32] but in any case it is based on assessments — not individuals — and does not separate out companies, unincorporated firms or local authorities from persons. Williamson's evidence based on Inhabited House Duty is more promising but, as Feinstein shows, his treatment of this data was in serious error in particular with regard to the estimation of values of houses below £20. Thus Feinstein shows that whilst Williamson estimates a Gini coefficient based on Inhabited House Duty of 0.451 in 1830, rising to 0.627 in 1871 and falling to 0.328 in 1911, when his errors are corrected a 'best guess' estimate would be 0.607 in 1830, rising to 0.667 in 1871 and falling to 0.553 in 1911.[33]

Using the social tables Williamson estimated Gini coefficients for England and Wales of 0.468 in 1688, 0.487 in 1759, 0.519 in 1801–3, 0.551 in 1867; 0.538 in 1867 and 0.502 in 1913 for the United Kingdom. Soltow's perspective was different mainly because he found a Gini of 0.551 for 1688 and 0.555 for 1801–3.[34] These data are based generally on only a few income classes and, given that, it should be said that even Williamson's estimates

31. Jackson, 'Structure of Pay', p. 567.
32. Williamson, *Did British Capitalism Breed Inequality?*, p. 63.
33. Feinstein, 'Rise and Fall', Table 5.
34. Williamson, *Did British Capitalism Breed Inequality?*, p. 68, and Soltow, 'Long Run Changes', p. 22.

(which differ from Soltow's mainly because of revised figures for occupations resulting from Lindert's work in sampling burial registers[35]) do not rule out the possibility that any changes in inequality were very slight.

While the revised social tables are independent estimates not affected by the problems which beset Williamson's calculations of pay ratios or his use of the Inhabited House Duty data, it should be said that it is certainly possible that his estimate of the Gini coefficient for 1688 at least is too low. There are two main reasons for this: Firstly, it appears that wages in the north of England were lower than in the south in 1700 — though not in the later years[36] — and this is not allowed for in the assignment of wages by occupation. Secondly, Lindert was unable to provide standard errors for his occupational estimates, but stated that he thought the margins of error for large groups could be as large as plus or minus 50 per cent.[37] Experimental calculations suggest that allowances for these two possible sources of error could easily raise the Gini coefficient by some five percentage points in 1688.

On balance, then it would seem probable there were some small increases in inequality in the first half of the nineteenth century but not the substantial change supposed by Williamson. It is certainly important, if possible, to supplement the Bowley-Wood wage data by obtaining reliable estimates of earnings of middle-class and service-sector occupations, and it may be that such estimates would reinstate some of Williamson's claims for the pay ratio — but at the moment we still await acceptable figures.

If, as seems likely on presently available and acceptable information, the pay ratio did not rise markedly in the period 1821–61, this would be inconsistent with the predictions of the general-equilibrium model constructed by Williamson to account for the phenomenon and would thus imply that the model and/or the assumptions about exogenous variables fed into the model are incorrect. As I have indicated elsewhere there are strong doubts on both the model and the data on exogenous variables used by Williamson.[38] In brief, Williamson's model fails to allow for the fact that exportable manufactures which had a rapid productivity improvement were only a small subset of industry as a whole, or that Britain was not a 'small country' in the sense of international-trade theory and cannot therefore be

35. P. H. Lindert, 'English Occupations, 1670–1811', Journal of Economic History, 40, 1980, 685–712.
36. See, for example, Gilboy, Wages in Eighteenth Century England; and E. H. Hunt, 'Industrialisation and Regional Inequality: Wages in Britain, 1760–1914', Journal of Economic History, 46, 1986, 935–66.
37. Lindert, 'English Occupations', p. 701.
38. Crafts, 'Some Difficulties of Interpretation', pp. 248–56, 260–4, and idem, 'Cliometrics', pp. 182–4.

satisfactorily modelled as facing parametric terms of trade. Moreover, many of the forces which play an interesting role in other treatments of nineteenth-century economic history, such as induced bias in technological progress, economic influences on fertility and migration or trade union growth are excluded *a priori*.

As for exogenous variables it is important to note that Williamson assumes quite arbitrarily both the rate of skills growth and the rates of agricultural- and industrial-productivity growth. Above all, it must be stressed that Williamson's claim that for 1821–61 'There is no evidence of significant productivity advance in British agriculture until very late in this period'[39] is completely false.

Firstly, the most careful recent study of data on the prices of outputs and inputs shown by Allen shows rapid increases in total factor productivity in early nineteenth-century south Midlands agriculture coming from rising yields and, especially, from an increasing size of farms.[40] Allen's results are displayed in Figure 4.2.

Secondly, Wrigley's careful reworking of the census data[41] confirms that the agricultural labour force grew at only 0.26 per cent per year between 1811 and 1851, and this (combined with what we know about imports, land and capital inputs) implies that total factor productivity in agriculture grew at 0.8 to 1.0 per cent per year in that period.[42] Based on the impact multipliers reported by Williamson, a value of 0.8 per cent for total factor productivity growth in agriculture would give a predicted rate of growth for the pay ratio of *minus* 0.42 per cent per year in 1821–61, assuming the model and all other exogenous variables were correct.[43] This compares with Williamson's own prediction of 0.78 per cent and his estimate that the actual change was 0.97 per cent, and with Feinstein's estimate that the actual change was 0.14 per cent.

Williamson's finding of a pronounced Kuznets Curve during British industrialisation is not therefore very persuasive. Indeed, it would appear that both data collection and modelling procedures have been heavily influenced by *a priori* assumptions and that the claims of a surge in inequality resulting from inbalanced productivity growth are, as they stand, com-

---

39. Williamson, *Did British Capitalism Breed Inequality?*, p. 247.
40. R. C. Allen, *The Agricultural Development of the South Midlands, 1600–1850*, Oxford, 1988, chapter 1.
41. E. A. Wrigley, 'Men on the Land and Men in the Countryside: Employment in Agriculture in Early Nineteenth Century England', in L. Bonfield, R. M. Smith and K. Wrightson (eds), *The World We Have Gained*, Oxford, 1986, p. 332.
42. Crafts, 'Some Difficulties of Interpretation', p. 253.
43. Williamson, *Did British Capitalism Breed Inequality?*, p. 146.

Figure 4.2 Total Factor Productivity in South Midland Agriculture

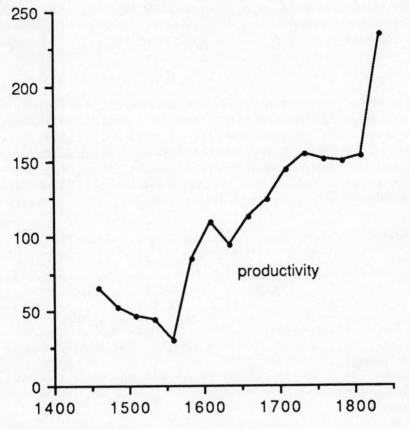

Source: Allen (1988).

pletely unsupported by reliable evidence. This need not, however, mean that there is no substance to Williamson's intuitions. Further data-gathering and a more refined model may yet produce results which are more plausible, since there certainly was unevenness in productivity growth within industry:[44] there are some signs of modest rises in inequality and, although Feinstein and Jackson have exposed the flaws in Williamson's data on skilled earnings, they failed to show there were no relative increases in high-wage service and professional earnings.

The past decade or so has been an exciting period in research on the

44. Crafts, '*Some Difficulties of Interpretation*', pp. 255, 262–3.

standard of living debate in general and on real wages and inequality in particular. What is now needed is a period of substantial effort to augment the existing database on wages and prices to see if the tentative hypotheses advanced in this paper can actually be sustained as more evidence becomes available.

Appendix 4.1

Two representative examples of budget studies for the period covered by the paper are reproduced in order to reinforce the point that the detail they embody is really quite modest. Table 4.9 is from F. M. Eden, *The State of the Poor*, London, 1797, and Table 4.10 is from W. Neild, 'Comparative Statement of the Income and Expenditure of Certain Families of the Working Classes in Manchester and Dukinfield in the Years 1836 and 1841', *Journal of the Statistical Society*, 4, 1841, pp. 330–4.

Table 4.9 Some Rural Budgets — DISS, NORFOLK, 1792 and 1794
Expences and Earnings of Four Families of Agricultural Labourers, by the Week, and by the Year.

Expences by the Week	No. 1. 4 Persons 1792.	1794.	No. 2. 6 Persons 1793.	1795.	No. 3. 7 Persons 1795.	No. 4. 8 Persons 1795.
	£. s. d.	£. s. d.	£. s. d.	£. s. d.	£. s. d.	£. s. d.
Bread, flour, or oat-meal	0 2 10	0 3 4	0 4 7½	0 8 0	0 9 4	0 10 8
Yeast and salt	0 0 1½	0 0 1½	0 0 2	0 0 2	0 0 3	0 0 4
Bacon, or other meat	0 0 0	0 0 0	0 0 3	0 0 3	0 0 2	0 0 0
Tea, sugar, and butter	0 0 5½	0 0 5¾	0 0 9¼	0 0 9½	0 1 4¾	0 1 6
Soap	0 0 1¾	0 0 2	0 0 2¼	0 0 2½	0 0 2½	0 0 4½
Candles	0 0 1¼	0 0 1¼	0 0 3	0 0 3	0 0 5	0 0 6¾
Cheese	0 0 2¾	0 0 3	0 0 5½	0 0 6	0 0 6	0 0 6
Beer	0 0 0	0 0 0	0 0 0	0 0 0	0 0 3	0 0 3
Milk	0 0 3½	0 0 3½	0 0 6	0 0 6	0 0 3½	0 1 0
Potatoes	0 0 3	0 0 3	0 0 6	0 0 6	0 0 2	0 0 6
Thread and worsted	0 0 1½	0 0 1½	0 0 2	0 0 2	0 0 2½	0 0 3
Total per Week	0 4 6	0 5 1½	0 7 10½	0 11 4	0 13 2¼	0 15 11¼
Total per Annum	11 17 3	13 6 6	20 9 6	29 9 4	34 5 9	41 8 9

Table 4.9 continued

Earnings per Week	No. 1. 4 Persons 1792.	No. 1. 4 Persons 1794.	No. 2. 6 Persons 1793.	No. 2. 6 Persons 1795.	No. 3. 7 Persons 1795.	No. 4. 8 Persons 1795.
The man	0 9 0	0 9 0	0 9 0	0 9 0	0 8 0	0 9 0
The woman	0 0 8	0 0 8	0 1 0	0 1 0	0 1 0	0 1 0
The children	0 0 0	0 0 0	0 1 6	0 1 6	0 0 3	0 3 0
Total Earnings per Week	0 9 8	0 9 8	0 11 6	0 11 6	0 9 3	0 13 0
Total Earnings per Annum	23 16 8	23 16 8	29 18 0	29 18 0	24 1 0	33 16 0
To the above amount of Expences, add Rent	2 10 0	2 10 0	3 3 0	3 3 0	3 3 0	2 12 0
Fuel	1 10 0	1 10 0	1 4 0	1 6 0	1 14 0	1 14 8
Cloaths	2 7 6	2 7 6	2 3 0	2 3 0	2 18 4	3 7 3
Births, burials, sickness	0 8 6	0 8 6	0 10 0	0 10 0	0 6 0	0 8 0
Total Expences per annum	18 13 3	20 2 6	27 9 6	36 11 4	42 7 1	49 10 8
Total Earnings per annum	23 16 8	23 16 8	29 18 0	29 18 0	24 1 0	33 16 0
Deficiency	0 0 0	0 0 0	0 0 0	6 13 4	18 6 1	15 14 8
Exceedings	4 3 5	3 14 2	2 8 6	0 0 0	0 0 0	0 0 0

No. 1. Man 33, woman 30; eldest child 3, youngest 1; man industrious; woman frugal; they use neither meat, sugar, nor beer. It now costs this family 1s. 2d. a-week more for barley, than it did in 1794 for wheaten, meal. No. 2. Man 38; woman 34; children, 10, 7, 5, and 2 years. Man works often by the piece; gets a good deal of firing in the course of his employment. Keeps a breeding sow; the profits of which help a little towards family expences. The parish allows this family 2s. a-week. They appear to be growing very poor. No. 3. Man 40, woman 28; he is a moderate workman; the woman, though healthy, not very diligent or attentive to her children. The ages of the children are 9, 7, 5, 3 and 1. This family is allowed 2s. a-week from the parish. No. 4. Man 42, woman 33; children 11, 9, 7, 5, 3, 2 and 1. He is a good workman. The parish allows this family 3s. a-week. The 1st, 3d and 4th families now live on barley bread; the 2d family on rye and wheat. The difference between the use of barley and wheat, to the two last families, is nearly 2s. per week. They did not adopt the use of barley during the scarcity of last year, which accounts in some degree for the great deficiency of those two large families. One Friendly Society in this parish — badly managed. Constant employment in the winter.

January, 1796.

Table 4.10(a) Some Urban Budgets, Dukinfield, 1836 and 1841
Average Income and House Expenditure for one week of Seven Families in Dukinfield.

15. Labourer; Family, 6 individuals.

	1836 (£ s. d.)	1841 (£ s. d.)
Income for each Individual per week	0 4 8	0 3 1½
Total Income of the Family	1 8 0	0 18 8
Total Expenditure of ditto	1 0 11½	1 4 3

Articles.	Weekly Expenditure of the Family. 1836	1841	Weekly Expenditure for each Individual. 1836	1841	Per Centage of Expenditure on the Total Income. 1836	1841
	£ s. d.	£ s. d.	£ s. d.	£ s. d.		
Rent	0 3 5	0 2 9	0 0 7	0 0 5	12.2	14.7
Flour or Bread	0 4 8	0 6 0	0 0 9¼	0 1 0	16.6	32.1
Meat	0 2 0	0 3 2	0 0 4	0 0 6½	7.1	16.9
Bacon	..	..	..	..	..	..
Nursing, Cooking, &c.	..	..	..	..	..	..

16. Card Room Hand; Family, 3 individuals.

	1836 (£ s. d.)	1841 (£ s. d.)
Income for each Individual per week	0 3 0	0 2 10½
Total Income of the Family	0 13 0	0 8 8
Total Expenditure of ditto	0 9 9	0 11 4

Articles.	Weekly Expenditure of the Family. 1836	1841	Weekly Expenditure for each Individual. 1836	1841	Per Centage of Expenditure on the Total Income. 1836	1841
	£ s. d.	£ s. d.	£ s. d.	£ s. d.		
Rent	0 1 7	0 1 3	0 0 6¼	0 0 5	12.2	14.4
Flour or Bread	0 2 3	0 2 11	0 0 9	0 0 11¾	17.3	33.6
Meat	0 0 9½	0 1 3	0 0 3¾	0 0 5	6.1	14.4
Bacon	0 0 3	0 0 4	0 0 1	0 0 1¼	2.	3.8
Nursing, Cooking, &c.	..	..	..	..	..	..

Oatmeal	0 0 7½	0 0 10	0 0 1¼	0 0 1¾	2.2	4.6	..	..	..	..	..	..
Butter	0 1 6	0 2 0	0 0 3	0 0 4	5.3	10.7	0 0 9	0 1 0	0 0 3	0 0 4	5.8	11.4
Eggs	0 0 6	0 0 6	0 0 1	0 0 1	1.8	2.6	..	..	..	..	..	..
Milk	0 1 6	0 1 6	0 0 3	0 0 3	5.3	8.1	0 0 8	0 0 8	0 0 2¾	0 0 2¾	5.1	7.7
Potatoes	0 1 0	0 1 6	0 0 2	0 0 3	3.6	8.1	0 0 4	0 0 6	0 0 1¼	0 0 2	2.5	5.8
Cheese	0 1 0	0 1 0	0 0 2	0 0 2	3.6	5.3	..	..	..	..	..	..
Tea	0 0 6	0 0 5	0 0 1	0 0 1	1.8	2.3	0 0 5	0 0 4½	0 0 1¾	0 0 1½	3.2	4.3
Coffee	0 0 3	0 0 3	0 0 0½	0 0 0½	.9	1.3	0 0 4½	0 0 4½	0 0 1½	0 0 1½	2.9	4.3
Sugar	0 0 9	0 1 0	0 0 1½	0 0 2	2.7	5.3	0 0 9	0 1 0	0 0 3	0 0 4	5.8	11.4
Treacle	0 0 2	0 0 3	0 0 0¼	0 0 0½	.5	1.3	0 0 2	0 0 3	0 0 0¾	0 0 1	1.2	2.9
Tobacco	0 0 6	0 0 6	0 0 1	0 0 1	1.8	2.6	..	..	..	..	..	..
Soap	0 0 9	0 0 9	0 0 1½	0 0 1½	2.7	4.	0 0 6	0 0 6	0 0 2	0 0 2	3.8	5.8
Candles	0 0 3	0 0 3	0 0 0½	0 0 0½	.9	1.3	0 0 1½	0 0 1½	0 0 0½	0 0 0½	1.	1.4
Salt	0 0 1	0 0 1	..	..	.3	.4	0 0 0½	0 0 0½	..	..	.3	.4
Coals	0 1 2	0 1 2	0 0 2½	0 0 2½	4.2	6.2	0 0 6	0 0 6	0 0 2	0 0 2	3.8	5.8
Yeast	0 0 4	0 0 4	0 0 0½	0 0 0½	1.2	1.8	0 0 3	0 0 3	0 0 1	0 0 1	2.	2.9
Total	1 0 11½	1 4 3	0 3 6	0 4 0½	74.7	129.6	0 9 9	0 11 4	0 3 3	0 3 9¼	75.	130.3

Table 4.10(b) Some Urban Budgets, Dukinfield, 1836 and 1841

Average Income and House Expenditure for one week of Seven Families in Dukinfield — continued.

17. Spinner; Family, 5 individuals.

	1836	1841
	£ s. d.	£ s. d.
Income for each Individual per week	0 3 10	0 2 10
Total Income of the Family	1 1 6	0 14 4
Total Expenditure of ditto	0 16 10	0 19 2

Articles.	Weekly Expenditure of the Family.		Weekly Expenditure for each Individual.		Per Centage of Expenditure on the Total Income.	
	1836	1841	1836	1841	1836	1841
	£ s. d.	£ s. d.	£ s. d.	£ s. d.		
Rent	0 3 6½	0 2 10	0 0 8½	0 0 7	16.5	19.8
Flour or Bread	0 3 6	0 4 6	0 0 8½	0 0 9¼	16.3	31.4
Meat	0 1 1	0 1 9	0 0 2½	0 0 4	5.	12.2
Bacon	0 0 5½	0 0 8	0 0 1	0 0 1¾	2.1	4.6
Nursing, Cooking, &c.	..	..	..	..	..	..

18. Warehouseman; Family, 4 individuals.

	1836	1841
	£ s. d.	£ s. d.
Income for each Individual per week	0 3 7½	0 2 8
Total Income of the Family	0 16 0	0 10 8
Total Expenditure of ditto	0 12 9	0 14 6

Articles.	Weekly Expenditure of the Family.		Weekly Expenditure for each Individual.		Per Centage of Expenditure on the Total Income.	
	1836	1841	1836	1841	1836	1841
	£ s. d.	£ s. d.	£ s. d.	£ s. d.		
Rent	0 2 6	0 2 0	0 0 7½	0 0 6	15.6	18.7
Flour or Bread	0 2 9	0 3 6	0 0 8¼	0 0 10½	17.2	32.8
Meat	0 0 9½	0 1 3	0 0 2½	0 0 3¾	5.	11.7
Bacon	0 0 5½	0 0 8	0 0 1½	0 0 2	3.	6.2
Nursing, Cooking, &c.	..	..	..	..	..	..

Oatmeal	0 0 4	0 0 5	0 0 $0\frac{3}{4}$	0 0 1	1.5	2.9	0 0 4	0 0 5	0 0 1	0 0 $1\frac{1}{4}$	2.	3.9
Butter	0 1 $1\frac{1}{2}$	0 1 6	0 0 $2\frac{3}{4}$	0 0 $3\frac{3}{4}$	5.2	10.5	0 0 9	0 1 0	0 0 $2\frac{1}{4}$	0 0 3	4.7	9.4
Eggs	..	..	..	..	..	..	..	..	..	..	..	..
Milk	0 1 4	0 1 4	0 0 $3\frac{1}{4}$	0 0 $3\frac{1}{4}$	6.2	9.3	0 0 $10\frac{1}{2}$	0 0 $10\frac{1}{2}$	0 0 $2\frac{1}{2}$	0 0 $2\frac{1}{2}$	5.4	8.2
Potatoes	0 0 6	0 0 9	0 0 $1\frac{1}{4}$	0 0 2	2.3	5.2	0 0 7	0 0 10	0 0 $1\frac{3}{4}$	0 0 $2\frac{1}{2}$	3.6	7.8
Cheese	..	..	..	..	..	..	..	..	..	..	..	..
Tea	0 0 $8\frac{1}{2}$	0 0 $7\frac{1}{2}$	0 0 $1\frac{3}{4}$	0 0 $1\frac{1}{2}$	3.3	4.3	0 0 6	0 0 5	0 0 $1\frac{1}{2}$	0 0 $1\frac{1}{4}$	3.1	3.9
Coffee	0 0 $4\frac{1}{2}$	0 0 $4\frac{1}{2}$	0 0 1	0 0 1	1.7	2.6	0 0 $4\frac{1}{2}$	0 0 $4\frac{1}{2}$	0 0 1	0 0 1	2.4	3.4
Sugar	0 0 $10\frac{1}{2}$	0 1 4	0 0 2	0 0 $3\frac{1}{4}$	4.	9.3	0 0 9	0 1 0	0 0 $2\frac{1}{4}$	0 0 3	4.7	9.4
Treacle	0 0 2	0 0 3	0 0 $0\frac{1}{2}$	0 0 $0\frac{3}{4}$	.8	1.8	0 0 2	0 0 3	0 0 $0\frac{1}{2}$	0 0 $0\frac{3}{4}$	1.	2.4
Tobacco	0 0 3	0 0 3	0 0 $0\frac{3}{4}$	0 0 $0\frac{3}{4}$	1.2	1.8	..	..	..	..	..	..
Soap	0 0 9	0 0 9	0 0 2	0 0 2	3.5	5.2	0 0 6	0 0 6	0 0 $1\frac{1}{2}$	0 0 $1\frac{1}{2}$	3.1	4.7
Candles	0 0 3	0 0 3	0 0 $0\frac{3}{4}$	0 0 $0\frac{3}{4}$	1.2	1.8	0 0 $1\frac{1}{2}$	0 0 $1\frac{1}{2}$	0 0 $0\frac{1}{2}$	0 0 $0\frac{1}{2}$	1.	1.1
Salt	0 0 1	0 0 1	0 0 $0\frac{1}{4}$	0 0 $0\frac{1}{4}$	.4	.6	0 0 $0\frac{1}{2}$	0 0 $0\frac{1}{2}$	..	..	.2	.4
Coals	0 1 3	0 1 3	0 0 3	0 0 3	5.8	8.7	0 1 0	0 1 0	0 0 3	0 0 3	6.2	9.4
Yeast	0 0 3	0 0 3	0 0 $0\frac{3}{4}$	0 0 $0\frac{3}{4}$	1.2	1.8	0 0 3	0 0 3	0 0 $0\frac{3}{4}$	0 0 $0\frac{3}{4}$	1.1	2.4
Total	0 16 10	0 19 2	0 3 5	0 3 10	78.2	133.8	0 12 9	0 14 6	0 3 $2\frac{1}{4}$	0 3 $7\frac{1}{4}$	79.3	135.8

D. MORSA

4.1 Is It Justified to Use Real Wages as a Standard of Living Index?

Professor Crafts's report shows the extraordinary productivity of British historians on the subject of real wages.[1] British scholars' interest in wages is probably not accidental since the British Isles were, as Peter Mathias puts it, the first industrial nation. The problem of wages is at the core of a debate with considerable implications.

However, Crafts remarks that we are far from reaching a consensus on the fluctuations of real wages in Great Britain for the years 1750–1850. The diverging results of recent studies are largely due to the indices chosen to express the cost of living. In this respect, one should mention the perspicacity of British researchers who, since E. H. Phelps Brown and S. Hopkins, have understood that plausible measures of real wages were only possible if nominal wages were related to weighted and composite cost of living indices. This rigorous approach contrasts strongly with the general attitude of French and Belgian historians who often — and wrongly — prefer an easier solution and merely deflate nominal wages by the price of an indispensable cereal or convert these wages in a weight of precious metal. These oversimplifying methods have not permitted much progress, and it is to be regretted that some historians still pursue this type of approach.

Crafts suggests that the construction of a relevant weighted cost of living index raises problems that have as yet not been solved. Of course, it is always possible to construct a weighted index for a given date on the basis of the budgets of a few average people. But historians are interested in change over time and know that the choice of a fixed basket of goods is open to criticism. In this respect, the increasing use of sugar in eighteenth-century England or the introduction of potatoes has a considerable impact.

1. The only objective of this short paper is to comment on Professor Crafts's contribution. This is why the notes which might have been redundant with the references quoted in this volume are reduced to a minimum. For explicit details see our article 'Salaire et salariat dans les économies préindustrielles (XVIe–XVIIIe siècle): quelques considérations critiques', *Revue belge de philologie et d'histoire*, LXV, 1987, 4, 751–94.

There is also the matter of custom, as a perceptive observer like Adam Smith realised:

> By necessaries, I understand not only the commodities which are indispensably necessary for the support of life but whatever the custom of the country renders it indecent for creditable people, even the lowest order, to be without. A linen shirt, for example, is strictly speaking not a necessity of life. The Greeks and Romans lived, I suppose, very comfortably though they had not linen. But in the present time . . . a creditable day-labourer would be ashamed to appear in public without a linen shirt, the want of which would be supposed to denote that disgraceful state of poverty.[2]

Consumption patterns chosen as the basis of the 'basket of commodities' are apt to undergo radical changes. Indeed, items of consumption are always interchangeable. Half a century ago, E. Labrousse observed that cyclical food shortages induced working classes to eat rye instead of wheat. But, at the same time, the fall of industrial prices enabled persons with sufficient income to increase their consumption of industrial or processed goods like cotton clothes. Last but not least, consumption models depend on income and personal characteristics. A young grown-up does not belong to the same category as an old man; consumption in rural areas is different from the prevailing habits in towns.

Even if the problems of constructing a cost of living index were solved, we would have to answer other questions; we would have the denominator of the fraction but not the numerator. What about the wages to be related to the cost of living index? Unfortunately, there is no satisfactory solution. Wages vary considerably according to regions and types of activities. Two approaches are possible:

a) The first is to use the wages paid for a given activity in a particular region, which are considered as representative of labour as a whole. Historians usually take the wages of building workers. But these salaries depend on specific economic circumstances described in numerous studies. The building trade represents a relatively low percentage of the active population in pre-industrial economic systems, when the textile sector employed the greater part of the proletariat.

b) Alternatively, information relating to several categories of labour may be combined to obtain an average figure for the whole active population. But the result has all the drawbacks of aggregates. In particular, a rise of average wages does not mean that all workers had better wages, although it probably does indicate that the workers who earned more money during

---

2. A. Smith, *An Inquiry into the Nature and Causes of the Wealth of Nations*, London, 1776, quoted in A. B. Atkinson, *The Economics of Inequality*, 2nd edition, London, 1983, p. 227.

the period studied outnumbered those whose financial situation deterio-
rated.

But there is a more fundamental question: is it justified to use real wages
as a standard of living index? Historians mostly use daily wages, although
workers were usually paid by the piece. Moreover, daily wages are not
relevant to the worker's or the family's income because they do not reflect
the number of active persons in a family or the rate of unemployment. In
fact, pre-industrial economic systems were characterised by a structural
underemployment (or hidden unemployment) in rural areas and losses of
jobs in towns on the occasion of wheat crises. Although mechanisation
created jobs, it probably intensified technological unemployment as some
crafts (like manual weaving) disappeared, and it accentuated cyclical unemployment because of frequent industrial crises. This is why the wage rate is
not very meaningful when one does not know the rate of unemployment.
One should always bear in mind that a daily wage rate is but a theoretical
index. Too few scholars try to discover the actual number of working days
of the workers whose salary they investigate. It is to be regretted that recent
British researchers reviewed and discussed by Crafts show hardly any
progress in this respect. Unfortunately, until the problem of the number of
days of inactivity is solved, our hypotheses concerning the level of the
wages will remain far from accurate.

Similarly, it is not advisable to use real wages while ignoring the impact
of taxes. Regional differences in taxation were considerable under the old
economic regime. In addition to state taxes, wage-earners had to pay local
taxes and sometimes taxes related to the handicraft. It is therefore impossible, without information on taxation, to say that wages paid in one
particular region or economic sector can be compared more or less favourably with others.

Researchers also have to be extremely cautious when studying proto-
industrialised regions. They should always remember that proto-industrial
workers at home did not receive wages in the strict sense of the term, for
they bought raw material from a merchant-manufacturer to whom they
subsequently sold processed goods. Moreover, the wages of proto-
industrial workers outside agriculture were merely a secondary income.
Besides, in every society — including pre-industrial communities and
society at the onset of the industrial revolution — there is always a group of
individuals who preferred inactivity (we would use the word leisure nowadays) to remunerated work. In the past, this phenomenon was most
obvious in areas where charitable institutions were well developed and
generous. Of course, the meaning of real wages is not the same for all
persons at work in the labour market. For workers, real wages represent the
quantity of goods they can buy with their nominal remuneration; for the

entrepreneurs, real wages (i.e. the real-labour cost) depend on the relation between their products and the nominal wage. Consequently, workers and entrepreneurs have a radically different interpretation of real wages.

Those are my reflections (not excessively systematised) on Crafts's stimulating survey. I have concentrated on the first part of his paper because I am convinced that it is impossible to tackle the questions of income inequality, and to solve the problem of the relative or absolute impoverishment of labour, without having reliable data. I have the impression — but it might be a wrong one — that recent research in Britain does not offer sufficient grounds for confidence in this respect. My conclusion is similar to Crafts's: we have to go on augmenting our database. Moreover, we should try to remain modest and collect as much data as possible in a restricted geographic area instead of elaborating macro-economic evaluations which will be refuted as soon as they are formulated. Historical demography indicates a method: the 'family card'. One should draw up a family-wages card mentioning the income of all the members of the families observed, the days of inactivity, the gifts (in money or in kind) from charitable institutions. This would enable us to study the yearly income of families, which is a much more significant variable than the individual daily salary. Once the sample is constituted it will be possible to extrapolate the results to a wider field.

I should also like to consider briefly a point which gives me the opportunity to discuss the second part of Crafts's paper. Strictly speaking, wages and income scarcely explain anything! One should devote special attention to several indicators which in some way measure the standard of living, such as death rates that would be reduced when income rose. A richer — or less poor — society protects itself more easily against malnutrition, acquires a greater number of medical facilities, and finances more public services connected with health (water supply, hospitals, town planning, cleansing works).

A reflection on the living standard should also be linked with a study of housing and food. Besides, the analysis of the income of a family is related to the issue of the participation of women and children in remunerated work. An increase in the population of women in paid work may, as L. Tilly and J. Scott have suggested, be due to a fall of family income *per capita* or, on the contrary, can be seen as an emancipation of women who find it less difficult to become integrated in the labour market.[3] Similarly, I would observe that studies based on the distribution of wealth, the Gini concentration curves or pay-ratios cannot measure the mobility of generations, nor understand the social mobility of some groups or persons.

3. L. A. Tilly, J. W. Scott, *Women, Work and Family*, New York, 1978.

The available real wage rates are still far from being completely reliable. But a preliminary question might be necessary: what would be the use of such real wages and what do they mean in the field of economic and social history?

J. LUCASSEN

4.2 The Standard of Living Debate and Social History: A Comment*

In his *The Economics of the Industrial Revolution*, published only four years ago, Joel Mokyr stressed the great leap forward made in the study of the Industrial Revolution — including the standard of living debate — mainly thanks to econometrists adhering to the New Economic History.[1] Professor Crafts offers a firm proof of this statement in his paper. As he puts it himself, 'Such has been the volume of literature that even the masterly surveys of the standard of living debate as those of Flinn and Taylor are now seriously out of date'.[2] I do hope for our students that Mokyr is not seriously out of date in the meantime. This is the kind of accumulation of knowledge which historians do not very often see. Besides, these results stem from a very lively debate.[3]

Among others, Lindert and Williamson, Schwarz, Botham and Hunt and most of all Crafts, have at last reached a stage at which we possess the general national basic data on wages and prices needed for a real standard of living debate on eighteenth- and nineteenth-century Britain.[4] Let us first

---

* In this short comment I shall restrict references only to recent debates on the British standard of living.
1. J. Mokyr (ed.), *The Economics of the Industrial Revolution*, London, 1985.
2. Whereas P. H. Lindert and J. G. Williamson, 'English Workers' Living Standards during the Industrial Revolution: A New Look', *Economic History Review*, 36, 1983, 1–25, still could recommend A. J. Taylor (ed.), *The Standard of Living in Britain in the Industrial Revolution*, London, 1975; and M. W. Flinn, 'Trends in Real Wages, 1750–1850', *Economic History Review*, 27, 1974.
3. E.g. Lindert and Williamson, 'A New Look'; commented upon by Flinn, 'English Workers' Living Standards during the Industrial Revolution: a Comment', *Economic History Review*, 37, 1984, 88–92; and N. F. R. Crafts, 'English Workers' Real Wages during the Industrial Revolution: Some Remaining Problems', *Journal of Economic History*, 45, 1985, 139–44. This was followed by Lindert and Williamson, 'Reply to Michael Flinn', *Economic History Review*, 37, 1984, 93–4; and, idem, 'English Workers' Real Wages: Reply to Crafts', *Journal of Economic History*, 45, 1985, 145–53; and is commented upon again by Crafts in this volume.
4. Although discussion about the content of the different baskets of goods is still open, at last the 'Silberling man' of Ashton now touches strong drink and pays

Figure 4.3 Real Wages Using 'Best Guess' Methods

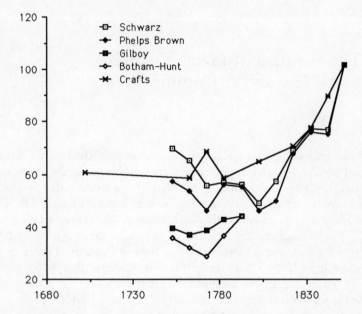

Legend:
- ⊟ Schwarz
- ◆ Phelps Brown
- ■ Gilboy
- ◇ Botham-Hunt
- ✳ Crafts

Sources: Table 4.3 for the 'South' according to Schwarz. Table 4.5 for Phelps Brown and for the 'North' according to Gilboy, and Table 4.6 for Botham and Hunt. Real Per Capita Consumption according to Crafts *British Economic Growth during the Industrial Revolution*, Oxford, 1985, p. 95, Table 5.2 (no data for 1790 and 1810.)

consider the compilation of recent research as presented by Crafts in his paper and given here as a graph (Figure 4.3). Although the evidence is limited to averages per decade and provides no detail for shorter periods, it is clear that in the long run the standard of living did not see much improvement, perhaps none at all between 1750 and Waterloo. Afterwards, an overall increase is undeniable. Of course, if we look at the evidence per decade, a more complicated picture is shown with a diminishing standard in the 1750s and, most probably, even in the 1760s, again in the 1790s and, to a lesser degree, in the 1830s. In the second place, the graph in Figure 4.3 gives an indication of income inequality, defined as the ratio between per capita income of all inhabitants and that of wage labourers. Again, the 1750s, 1760s and 1830s show a surge in inequality.[5]

---

his rent. Cf. Ashton in F. W. Botham and E. H. Hunt, 'Wages in Britain during the Industrial Revolution', *Economic History Review*, 40, 1987, p. 385.

5. In my view, pay ratios in Table 4.8 of Crafts's paper do not contribute as much

These are the main results. Here I come to a difficult point in my comment. As may be concluded already from Mokyr, the standard of living debate has shifted in the last decade from — roughly speaking — social historians to economic historians. It may be underlined in this respect that most contributions to the discussion have been published by the *Journal of Economic History* and by the *Economic History Review*. As a rank-and-file social historian, I therefore do not feel qualified to comment on the value of separate price and wage series. So unfortunately I cannot do justice to the efforts of Crafts and his colleagues in this field. The only thing I will do here is to make some remarks on the consequences of the above-mentioned results for social history.

Firstly, what do the real wages of Figure 4.3 really have to say? There are many reasons to believe that many aspects of expenditure and income do not receive due attention in this kind of approach. I will dwell only briefly on the expenditure side. Expenditures in this kind of analysis rely exclus- ively upon purchasing at the market place and in the shop. Consequently, wage labourers living in the countryside, with a garden or even a plot of their own, keeping a sow, a goat, chickens and so on, may have been better off in periods of price surges than may be seen from this graph. Of course, this applies more to the eighteenth-century countryside than to nineteenth- century cities, but still it does have relevance.[6]

I think more has to be said about the income side. As Crafts puts it clearly, 'real-wage rates' are not equal to 'real earnings'.[7] Besides, human beings do not produce and consume as individuals but as households. From both statements may follow optimistic as well as pessimistic corrections. Let us start with some optimistic corrections:

Many a proletarian family did have — or even was obliged to have — sources of income supplementary to its industrial money-wage income. To mention a few: seasonal work, e.g. the famous hop-picking, Benson's penny capitalism, Schwarz's 'perquisites', the 'chips' on the London ship- yards and the 'earnest' in Staffordshire potteries.[8]

---

to the problem of social and political consequences of income inequality as they both concern wage labour. And neither do the estimated Gini coefficients for England and Wales in 1688, 1795, 1801 to 1803, 1867 and 1913, as they cover periods of half a century or more and therefore do not give sufficient detail.

6. Cf. G. Malmgreen, *Silk Town: Industry and Culture in Macclesfield 1750–1835*, Hull, 1985, especially pp. 73–5.
7. Crafts, 'Some Remaining Problems', p. 144; cf. also Botham and Hunt, 'Wages in Britain', the conclusion.
8. J. Lucassen, *Migrant Labour in Europe 1600–1900: The Drift to the North Sea*, London, 1987; J. Benson, *The Penny Capitalists: A Study of Nineteenth-century Working-class Entrepreneurs*, Dublin, 1983; L. D. Schwarz (Chapter 2 in this

Table 4.11 Nominal Wages of Different Groups of British Bricklayers and Carpenters, 1843–1860, in Shillings (pennies in decimals)

	1843	1846	1849	1851	1855	1857	1860
Bricklayers: London daily rates	5.00	5.00	5.00	5.00	5.50	5.50	5.50
Navvies average weekly wage	21.0	30.0**	24.0	21.0	25.5	22.5	22.5
Cost of labour per cubic yard of brickwork	2.25	3.75	2.75	2.50	2.50	2.50	2.33
Carpenters: London daily rates	5.00	5.00	5.00	5.00	5.50	5.50	5.50
Navvies* average weekly wages	21.0	30.0**	24.0	21.0	25.5	22.5	22.5

* carpenters and blacksmiths.
**plus beer
Sources: London: Schwarz, 1985, p. 38; Navvies: Coleman, 1968, p. 67.

But it is probable that more income corrections of a pessimistic kind have to be made, the most important of which are, of course, due to unemployment. We do not have much systematic information on this point.[9] If we return to Figure 4.3, we may discern periods of massive unemployment, not only in decades in which real wages are already falling (e.g. the 1790s) but also in decades showing an overall improvement in the standard of living, e.g. the years around 1815, the 1820s and the early 1840s.[10]

Corrections — in themselves neither optimistic nor pessimistic, but nevertheless corrections — have to be made in connection with the way wages were paid. Wages were paid per hour or per day — in short, by time-unit or for piecework. Here it must be stressed that nearly all wages discussed in the standard of living debate are time-wages. However, time-wages may not have been the rule. Crudely speaking, maybe only people (workers cooperating with employers) able to influence the labour market could afford themselves this luxury: mainly craftsmen in cities, controlling

volume); Botham and Hunt, 'Wages in Britain'. Cf. also M. Huberman, 'Invisible Handshakes in Lancashire: Cotton Spinning in the First Half of the Nineteenth Century', *Journal of Economic History*, 46, 1986, 987–98, for employers' policies in Lancashire cotton spinning; and G. R. Boyer, 'The Poor Law, Migration and Economic Growth', *Journal of Economic History*, 46, 1986, 419–30, for a new interpretation of the Poor Law.

9. The only systematic effort, although very rough, in Lindert and Williamson, 'A New Look', (last table).
10. L. D. Schwarz, 'The Standard of Living in the Long Run: London, 1700–1860', *Economic History Review*, 38, 1985, p. 32; Crafts, 'Some Remaining Problems', p. 144; and R. A. Leeson, *Travelling Brothers: The Six Centuries' Road from Craft Fellowship to Trade Unionism*, London, 1979, pp. 171–82.

their own segment in the local labour market. However, many — maybe the majority of money-wage labourers — were paid for piecework, like spinners and weavers, navvies, fishermen and brickmakers. Many also were subcontractors or, being dependent on those people, subcontracting others in their turn. Wages did fluctuate much more for these labourers than they did for craftsmen in the cities (see Table 4.11).

How did these people meet price fluctuations? Many strategies are known to have been applied. Handloom weavers worked more and more hours, as did the Staffordshire potters.[11] Dutch navvies and peatworkers made a tougher stand in wage negotiations.[12] Tramping could change in intensity as could female participation in the labour market.[13] It should be clear that many possibilities were available. What the historian needs is a framework which encompasses at least three elements: the way wages were paid, the organisation of labour and the availability of other flexible survival strategies. To sum up: 'real wages', as presented in many studies and condensed in Figure 4.3, were not earned by many labourers. This does not mean that we have to start again from scratch. The only conclusion I want to draw is that labour market studies ought to move to the centre of the standard of living debate.

Secondly, there is another reason why the labourer, as represented in Figure 4.3, does not exist. This argument is not new, as is shown, e.g. in Crafts's paper. I mean the call for diversification as regards regions and separate labour markets, or, as Ashton already put it in 1954, 'we require not a single index, but many . . . each relating to a single area, perhaps even to a single social or occupational group'.[14] Recently, Hunt has done important work in this field.[15] However, this diversification is not always as necessary as it seems to be. Especially in periods of price surges (as in the 1790s) and in periods of massive unemployment (both in the 1790s and in the 1840s), nationwide deterioration may affect such a great part of the labour force that industrial disputes will arise, which are serious enough to cause political problems. This may be exemplified by the 1790s, as is shown by Dobson's rough statistics of labour disputes, by the Combination Acts of 1799–1800 and also by the Reform and Chartist movements in the 1830s

11. Botham and Hunt, 'Wages in Britain', pp. 396–7.
12. E.g. A. Geelhoed, 'Spades are Trumps. Strikes of Navvies at the Construction of the Utrecht-Arnhem Railway, 1840–1843', L. Heerma van Voss and H. Diederiks (eds), Industrial Conflict: Papers Presented to the Fourth British–Dutch Conference on Labour History, Amsterdam, 1988, pp. 147–64.
13. Leeson, 'Travelling Brothers'.
14. As quoted in Botham and Hunt, 'Wages in Britain', p. 385.
15. E. H. Hunt, 'Industrialization and Regional Inequality: Wages in Britain, 1760–1914', Journal of Economic History, 46, 1986, 935–61.

and 1840s.[16]

Thirdly and last, as the events of, for example, the 1790s have already shown, what matters most when looking for the missing links between social history and economic history, is the length of the periods analysed. Decades say more about the problems wage-earners faced than do periods of half a century, and years say more than decades. Labourers had to find a reply on the short term, either individually or collectively; they had to find an economic, a social or a political answer — or all at the same time. After all, in the long run all of us can easily afford to be optimistic in the standard of living debate. What matters for social history in this case is also the short run. It may be clear: my priorities for research would be different from those pointed out by Crafts. I would not stress the need to 'augment the existing database on wages and prices'. For in my opinion the study of the labour market should be given priority, both for economic and social historians[17].

16. C. R. Dobson, *Masters and Journeymen. A Prehistory of Industrial Relations 1717-1800*, London, 1980, of course only gives the tip of the iceberg, but still mentions seventy-six disputes between 1790 and 1795, as compared with thirty-one between 1785 and 1789.

17. Cf. the discussion between J. G. Williamson, 'The Impact of the Irish on British Labor Markets during the Industrial Revolution', *Journal of Economic History*, 46, 1986, 693–720; and R. V. Jackson, 'The Structure of Pay in Nineteenth-century Britain', *Economic History Review*, 40, 1987, 561–70.

V. ZAMAGNI

5. An International Comparison of Real Industrial Wages, 1890–1913: Methodological Issues and Results

After many years of intermittent work on the wages of various categories of workers in Italy,[1] I tried in my last essay[2] to set up an international comparison. This attempt raised innumerable methodological problems. I then became interested in finding out whether it would be possible to improve upon such comparisons, and in examining the interpretative relevance such comparisons might have especially in terms of illustrating the development path of the European economies in the nineteenth century. I therefore extended my research mainly along methodological lines, around the following three questions which are the subject of this paper:

I.   The construction of wage series by country
II. The measurement of industrial workers' living standards
III. Wages and productivity

The issues involved are many and complex; most of the conclusions reached can only be provisional. This is due partly to theoretically unresolved controversies and partly to wild empirical discrepancies. As far as both of these problems are concerned, I am absolutely convinced that, if we are going to make a real leap forward, the only truly viable solution is an international research project that would fill in existing gaps using common methods. The remarks offered in the following pages could form the basis for the agenda of such an international project. Some of them, however, are generally relevant for inter-country comparisons of per capita income and welfare estimates.

1. 'La dinamica dei salari nel settore industriale', in P. Ciocca and G. Toniolo (eds), *L'economia italiana nel periodo fascista*, Bologna, 1976; 'Distribuzione del reddito e classi sociali fra le due guerre', *Annali*, Feltrinelli, XX, 1980; 'Le alterazioni nella distribuzione del reddito in Italia nell'immediato dopoguerra (1919–1922)', in P. Hertner and G. Mori (eds), *La transizione dall'economia di guerra all'economia di pace in Italia ed in Germania dopo la prima guerra mondiale*, Bologna, 1983.
2. 'The Daily Wages of Italian Industrial Workers in the Giolittian Period (1898–1913)', *Rivista di storia economica*, 1984, I, International Issue.

Industrial Wages and Cost of Living Series

There are at present two available sources offering industrial wage series for more than one country: the fundamental work by Phelps Brown,[3] which gives series of real and money wages for France, Germany, the UK, Sweden and the USA for the period 1869–1960; and the statistical collection published by Mitchell,[4] which supplies money wage series and cost of living indices for a number of European countries, including (for the period under consideration here) Belgium, France, Germany, Italy, Sweden and the UK.

A collection of data from these two sources, along with some from other sources when available, is presented in Tables 5.9–5.14 of appendix 5.1. From these, the following remarks can be derived:

1. *France.* The four wage series available differ only marginally as far as their trend is concerned; they are all based on very piecemeal data of hourly or daily rates. The only good source of cost of living data is the work by Singer-Kérel, but that only processes Paris data. Of the three indices she offered, I consider the '213 items' one the most appropriate; in any case, they all show 'la fameuse crise de vie chère, génératrice de troubles importants'[5] of the years 1911–12, which severely cut down the rising trend of real wages. Phelps Brown's wage series has been retained, recalling that it has fixed 1905 employment weights.

2. *Germany.* In the case of Germany, too, four money wage series are available, but two are the basic series (Kuczynski and Desai), of which the other two (Bry and Hoffmann, respectively) are slight variations. Desai's series grows considerably more over the period (about 20 per cent more) and appears to be constructed with great care. It is an annual wage series derived from excellent sources. The four price series are all very similar up to 1910. Kuczynski then reports a burst of inflation similar to the French one, while the other series give a much less pronounced inflation. Hoffmann's implicit deflator of private consumption (corresponding to the French, '214 items' index) cannot be used to deflate wage data. Desai and Orsagh's cost of living series are very similar. In conclusion, Desai's wage

---

3. E. H. Phelps Brown with M. H. Browne, *A Century of Pay*, London, 1968.
4. B. R. Mitchell, *European Historical Statistics, 1750–1970*, London, 1968. The quality of the Belgian series is so poor that it has not been taken into consideration here.
5. 'Les classes populaires urbaines', in F. Braudel and E. Labrousse (eds), *Histoire économique et sociale de la France*, Paris, 1979, IV, vol. I, 493. Other works on French wages do not add new data. See J. Lhomme, 'Les enseignements théoriques à retirer d'une étude sur les salaires dans la longue période', *Revue économique*, 1965; J. Rougerie, 'Remarques sur l'histoire des salaires à Paris au XIX siècle', *Mouvement social*, 1968.

series and Orsagh's cost of living series appear to be the best choice.

3. *Italy*. The *Cassa Infortuni*'s series used by Mitchell and by many other statistical collections were criticised in my last essay, while the implicit deflator of private consumption cannot substitute ISTAT's time-honoured cost of living series,[6] which is therefore retained here. In my last essay I gave daily wages in several industries with moving employment weights.

4. *Sweden*. The wage series is an average of annual wages in several industries, with fixed 1913 employment weights; the cost of living series is constructed with weights taken from national consumption 1881–90.

5. *UK*. The Wood-Bowley series have won wide acceptance, as the recent contribution by Gourvish recognised[7]; we retain them in Phelps Brown's more accurate version. The money wage series is built on weekly wages, with variable employment weights. The cost of living series has variable weights as well.

6. *USA*. The two annual money wage series do not differ much, while the cost of living series show wide discrepancies; Rees's series, employed by Phelps Brown, appear more solid.

The selected money wage and cost of living series, and the resulting real-wage series, have been reported in Figures 5.1–5.6 to allow a visual appreciation of their behaviour. Some overall remarks are now in order.

Money wages. It is possible to identify three pairs of countries behaving somewhat similarly. France and UK form the first pair, with slowly growing wages and a very similar trend. USA and Germany form the second pair, with a very similar growth of wages after 1900, but a dissimilar performance in the preceding decade. Considering the whole span 1890–1913, the German behaviour would actually be more comparable to that of the third pair of countries, namely Italy and Sweden. This last pair

6. Since I wrote my essay, I had the possibility of seeing a work on wages that I had not examined (M. Berra and M. Revelli, 'Salari', in *La Storia d'Italia, Il mondo contemporaneo*, La Nuova Italia, 1978, vol. I, 3), but the authors quote the usual wage series employed by everybody, though they advance some interpretative reservations. Of the three new articles published, two provide a confirmation of my results: C. Biffoli and M. Lungonelli, 'Una classe operaia in formazione: i Siderurgici di Portoferraio, 1901–1905', *Studi storici*, 1985, n. 1; and G. Barberis, 'Torchi e meccanica. Appunti per una storia della Negro', *Rassegna economica della provincia di Alessandria*, 1985, n. 4. The third one (A. Dewerpe, 'Modi di retribuzione e organizzazione produttiva all'Ansaldo (1900–1920)', *Studi storici*, 1985, n. 1) analyses wages by categories and the use of new forms of remuneration, but does not offer quantitative elaborations that could be used.
7. In his essay, T. R. Gourvish, 'The Standard of Living 1890–1914', in A. O'Day (ed.), *The Edwardian Age: Conflict and Stability 1900–1914*, London, 1979, reports a few additional regional wage series confirming the stationary trend of the national series. Interesting are the 'qualitative' observations offered.

Figure 5.1 Wage Indices for France, Germany and Italy

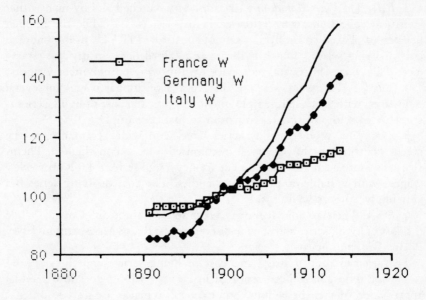

Figure 5.2 Wage Indices for Sweden, the UK and the USA

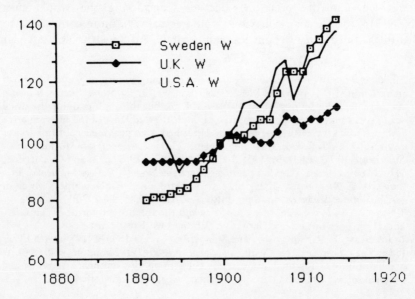

Figure 5.3 Cost of Living Indices for France, Germany and Italy

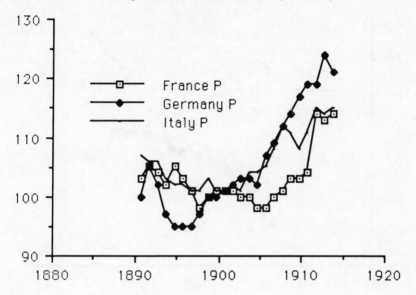

Figure 5.4 Cost of Living Indices for Sweden, the UK and the USA

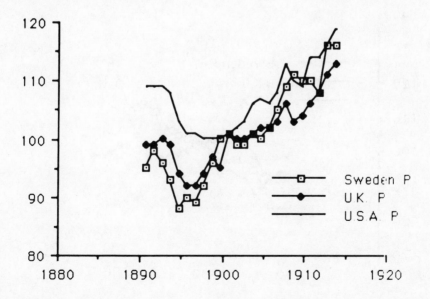

Figure 5.5 Real Wage Indices for France, Germany and Italy.

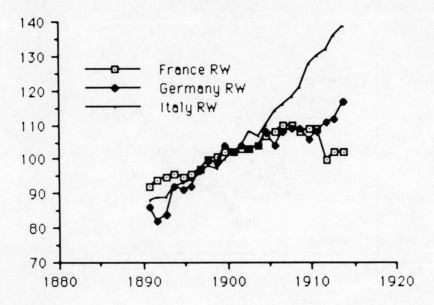

Figure 5.6 Real Wage Indices for Sweden, the UK and the USA.

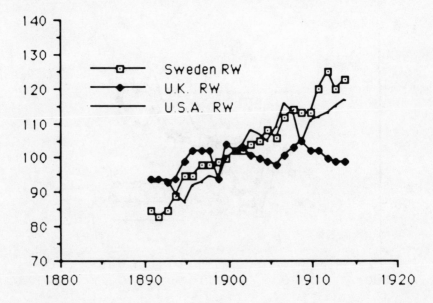

shows a very dynamic wage trend, slightly more so in Sweden than in Italy over the whole period (78 per cent increase against 71 per cent), but with a different growth path, more rapid in Sweden in the 1890s and in Italy after the 1907 crisis. Concerning the effects of the 1907 crisis, they can clearly be noticed in the USA and UK, less so in Sweden and Germany; Italian and French wages do not seem to have suffered appreciably.

Cost of Living. While in Figure 5.1 I had to stick to the same pairs identified for the comparison of money wages, the performance of the six cost of living series is everywhere broadly similar: a fall in the 1890s followed by a rise to the 1907 crisis, a second short-lived fall (with the exception of Germany) and a final rise. However, the amplitude of the cycles and the timing of the turning points differ.

Real Wages. The grouping of countries in three pairs has retained some meaning: the ranking of real-wage performance is the same as for money wages but for the two fast-growing countries: Italy has outstripped Sweden, as a result of the stronger Swedish inflation in the period. More detailed comments are in order, however. UK wages show some increase in the first half of the 1890s followed by cyclical stagnation; French real wages, on the other hand, show a continuous rising trend up to 1906, followed by four years of near stagnation and then by an abrupt fall. Both American and German real wages are highly cyclical on a clearly upward trend, more marked in the German case. The effects of the 1907 crisis on the American real wages appear quite devastating.

Finally, Swedish real wages are more dynamic than the Italian ones in the 1890s (and similar to the German wages), but show years of standstill (and even reversal) after 1900. An inflationary outburst similar to that of the French is responsible for Swedish real wages losing touch with the Italian trend in the very final years of the period.

On average, the yearly growth rate of real wages between 1890 and 1913 is the following: UK 0.2 per cent; France 0.5 per cent; USA 1.0 per cent; Germany 1.4 per cent; Sweden 1.6 per cent; Italy 2 per cent.

The conclusions reached are open to revisions on a number of accounts, the most important of which are now briefly mentioned:

i)   Annual wages are often the result of elaborations based on the daily (or weekly) rates mutliplied by a fixed coefficient. This is, for example, the case with UK (weekly wages multiplied by 49 weeks), France (daily wages multiplied by a factor of 5.4 to get weekly wages and then by 49 weeks) and Italy (daily wages multiplied by a factor of 6 and then by 49 weeks). It would be possible to be more precise on the length of the working week,[8] but not on that of the working year for those countries

8. Information on hours of work per week can be found in Phelps Brown (pp. 55–6,

not having direct figures for annual wages.

ii) Wage series by industries are sometimes combined into on overall average by means of fixed employment weights; this has been so with France and Sweden. In this case, the effects of structural change are not captured and the growth rates of wages are usually understated;

iii) Short-time and overtime, as well as piece-rates and other forms of remuneration, are generally not taken into account. Only data coming from single firms' bookkeeping can provide such detailed information. Unemployment and underemployment also become an issue when wages are used to construct wage bills, annual wage rates usually referring to a 'normal' full year of work.

iv) Price series are usually of the cost of living type, but their coverage, the weight of the items included as well as the type of index-number formula used are unknown, more often than not. Their importance for a correct evaluation of real-wage rates cannot be overemphasised.[9]

The International Comparison of Industrial Workers' Living Standards

The basis on which to build an international comparison of the standard of living of industrial workers might be considered easily defined: the average workers' remuneration in the national currency, with reference to some agreed-upon span of time (day/week/year). But here again things are ambiguous. First of all, *average* wages should (although for empirical limitation they do not always) include all sectors — skilled as well as unskilled workers, women, apprentices and youth, large as well as small firms. My experience suggests that small firms, apprentices and youth, and more traditional sectors with very high and very low wages are usually under-represented. (I comment upon this in the case of Italy in my last essay, see especially footnotes 20, 21, 26.) This tends in general to overstate average wages.

Secondly, it must be remembered that average wages rise or fall not only as a result of rising or falling basic rates, but also as a result of more weight acquired by high-wage sectors, by skilled versus unskilled workers, by high-wage regions. Wage data that do not mirror this structural change

---

207), in the Board of Trade *Reports* (quoted in my essay on p. 92) and in various other works quoted here; they have never been systematically studied. See also Table 5.1 in the text.

9. An example of the strategic importance of a different cost of living index is given in the recent essay by P. Scholliers, 'A Methodological Note on Real Wages During the Interwar Years', *Historical Social Research*, January 1987, n. 41.

usually tend to show lower growth rates, as has already been mentioned. However, if one wants to evaluate the progress in welfare of single categories of workers, wages by profession should be used. In international comparisons, too, it might be of interest to compare the earnings of workers in the same industry, as Scholliers has done.[10] An example of what could be done in this direction is provided in Table 5.1, where I have gathered weekly wage rates in three industries (building, engineering and printing) for six countries in 1905. All wage figures come from the British Board of Trade (BOT) reports,[11] with the exception of the Italian figures, derived from the sources quoted in my last essay.

In Table 5.1 it is possible to detect a ranking of each country in comparison with Britain. If Britain = 100, USA ranks more than 200, Germany around 80, France around 70, Belgium around 60 and Italy around 45, but differentials differ by industry and by country. The ratio of unskilled to skilled workers' wages ranges from 0.59 to 0.72 (with the exception of American labourers/bricklayers, which is 0.50). It appears highest in Germany and lowest in the USA.

Using the figures for engineering wages quoted in Scholliers[12] and the corresponding figures of Table 5.1, one can draw the picture of the trend in relative wages 1850–1905, appearing in Table 5.2. The gap with Great Britain was progressively closing, very rapidly for Germany (which started from a low level).

Having analysed average wages in the first section of this papers an international comparison of average wages will now be my main concern. It will be done with reference to the same year — 1905 — already used in Table 5.1, because of the availability of cost of living data from BOT. In Table 5.3 I have gathered annual earnings for seven countries: Germany, Sweden, GB and USA come from Phelps Brown; France comes from Phelps Brown as well, but the figure has been put up 11 per cent to correct what I consider to be an inconsistency in Phelps Brown's estimation procedure.[13] The Italian estimate derives from daily rates multiplied by

10. P. Scholliers, *Industrial Wage Differentials in 19th Century Belgium*, mimeo, August 1986.
11. Besides the Board of Trade *Reports* quoted in my essay on p. 92, I have also used *Report of an Inquiry by the Board of Trade into Working Class Rents, Housing and Retail Prices, together with the Rates of Wages in Certain Occupations in the Principal Industrial Towns of Belgium*, London, 1910.
12. P. Scholliers, *Industrial Wage Differentials*, table 4 and table 7.
13. The French weekly rate estimated by him on the basis of daily rates results from the use of 54 hours of work per week, while all sources (and, strangely enough, Phelps Brown himself) agree that the French working week was still of 60 hours before the First World War. There are other reasons suggesting that Phelps Brown's estimate, even after the present adjustment, might still be too low. In

Table 5.1 Wages and Hours of Work in Certain Industries and Occupations in 1905 (shillings per week, hours per week)

	Wage Rates												Hours of Work					
	Great Britain		Germany		France		Belgium[a]		Italy		USA[b]		GB	Germany	France	Belgium	Italy	USA
		index GB = 100		index GB = 100		index GB = 100		index GB = 100		index GB = 100		index GB = 100						
	(1)	(2)	(3)	(4)	(5)	(6)	(7)	(8)	(9)	(10)	(11)	(12)	(13)	(14)	(15)	(16)	(17)	(18)
Building																		
bricklayers	39	100	29	74	25	64	22	56	14	36	117[c]	300	53	59	64½	67½	60	47
labourers	26	100	21	81	18	69	16	62	9	35	59	227						
Engineering																		
fitters	34	100	29	85	26	76	21	62	17	50	68	200	53	59	60½	60½	60	56
labourers	20	100	20	100	17	85	14	70	12	60	40	200			60½	60½		
Printing																		
compositors	30	100	25	83	24	80	21	70	19	63	75	250	52½	54	59½	59¾	54	49

(a) Data refer to June 1908; a footnote in the BOT report for Belgium (p. xxxiv) warns, however, that rates in the industries considered had not changed since 1905.

(b) Data refer to February 1909. From table A.6 US money wages appear at this date to be at a level not substantially different from that reached in 1905, after two years of rise and a sharp fall in 1908, following the 1907 crisis.

(c) The BOT Report comments upon the very high comparative level of US bricklayers' wages.

Sources: BOT Reports for all countries, except Italy; my own sources for Italy.

Table 5.2 Relative Wages in Engineering (Great Britain = 100)

	1850	1896	1905*
Great Britain	100	100	100
France	42	61	78
Belgium	36	52	64
Germany	28	59	89

*Fitters 2/3; labourers 1/3

6×49, which is probably too 'full' a working year for Italian industrial workers; the Belgian estimate is an extrapolation to 1905 of a 1913 estimate in Baudhuin (see description of procedure in Table 5.3). The ranking of Belgium and France with reference to Great Britain is very similar to that already established above for engineering wages alone, while the German average index is 14 percentage points lower, signalling that the wage of the industries selected by BOT (see column 5 of Table 5.3) was comparatively higher in Germany. A similar comment applies to the USA where, as has been commented in a footnote in Table 5.1, bricklayers' wages were abnormally high. It can therefore be seen that the comparison of average wages offers a comprehensive view that is not adequately conveyed by wage comparisons for single industries.

However, a simple conversion of wage rates (expressed in national currencies) into one common monetary standard through official exchange rates does not give a reliable picture of the relative purchasing power of wages (as well as that of income). I refer the reader to the relevant technical literature for the debate on the causes of this.[14] It is clear that, while the use of official exchange rates in a period of exchange-rate stability (like the one under consideration in this paper) at least does not produce the same

the essay by L. A. Vincent, 'Les comptes nationaux', in A. Sauvy, *Histoire économique de la France entre les deux guerres*, vol. 3, Paris, 1972, p. 332, a 'salaire par tête et par an', for the industrial sector is reported for 1913. It is equal to F. F. 1620, i.e. 44 per cent higher than the yearly wage that can be arrived at applying the index of Phelps Brown's monetary wages to the corrected value in Table 5.1. It must be noted that Vincent's estimates include white-collar workers and foremen; but even so, it seems to imply a higher average wage. Also, Phelps Brown has used, with one exception only, non-Paris rates, which are reported in all sources to have been much lower (sometimes as much as half) than Paris rates, perhaps ending up with playing down too much the weight of Paris workers in the aggregate.

14. See especially I. B. Kravis and R. E. Lipsey, 'Toward an Explanation of National Price Levels', *Princeton Studies in International Finance*, Nov. 1983, n. 52, and I. B. Kravis, 'Comparative Studies of National Incomes and Prices', *Journal of Economic Literature*, XXII, March 1984.

Table 5.3 Average Industrial Wages in 1905

	Yearly wages in national currencies (1)		Exchange rate of the £ (2)		Yearly wages in £ (3)	Index of (3) GB = 100 (4)	BOT index GB = 100 (5)
Belgium	907	B.Fr.	25.40	B.Fr.	35 14s	64	63
France	1021	F.Fr.	25.15	F.Fr.	40 12s	72	75
Germany	856	M.	20.45	M.	41 17s	75	83
Italy	623	lire	25.15	lire	24 15s*	44*	–
Sweden	851	Kr.	18.16	Kr.	46 17s	84	–
GB	56	£	–		56 2s	100	100
USA	487	$	4.86	$.	100 4s	179	232

*A slight imprecision in the original version has been corrected
Sources: Col. 1 Germany, Sweden, GB and USA are from Phelps Brown; France also comes from Phelps Brown, but using a working week of 60 hours; Italy comes from my own computations. Belgium's estimate has been derived as follows: from F. Baudhuin, *Histoire économique de la Belgique 1914–1939*, vol. 1, Bruxelles, 1946, p. 409, I have taken the yearly wage for 1913 (1125 B. Fr.), which has been reported to 1905 using Mitchell's money wage index.

volatility of results as in times of fluctuating exchange rates, nevertheless the purchasing-power parity issue has to be tackled.

The Purchasing Power Parity (PPP) Approach

A working class budget, calculated first using the prices of one country and then the prices of a second country, can provide a ratio, through which it is possible to determine an exchange rate that allows a bilateral comparison of wages based on PPP. Given that such a procedure can be applied taking both countries' budgets in turn, two estimates of such PPP exist. While I refer the reader to Appendix 2 of my last essay for the steps and the sources needed for the application of this procedure, I have reported the results,[15] with the addition of Belgium, in Table 5.4. It can be seen that 'real' average wages in 1905 would appear to be very close in Belgium, France and Germany, substantially higher in Sweden, substantially lower in Italy. Great Britain would still be firmly ahead of all the European countries, but not ahead of the USA.

15. In Appendix B of my last essay, I had used, to estimate the Italian diet, quantities that were the average quantities consumed in the nation. I can now substitute quantities derived from the enquiry made by Pugliese in July 1913 on fifty-one Milanese working-class families with 210 members, which yields the results gathered in Table 5.5.

Table 5.4 Comparison of Industrial Wages in 1905 and 1913 Based on Purchasing Power Parities

	Yearly wages in 1905 at the official exchange rate in £ (1)	Index of (1) GB = 100 (2)	Cost of living index[a] GB = 100 (3)	Index of real wages in 1905 GB = 100 (4)	Index of real wages in 1913[b] GB = 100 (5)
Belgium	35 14s	64	91–95	67–70	65–68
France	40 12s	72	104–112	64–69	60–64
Germany	41 17s	75	107–117	64–70	68–75
Italy	24 15s	44	108–117[c]	38–41	45–49
Sweden	46 17s	84	103–115	73–81	82–92
GB	56 2s	100	100	100	100
USA	100 4s	179	143–153[d]	117–125	126–134

(a) only foodstuffs and rents, excluding coal
(b) applying the indices from Tables 5.9–5.14
(c) corrected through the use of working-class budgets (see footnote 15)
(d) the cost of living comparison GB/USA refers to 1909, but the change in prices in the two countries between 1905 and 1909 was similar and therefore the comparison can be considered valid for 1905 as well.
Sources: Table 5.1, my calculations, Board of Trade report for cost of living in Belgium (rents have been combined with cost of foodstuffs with a weight of 16.7 per cent).

A refinement of this approach could be obtained by applying the devices suggested by UN researchers.[16] These devices have found wide acceptance,[17] although there is a less than general consensus on the meaning of the 'international dollar' built to value the GNP of each country, and other methods have been suggested.[18] After a deep inspection of the UN method it has seemed to me that the extensive computations necessary to apply it to

16. I. B. Kravis, A. Heston, R. Summers, *World Product and Income. International Comparisons of Real Gross Product*, Washington, D.C., 1982.
17. R. Marris, 'Comparing the Incomes of Nations: a Critique of the International Comparison Project', *Journal of Economic Literature*, XXII, March 1984, states that the 'work by Kravis, Heston and Summers . . . represents one of the great contributions to applied economics' (p. 40). N. F. R. Crafts, 'Gross National Product in Europe 1870–1910: Some New Estimates', *Explorations in Economic History*, 1983, n. 4 bases on it a set of backward extrapolations to revise Bairoch's estimates of income per capita in the European countries before the First World War.
18. P. Pashardes, *True Purchasing Power Parities and Real Consumption Comparisons with an Application to EEC Countries*, Birkbeck College paper, London, 1984 suggests a method that explicitly embodies at least part of the substitution effects, while A. Maddison, 'A Comparison of Levels of GDP per Capita in Developed and Developing Countries, 1700–1980', *Journal of Economic History*, March 1983 declares himself in favour of quantity estimates (rather than value estimates) à la Usher.

Table 5.5 Average Food Consumption of Milanese Working-class Families in 1913

	Unit prices in lire		British Budget			Italian Budget		
	GB	Italy	Kg. or l. consumed	Cost at British prices (lire)	Cost at Italian prices (lire)	Kg. or l. consumed	Cost at British prices (lire)	Cost at Italian prices (lire)
	(1)	(2)	(3)	(4)	(5)	(6)	(7)	(8)
Bread	.29	.36	9.98	2.89	3.59	9.20	2.67	3.31
Flour	.30	.38	4.54	1.36	1.73	.47	.14	.18
Potatoes	.10	.12	7.71	.77	.93	2.39	.24	.29
Beef	1.56	1.90	2.04	3.18	3.88	1.80	2.81	3.42
Pork	1.85	1.68	.23	.43	.39	.60	1.11	1.00
Lamb	1.48	1.37	.68	1.01	.93	.20	.30	.27
Butter	3.06	2.80	.91	2.78	2.55	.35	1.07	.98
Milk	.32	.24	5.65	1.81	1.36	5.50	1.76	1.32
Cheese	1.62	1.30	.34	.55	.44	.49	.79	.64
Sugar	.46	1.49	2.42	1.11	3.61	.74	.34	1.10
Bacon	1.85	1.60	.68	1.26	1.09	.53	.98	.85
Totals				17.15	20.50		12.21	13.36

The ratio of the total of column (8) to the total of column (7) yields 109, rather than 111 as stated in my last essay.

Sources: (1)–(5) from Table B.1 in my last essay.
(6) from A. Pugliese, 'L'alimentazione della famiglia operaia milanese durante la guerra', in P. Albertoni and A. Pugliese, *Studi sull'alimentazione*, Naples, 1937, p. 455.

my inter-country wage comparisons could not yield any new insight. The whole exercise, in fact, basically amounts to an averaging out of the prices prevailing in the countries considered for each of the items included in the budget, with country-weights decided *a priori*. This would allow a multilateral rather than a bilateral comparison of real wages based on PPP. It would only be worth reconsidering the issue if wages from many more countries would be available for comparison, and if the quality of the data could be improved and standardised. In addition, we must not forget the theoretical shortcomings of this approach stemming from the use of the time-honoured consumer's theory which has recently been very seriously criticised.[19] These considerations have pushed me to take into consideration the heuristic validity of other approaches.

The 'Basic Needs' Approach

This approach in its 'recommended food allowances' version still appears relevant in a context of widespread poverty like the one prevailing in early twentieth-century Europe, although it would be much less acceptable in present-day Europe (in fact, today it is used mainly in the analysis of LDCs). The main difficulties in its use lie in the quantitative determination of a subsistence diet, which varies at least according to age, sex, body, size, climate, type and intensity of work,[20] and also according to the various biological theories in use.[21] For the period under consideration here, a relevant study can be cited. It was produced for the *Commission scientifique interalliée du ravitaillement* (CSIR), an organisation formed in Paris in 1917 to assist governments of the Allied countries in the adoption of correct measures to provide enough food for their populations.[22] The study was

19. My theoretical referee is here, (as in my section on the 'capabilities' approach in this paper), A. Sen. In particular, A. Sen, 'The Welfare Basis of Real Income Comparisons: a Survey', *Journal of Economic Literature*, XVII, March 1979.
20. In an article by C. Gini, 'Sui confronti internazionali dei salari reali', *Rivista di politica economica*, Jan. 1927, the author, after having reviewed the issue, concluded that 'the adoption of the calories approach gives . . . more troubles than advantages in comparison to the budget approach' (p. 12, my translation).
21. Daily recommended allowances in terms of calories appear to have been revised substantially downwards over time, while their requirements of vitamins and other nutrients have been more explicitly stressed.
22. The works of CSIR took place in six sessions between March 1918 and April 1919. The CSIR calculated the food requirements of the human and animal population of the Allies, the energetic content of national production and the ensuing import needs. CSIR suggestions were obviously consultative; Italy, for example, is said never to have been able to guarantee the recommended food imports, although the diet of the Italian population did not deteriorate appreciably during the war.

presented by the well-known Italian statistician, Corrado Gini, at the fifth session of the CSIR (December, 1918).[23] It aimed at the quantitative assessment of the differences, if any, in the recommended allowances for each of the three countries considered (France, Great Britain and Italy).

Starting with the assumption of 3,300 gross calories (3,000 net) as the daily recommended allowances for an average adult male, Gini develops a set of convincing arguments,[24] leading to the conclusion that Italy and Great Britain needed 2,650 calories per capita and France needed 2,740. We could easily extend his argument to the Belgian and German populations, but the more rigid climate and some types of very heavy forest work might indicate a need to raise the average for Sweden.

At this point, the problem becomes one of availability of historical material useful for this line of research. For Italy, there are plenty of works allowing us to go further in this direction. There is, for instance, a very accurate work by L. Spina calculating the overall calories available to the Italian population in 1910–14.[25] The main results of such work have been arranged in Table 5.6, together with a similar analysis developed by Pugliese on a sample of fifty-one Milanese working-class families. The following can be noted:

a) On average, the Italian population in 1910–14 barely reached the daily recommended allowances, if we accept the above cited estimation by Gini, or was just under it, if we adopt the estimate by Spina (Table 5.6, Column 3). In any case, the weight of proteins derived from vegetable-food was higher, and that of proteins derived from animal-food much lower, than the recommended weight;

b) The diet of the Milanese working-class family offered substantially

---

23. C. Gini, 'Sull'influenza di alcuni fattori sopra il fabbisogno Alimentare del uomo medio', *Problemi sociologici della guerra*, Bologna, 1921.

24. The daily recommended allowances were so specified by Gini by age, sex and type of work:

Children 0–5 years			Calories	1,500
Boys/Girls 5–15 years			"	2,400
Employed in agriculture		males	"	3,500
		females	"	3,250
Employed in heavy jobs	—	males	"	3,900
Employed in less heavy jobs		males	"	3,250
		females	"	3,000
Employed in sedentary jobs		males	"	2,450
and non-working		females	"	2,300

25. The computation of calories and nutrients in the average Italian diet has been subsequently extended to all the years from 1861, with a variable degree of reliability due to the different quality of the basic data. Cf. ISTAT, *Sommario di statistiche storiche dell'Italia*, Rome, 1958.

Table 5.6 The Italian Daily Food Allowances in the Prewar Years

	Recommended allowances per adult male (1)	Actual allowances of the Italian population 1910–14 per capita (2)	per adult male (3)	Actual allowances of 51 Milanese families 1913, per adult male (4)
Calories	3300	2696	3220[a]	2853[b]
Proteins { Vegetable (g.)	58	61.42	73.38	45.18
Animal (g.)	42	20.00	23.81	39.39
Fats (g.)	75	53.03	63.34	70.92
Carbohydrates (g.)	540	412.39	492.70	411.12
Average cost (lire)	–	.64[c]	.76[c]	1.07[d]

(a) of which 273 calories are from wine
(b) of which 240 calories are from wine
(c) bread and pasta have been included at the cost of flour
(d) the cost has been calculated by me using average prices reported in L. Spina, op. cit.: for bread and pasta prices come from *Idea cooperativa*, Milan, 30 July 1911, n. 233. The difference between the cost of the diet of the Milanese working-class families and the cost of the average Italian diet is large because in the former more animal proteins appear (which are dearer than vegetable proteins), and because bread and pasta are bought ready-made (and are therefore more costly than their flour content).
Sources: (1)–(3) L. Spina, 'I consumi alimentari della popolazione italiana nell'anteguerra (1910–14) e negli ultimi anni (1926–30)', *Metron*, 1932, n. 1–2.
(4) A. Pugliese, 'Il bilancio alimentare di 51 famiglie operaie milanesi' and 'L'alimentazione della famiglia operaia milanese durante la guerra', in P. Albertoni and A. Pugliese, *Studi sull'alimentazione*.

fewer calories than recommended, though animal proteins were present in a higher amount compared to the average for Italy.[26] It must be underlined that the families surveyed by Pugliese were admittedly selected from among the least poor of the Milanese proletariat!

Data referring to the cost of the average Italian diet (Table 5.6, columns 2 and 3) and of the Milanese working class diet (Table 5.6, column 4) are also interesting. Though the former is in agreement with other estimates given at the time, it does not represent the minimal cost of a diet offering the same amount of calories and nutrients. (Such a minimal cost diet could be easily computed and compared with the actual one.) The extra cost of the

26. Milan was known to be the Italian town where more meat per capita was consumed (157 gr. per day before the First World War), 30 per cent more than Turin and Genoa, 40 per cent more than Rome, double the consumption in Naples and three times the consumption in Bari and Catania.

working-class diet exemplifies this problem even further, showing how the purchase of ready-made bread and pasta rather than flour — plus an extra amount of more costly animal proteins and sugar — can make a lower calories diet 41 per cent dearer.

How does the cost of such diets compare with average wages? A simple (though not completely exact) answer could be given by comparing the cost of an adult male diet with the going average male wage.[27] This can be done by drawing upon one of my students' work[28] which gives an estimate for female wages of 1.50 lire[29] per day in 1911. Given that the overall average wage was 2.67 lire for the same year and the percentage of female workers in the total was 32.74 per cent, it follows that an average male wage was 3.25 lire per day. Reduced by a factor of 0.805 (294 days of work out of 365) or, more realistically, 0.712 (260 days of work out of 365), the daily wage rate becomes the daily disposable income (2.62 lire or 2.31 lire) of an Italian male industrial worker in 1911 (no direct taxation existed on wages at the time). Using Gini's recommended allowances (footnote 24), a male worker (1) with a housewife (0.9) and two children 5–15 years of age (0.7 each) would spend 2.51 lire each day in food, using the lower-cost diet (and 3.53 lire using the higher cost one!). Everyone can see that one male wage was not enough to support even a modest family. Two or more wages[30] or no children[31] was necessary to cross the threshold of dire misery. Once again, family incomes and dependency ratios appear crucial. This last remark paves the way to a brief discussion of a third approach.

27. The inexactness is given by the presence in the average male wages of the wages of youth less than 15 years old, which, in 1911, formed 10 per cent of the male labour force. An appropriate adjustment could be to put up the male adult wage to 3.40–3.50 lire.
28. M. Giovanna Incerti Dal Monte, *Il lavoro femminile in età giolittiana*, thesis defended in 1984, University of Florence, a brief summary of which has been published in *Rivista di storia economica*, 1985, II, 3.
29. It can be noted in passing that female wages were 46 per cent of male wages in Italy in 1911, while they were 44.4 per cent in Great Britain (see R. C. O. Matthews, C. H. Feinstein, J. C. Odling Smee, *British Economic Growth 1856–1973*, Oxford, 1982, p. 630).
30. The existence or non-existence of residual ties with the land, as well as the diffusion of female employment, become relevant issues in this context. For example, the widespread female employment in textiles, coupled with the presence of engineering and metal sectors, made the industrial working class in Lombardy definitely more prosperous (than in, say, Liguria, where textiles were unimportant), as a result of higher *family* incomes.
31. A. Pugliese, 'Il bilancio alimentare', p. 380, notes that fourteen out of his fifty-one families were without children and fourteen had only one. He comments, 'The idea that it is convenient to limit the number of children born has already . . . penetrated the Milanese working class' (my translation).

The 'Capabilities' Approach

The limitations shown by the PPP and basic needs approaches have led me to the study of the theory developed by A. Sen in the last ten years.[32] He has underlined first the necessity of using income distribution to evaluate correctly income per capita figures — the *entitlement* approach[33] — and then, through a sweeping critique of utility theory, he has moved his emphasis from measurement of commodity bundles to the illustration of functionings — *capabilities* — as better suited to measure and compare, objectively, levels of welfare reached. In referring the reader to Sen's writings for a demonstration of this approach, I have to say that I find the implications of it — the use of non-market indicators — very interesting.

Indicators such as life expectancy, infant mortality, child death rates, adult literacy, schooling, malnutrition and the like were already used in the past, either under the generic heading of the 'quality' of life or, instrumentally, to help fill the gaps of income statistics.[34] They could be used more extensively and systematically today, if some sort of ranking and/or a well-specified connection with the welfare of a society could be identified.

Wages and Productivity

One of the interesting exercises that are possible with industrial wage rates is a comparison with productivity in industry (Y_I/L_I), something already tried by Phelps Brown and various other authors.[35] The trouble is that, if the assessment of wage rates is difficult, an estimate of productivity in industry is not easier. I have gathered the most recent estimates of overall productivity (GNP/L) around 1913 in Table 5.7, and I have tried in Table 5.8 to derive Y_I/L_I. Here is a brief commentary on the results, by country:

32. A. Sen, *On Economic Inequality*, Oxford, 1973; idem; *Poverty and Famines, An Essay on Entitlement and Deprivation*, Oxford, 1982; idem, *Resources, Values and Development*, Oxford, 1984; idem, *Commodities and Capabilities*, Amsterdam, 1985.
33. An application of the distributive emphasis suggested by Sen to the wage field would be the analysis of wages by categories, age, skill, male, female, regions, etc.
34. See, for example, S. L. Barsby, 'Economic Backwardness and the Characteristics of Development', *Journal of Economic History*, XXIX, 1969 and N. F. R. Crafts, op. cit.. The Chenery-Syrquin approach (H. B. Chenery and M. Syrquin, *Patterns of Development*, Oxford, 1975) adopted by N. F. R. Crafts, 'Patterns of Development in Nineteenth Century Europe', *Oxford Economic Papers*, XXXVI, 1984, is a more skilful (but not substantially different) variation along the same lines.
35. Among them, P. O'Brien and C. Keyder, *Economic Growth in Britain and France 1780–1914. Two Paths to the Twentieth Century*, London, 1978, and N. F. R. Crafts, 'Economic Growth in France and Britain, 1830–1910: A Review of the Evidence', *Journal of Economic History*, March 1984.

Table 5.7 Estimates of Output per Worker around 1910–13

	Crafts 1910					Maddison 1913					Bairoch 1913				
	GNP/P 1970 $	Index of (1) GB = 100	% active population	active GNP/L 1970 $	index of (4) GB = 100	GNP/P 1970 $	index of (6) GB = 100	% active population	active GNP/L 1970 $	Index of (9)[b] GB = 100	GNP/P 1960 $	Index of (11) GB = 100	% active population	active GNP/L 1960 $	index of (14) GB = 100
	(1)	(2)	(3)	(4)	(5)	(6)	(7)	(8)	(9)	(10)	(11)	(12)	(13)	(14)	(15)
USA	–	–	–	–	–	1810	116	43	4150	117	–	–	–	–	–
France	883	68	52	1698	59	1177	76	50	2331	66	695	70	52	1337	60
Germany	958	74	44	2177	75	1073	69	43	2466	70	781	78	44	1775	80
Italy	548	42	45	1218	42	836	54	46	1829	52	441	44	45	980	44
Sweden	763	59	40[a]	1907	66	994	64	46	2147	61	680	68	40	1770	77
GB	1302	100	45[a]	2893	100	1555	100	44	3533	100	996	100	45	2213	100

(a) from R. C. O. Matthews, C. H. Feinstein, J. C. Odling Smee, pp. 222–3.
(b) the index of GDP per man hours calculated by Maddison, p. 98 practically coincides.

Sources:
(1) N. F. R. Crafts, 'Gross National Product'.
(3), (13) from Mitchell.
(6), (8) from A. Maddison, *Phases of Capitalist Development*, Oxford, 1982 Appendices A, B, C.
(11) from P. Bairoch, 'Europe's Gross National Product: 1800–1975', *Journal of European Economic History*, 1976, n. 2.

Table 5.8 Estimates of Output per Worker in Industry around 1910–13

	L_1/L 100	Y_1/Y 100	Y_1/L_1 Crafts 1910 1970 \$	Y_1/L_1 Maddison 1913 1970 \$	Bairoch 1913 1960 \$	PB 1913 current \$	PB 1913 ppp \$	Index of Y_1/L_1 GB = 100 (3)	(4)	(5)	(6)	(7)	Index of Real Industrial Wages in 1913 GB = 100
	(1)	(2)	(3)	(4)	(5)	(6)	(7)	(8)	(9)	(10)	(11)	(12)	(13)
USA	29	27	–	3864	–	944	638	–	120	–	195	132	126–134
France	29(32)	36(41)	2108(2176)	2896(2988)	1660(1714)	–	–	80(83)	90(93)	83(85)	–	–	60–64
Germany	41	43	2283	2588	1863	442	395	87	81	93	91	81	68–75
Italy	24	24	1218	1829	980	–	–	46	57	49	–	–	45–49
Sweden	26	31	2278	2559	2026	504	462	87	80	101	104	95	82–92
GB	44	40	2630	3212	2012	485	485	100	100	100	100	100	100

Sources: (1)–(2) data come from Mitchell, with the exception of: figures in parenthesis for France, which are revisions suggested by F. Caron, *An Economic History of Modern France*, London, 1979; figures for Italy, which come from P. Ercolani, 'Documentazione statistica di base', in G. Fuà (ed.), *Lo sviluppo economico in Italia* Milan, 1969, vol. III; figures for Great Britain, which are taken from R. C. O. Matthews, C. H. Feinstein, J. C. Odling Smee, op.cit.; and figures for USA, which come from A. Maddison 'Growth and Slowdown in Advanced Capitalist Economies: Techniques of Quantitative Assessment', *Journal of Economic Literature*, June 1987.

(3)–(5) my elaborations on the basis of (1), (2) and data in Table 5.6

(6) from Phelps Brown

(7) (6) made comparable at PPP price through the index of Column (3), Table 5.4

(13) from Table 5.4

USA: The two estimates of Y_1/L_1 available rank the USA at the same
            level with respect to Britain as real wages.

France: The estimates of French industrial productivity range from 83
            per cent to 93 per cent of the British level, while real wages stand
            at 60 to 64 per cent. The gap seems to me very wide indeed, and
            I consider this one further piece of evidence that French wages
            are undervalued.

Germany: In this case we have four estimates of industrial productivity
            ranging between 81 and 93 per cent of the British level, again in
            presence of wages distinctly lower in comparative terms, al-
            though not so distant as in the French case. As there is no reason
            to doubt the quality of German wage data, we might be inclined
            to advance the hypothesis of a real competitive advantage in the
            cost of labour on the part of German industry.

Italy: The ranking of industrial productivity and wage rates broadly
            agree.

Sweden: Industrial productivity estimates range between 80 and 101 per
            cent. With the exception of Bairoch's estimate, which is dis-
            tinctly higher, they are in line with the ranking of wages.

A better quality of industrial productivity data and their availability at more
than one date would allow a comparison between rates of growth of productivity
and rates of growth of wages (as I have done in the case of Italy
1898–1913 in my last essay). Also, the trend in strikes and profits could be
compared with that of wages, when such data are available.

Appendix 5.1: Money Wages and Cost of Living Series 1890–1913

All figures reported in the tables are indices 1900=100.

Appendix 5.2: Construction of the Money Wages Series for Italy, 1890–7

The construction of the average money wage rates series for Italy 1890–7
has followed a two-stage approach. First, the series for individual industries
have been built extrapolating the 1898–1913 series (already available in my
earlier essay) on the basis of the trend in wages in various firms available in
ASI 1895, 1900, 1905/7, and in A. Geisser and E. Magrini, 'Contribuzione
alla storia e statistica dei salari industriali in Italia nella seconda metà del
secolo XIX', La riforma sociale, 1904. Next, a weighting system has been
devised that assigns more weight to textiles (and to silk in particular) in
1890, less weight to mining and chemicals, less to building (which had a
deep crisis at the beginning of the 1890s) and a cyclical performance to

metal-engineering. Quarrying has been embodied into mining; bricks and tiles, gas (very small before 1898) and tobacco have been combined into chemicals for lack of direct information. The details of the computation are collected in Table 5.15.

Table 5.9 Money Wages and Cost of Living — France 1890–1913

	Money Wages				Cost of Living				Real Wages
	Singer-Kérel				Singer-Kérel				(3):(6)
	All France	Paris	Phelps Brown	Kuczynski	Ouvrier A	213 items	214 items	Kuczynski	× 100
	(1)	(2)	(3)	(4)	(5)	(6)	(7)	(8)	(9)
1890	94	96	92	92	108	102	102	105	90
1891	94	96	94	92	110	104	102	107	92
1892	94	96	94	93	111	103	101	101	93
1893	94	96	94	93	104	101	100	99	94
1894	95	98	94	93	106	104	101	102	93
1895	95	98	94	93	105	102	100	101	94
1896	96	100	95	94	103	100	100	100	95
1897	96	100	96	95	104	97	98	100	98
1898	97	100	98	97	106	99	99	101	99
1899	98	100	100	100	103	100	99	99	100
1900	100	100	100	100	100	100	100	100	100
1901	101	100	101	99	101	100	100	94	101
1902	101	100	100	97	101	99	100	92	101

1903	102	100	99	103	99	99	100	102
1904	103	100	99	101	97	99	98	105
1905	105	100	99	103	97	99	94	106
1906	109	101	104	104	99	100	93	108
1907	111	103	105	104	100	101	98	108
1908	112	103	108	103	102	102	100	106
1909	113	106	109	106	102	102	99	107
1910	106	107	111	110	103	103	103	107
1911	106	110	113	114	113	108	112	98
1912	107	111	114	119	112	108	116	100
1913	108	113	115	118	113	108	113	100

The consumer price series in A. Maddison, op. cit., table E 2, is the one reported here in 6. It must be noted, however, that Maddison must have reported his series from p. 105 of the book by Singer-Kérel where, as a result of a quite apparent printing mistake, the figure for 1910 has been interchanged with the figure for 1911.

Sources: Phelps Brown: Wages are an estimate from various sources, detailed at p. 363; Prices: index for ouvrier A constructed by J. Singer-Kérel, *Le coût de la vie à Paris 1840–1954*, Paris, 1961. Mitchell: Wages from unspecified source (not reported here because incomplete); Prices: same sources as Phelps Brown, but it is the index 'coût de la vie 214 articles' (column 7) including wages of servants and using 'bourgeois' weights. Kuczynski: J. Kuczynski, *Die Geschichte der Lage der Arbeiter unter dem Kapitalismus*, vol. 33, *Darstellung der Lage der Arbeiter in Frankreich seit 1848*, Berlin, 1967. The author comments at p. 170 on the discrepancies between his indices and those calculated by Singer-Kérel.

Table 5.10 Money Wages and Cost of Living — Germany 1890–1913

	Money Wages				Cost of Living				Real Wages (3):(6) (9)
	Kuczynski (1)	Bry (2)	Desai (3)	Hoffmann (4)	Kuczynski (5)	Orsagh (6)	Desai (7)	Hoffmann (8)	
1890	91	87	83	84	97	99	96	98	84
1891	91	87	83	86	100	104	100	99	80
1892	91	87	83	85	99	101	99	93	82
1893	91	87	86	86	97	96	95	92	90
1894	91	87	84	86	96	94	94	91	89
1895	91	87	85	88	95	94	94	93	90
1896	92	91	89	89	94	94	94	95	95
1897	93	91	94	92	96	96	96	95	98
1898	96	95	96	95	99	99	98	95	97
1899	99	97	101	97	99	99	96	97	102
1900	100	100	100	100	100	100	100	100	100
1901	100	99	103	100	101	101	101	100	102
1902	100	99	103	101	101	102	102	100	101
1903	101	100	104	104	101	102	102	100	102

Year									
1904	104	103	107	107	103	101	103	101	106
1905	107	107	108	110	106	106	106	104	102
1906	112	112	114	115	113	108	109	110	106
1907	116	119	119	121	114	111	112	109	107
1908	116	117	121	121	114	113	114	108	107
1909	117	119	121	122	117	116	116	112	104
1910	120	121	125	125	119	118	117	117	106
1911	122	124	129	130	123	118	118	116	109
1912	126	128	135	134	130	123	124	118	110
1913	132	133	138	137	130	120	122	118	115

Phelps Brown uses Desai's series; Mitchell uses Kuczynski's; A. Maddison (op. cit., table E 2) uses Hoffmann's. Three recent works of interest have appeared: R. Gömmel, *Realeinkommen in Deutschland. Ein internationaler Vergleich 1810–1910*, Nürnberg, 1979, where Desai's series are used; the more comprehensive and detailed E. Wiegand, 'Zur historischen Entwicklung der Löhne und Lebenshaltungskosten in Deutschland', in E. Wiegand and W. Zapf (eds), *Wandel der Lebensbedingungen in Deutschland*, Frankfurt–New York, 1982, where a full discussion of all series available is provided; and T. Pierenkemper, 'The Standard of Living and Employment in Germany, 1850–1980: An Overview', *Journal of European Economic History*, Spring 1987, where Wiegand's elaborations are reported without further comment.

Sources: A. V. Desai, *Real Wages in Germany 1871–1913*, Oxford, 1968; G. Bry, *Wages in Germany 1871–1945*, Princeton, 1960 (slightly revised version of Kuczynski's series); J. Kuczynski, *Die Geschichte der Lage der Arbeiter in Deutschland von 1789 bis in die Gegenwart*, Berlin, 1954; W. G. Hoffmann, *Das Wachstum der deutschen Wirtschaft seit der Mitte des 19. Jahrhunderts*, Berlin, 1965 (the cost of living series is the implicit deflator of private consumption); T. J. Orsagh, 'Löhne in Deutschland 1871–1913. Neuere Literatur und weitere Ergebnisse', *Zeitschrift für die gesamte Staatswissenschaften*, 125, 1969, p. 481.

Table 5.11 Money Wages and Cost of Living—Italy 1890–1913

	Money Wages		Cost of living		Real
	Cassa Infortuni	ZM	ISTAT	Implicit deflator of private consumption	Wages (2):(3) ×100
	(1)	(2)	(3)	(4)	(5)
1890	–	91	106	102	86
1891	–	91	105	102	87
1892	–	91	105	97	87
1893	–	92	102	96	90
1894	–	92	101	95	91
1895	–	93	101	99	92
1896	–	94	100	95	94
1897	–	96	100	96	96
1898	100	97	102	102	95
1899	100	98	100	99	98
1900	100	100	100	100	100
1901	100	103	101	96	102
1902	103	106	100	94	106
1903	104	108	103	101	105
1904	104	112	103	98	108
1905	102	116	104	99	112
1906	106	122	107	104	114
1907	119	129	111	104	116
1908	119	131	110	103	119
1909	134	135	107	106	126
1910	131	141	110	113	128
1911	133	148	114	115	130
1912	137	152	113	119	134
1913	143	156	114	120	137

Sources: For wages, see all references in my last essay. For the years 1890–7, see Table 5.15; Mitchell uses the *Cassa Infortuni* series; ISTAT's cost of living series has never been challenged by any other estimate; the implicit deflator of private consumption reported in column 4 comes from P. Ercolani, op. cit., table XII.4.4 and is used by A. Maddison, op. cit., table E2. I do not think its use is correct in this context, as it has been argued already in the case of France and Germany.

Table 5.12 Money Wages and Cost of Living—Sweden 1890–1913

| | Money Wages | | Cost of Living | Real Wages (1):(3) ×100 |
	Phelps Brown (1)	Mitchell (2)	(3)	(4)
1890	78	74	94	83
1891	79	75	97	81
1892	79	76	95	83
1893	80	78	92.	87
1894	81	79	87	93
1895	82	80	89	93
1896	85	83	88	96
1897	88	87	91	96
1898	92	92	95	97
1899	97	96	99	98
1900	100	100	100	100
1901	98	100	98	100
1902	100	102	98	102
1903	103	103	100	103
1904	105	107	99	106
1905	105	110	101	104
1906	114	116	104	110
1907	121	122	108	112
1908	121	125	110	111
1909	121	129	109	111
1910	129	135	109	118
1911	132	137	107	123
1912	136	142	115	118
1913	139	144	115	121

It appears that at p. 441, column 1 of Phelps Brown there is a printing mistake (891 rather than 981), which I have corrected.

Sources: Both Phelps Brown and Mitchell have used G. Bagge, E. Lundberg, I. Svennilson, *Wages in Sweden*, London, 1933. Cost of living universally used comes from G. Myrdal and S. Bouvin, *The Cost of Living in Sweden 1860–1930*, London, 1933.

Table 5.13 Money Wages and Cost of Living—United Kingdom 1890–1913

	Money Wages		Cost of Living		Real Wages (1):(3) ×100
	Phelps Brown (1)	Mitchell (2)	Phelps Brown (3)	Mitchell (4)	(5)
1890	91	91	98	–	92
1891	91	92	98	–	92
1892	91	90	99	103	91
1893	91	91	98	99	92
1894	91	90	93	94	97
1895	91	89	91	92	100
1896	91	90	91	91	100
1897	93	91	93	96	100
1898	94	93	96	99	92
1899	96	96	94	94	102
1900	100	100	100	100	100
1901	100	99	99	100	101
1902	98	98	99	101	99
1903	98	97	100	102	98
1904	97	97	101	102	97
1905	97	97	101	102	96
1906	101	99	102	101	99
1907	106	102	105	104	101
1908	105	102	102	107	103
1909	103	100	103	107	100
1910	105	101	105	109	100
1911	105	101	107	109	98
1912	107	104	110	114	97
1913	109	107	112	114	97

Sources: The money wages series come from G. H. Wood, 'Real Wages and the Standard of Comfort since 1850', *Journal of the Royal Statistical Society*, March 1909 and A. L. Bowley, *Wages and Income in the United Kingdom since 1860*, Cambridge 1937. Mitchell appears not to have excluded agricultural workers. The Phelps Brown cost of living series is from Bowley, op. cit.; the Mitchell cost of living series is from the eighteenth *Abstract of Labour Statistics*.

Table 5.14 Money Wages and Cost of Living—United States 1890–1913

	Money Wages		Cost of Living		Real Wages (1):(3) (1):(3) ×100
	Phelps Brown	Abstract	Phelps Brown	Douglas	
	(1)	(2)	(3)	(4)	(5)
1890	98	101	108	98	91
1891	99	102	108	95	91
1892	100	103	108	96	92
1893	95	97	107	94	88
1894	87	89	102	92	85
1895	91	96	100	92	90
1896	91	93	100	93	91
1897	91	94	99	94	93
1898	91	95	99	94	92
1899	97	98	99	96	98
1900	100	100	100	100	100
1901	103	105	101	102	102
1902	110	109	102	105	106
1903	111	112	105	109	105
1904	109	110	106	108	103
1905	113	114	105	108	107
1906	122	116	107	112	114
1907	125	120	112	119	111
1908	112	109	109	114	102
1909	119	119	108	114	109
1910	125	128	113	121	110
1911	126	123	113	125	111
1912	131	126	115	125	113
1913	135	133	118	129	115

Sources: Phelps Brown's annual money wage series in manufacturing comes from A. Rees, *Real Wages in Manufacturing 1890–1914*, Princeton, 1961. The other series comes from the US Department of Commerce, *Historical Statistics of the United States*, Washington, 1961, series D 605 (from P. H. Douglas, *Real Wages in the United States 1890–1926*, Boston, 1930).
Phelps Brown's cost of living series comes from Rees and is more reliable than Douglas's series reported in the US Department volume, which is too heavily built with wholesale prices.

Table 5.15 Daily Wage Rates in Italian Industry 1890–1897 (lire)

	Metal-Engineering		Chemicals, Etc.		Wool		Cotton		Silk		Textiles Average		Paper	
	rates (1)	weight (2)	rates (3)	weight (4)	rates (5)	weight in textiles (6)	rates (7)	weight in textiles (8)	rates (9)	weight in textiles (10)	rates (11)	weight (12)	rates (13)	weight (14)
1890	2.85	15	2.0	10	1.75	5	1.40	20	1.00	75	1.12	50	1.25	2
1891	2.80	14	2.0	11	1.75	5	1.45	20	1.00	75	1.12	50	1.28	2
1892	2.75	14	2.0	11	1.78	6	1.45	21	1.00	74	1.14	49	1.28	2
1893	2.80	14	2.0	12	1.80	6	1.48	21	1.00	73	1.15	48	1.30	2
1894	2.85	13.5	2.0	12	1.80	7	1.50	23	1.00	70	1.17	48	1.30	2
1895	2.90	13.5	2.0	12	1.80	7	1.52	25	1.00	68	1.19	47	1.30	2
1896	2.90	13.5	2.0	12	1.82	8	1.55	25	1.00	67	1.20	46	1.30	2
1897	2.90	13.5	2.0	13	1.82	8	1.58	26	1.00	66	1.22	45	1.32	2

| | Printing | | Leather | | Mining, Etc. | | Building | | Average Money Wage | Cost of Living Index 1913=1 | Average Real Wages 1913/lire | Index 1900 = 100 of (23) (25) | |
	rates (15)	weight (16)	rates (17)	weight (18)	rates (19)	weight (20)	rates (21)	weight (22)	(23)	(24)	(25)	(26)	(27)
1890	3.00	2.5	1.90	2.5	1.80	8	1.80	10	1.66	1.0730	1.78	91.2	86.4
1891	3.20	2.5	1.90	2.5	1.90	8	1.80	10	1.66	1.0764	1.79	91.2	86.9
1892	3.20	2.5	1.90	2.5	1.95	8	1.70	11	1.66	1.0858	1.80	91.2	87.4
1893	3.20	2.5	1.90	2.5	1.90	8.5	1.70	11	1.67	1.1099	1.85	91.8	89.8
1894	3.20	2.5	1.90	2.5	1.80	9	1.70	11	1.68	1.1148	1.87	92.3	90.8
1895	3.20	2.5	1.90	2.5	1.70	9	1.70	12	1.69	1.1211	1.89	92.9	91.7
1896	3.20	2.5	1.90	2.5	1.90	9	1.70	12	1.71	1.1261	1.93	94.0	93.7
1897	3.20	2.5	2.00	2.5	1.95	9	1.70	12.5	1.75	1.1287	1.98	96.2	96.1

(24) from ISTAT, Il valore della lira dal 1861 al 1956, Rome, 1966.

R. LEBOUTTE

5.1 Passing through a Minefield:
International Comparisons of 19th-century Wages

Professor Zamagni raises important methodological problems. Some of these are well known, but they bear repetition as the basis for improving our knowledge of wages in the past.

Annual wages are often derived by multiplying daily or weekly rates by a fixed coefficient, which may be set at anything between 200 to 300 working days per year. The figure which is chosen may not reflect the actual number of days worked in the nineteenth century, for we have no idea of periods of unemployment or of overtime, not to mention traditional days off such as Easter Monday or Saints' days.

Wages series by branches of industries are sometimes combined into an overall average by means of fixed employment weights. In this case, the effects of structural changes are not taken into account and the rate of wage growth is usually understated. Moreover, we do not always know how the price series in different countries have been constructed. Finally, the annual wage series only deals with workers who were paid by the day, week or fortnight. We must remember that, in the past, a large portion of workers were paid by other means: by piecework, or by contract. For instance, an inquiry carried out in October 1903 among male workers in the Belgian metallurgical industry showed that while 82.4 per cent were paid by the hour (47.9 per cent) or by the day (33.8 per cent) or even by the week (0.7 per cent), 17.6 per cent were paid by piecework. Moreover, 19.4 per cent received premiums or fines.[1] Are these extra wages also taken into account in nominal or real wages calculations? It is not at all clear.

Zamagni is well aware of these problems, and she stresses the general problem of using average wages. The central values of the distribution (mean, median, mode) must be completed by estimates of dispersion

---

1. Ministère de l'industrie et du travail. Office du travail — section de la statistique, 'Salaires et durée du travail dans les industries des métaux au mois d'octobre 1903', Brussels, 1907, p. 25. The total number of male workers who were over 16 amounted to 84,185.

(standard variation, coefficient of variation, and so on). Let us consider as an example the distribution of wages in a coal mine near the city of Liège in 1888. The average wage per day was 2.85 francs and the modal wage was 3.50 francs; the standard deviation (0.81) and the coefficient of variation (28.5 per cent) indicate a large dispersion, and daily wages in fact varied between 1 and 4.60 francs.[2] Thus, variations in nominal wages moved according to the number of skilled versus unskilled workers, and to the structure of the workforce by age and by sex. As Zamagni notes, the structure of the working class is a crucial factor. Average wages rise or fall not only as a result of rising or falling basic rates, but also as a result of a greater weight acquired by high-wage sectors, or by high-wage regions.

More could be said about technical questions such as these, but let us turn to other areas considered in Zamagni's paper. As far as the 'basic needs' approach and household budgets are concerned, we might mention recent studies by historians of the family. Thanks to the work of L. Tilly and J. Scott,[3] we are well aware of the role of secondary and non-monetary incomes in the household budgets in the past. More recently, R. Wall has introduced the concept of the 'adaptive family economy', by which he takes into account both occupational diversity among members of the household and non-money jobs.[4] In the same way, G. Alter has indicated the impact of female wages (especially of married women) upon the budget of households in Belgium in the second half of the nineteenth century.[5] He shows a strong decline in the participation of married women in the labour force between 1853 and 1891, which seems to be related to a dramatic increase of real wages over the same period. He also stresses the role of secondary incomes from small business or trade (cabarets, garden-plots, small handicrafts). All of these jobs were generally managed by married women.

As far as the 'capabilities approach' is concerned, it is important to remember how useful non-market indicators are in measuring welfare levels. We might mention life expectancy, infant mortality, adult literacy. We might also consider the stature of recruits in the army, on which historians have considerable archival material at their disposal. The archives give not only the height but also the occupation of the recruit and of his father, diseases, level of literacy, and even household composition. Signifi-

---

2. R. Leboutte, *Evolution des salaires au charbonnage de la Grande-Bacnure (Herstal) au XIXe siècle* (forthcoming).
3. L. Tilly and J. Scott, *Women, Work, and Family*, New York, 1978.
4. R. Wall, 'Work, Welfare, and the Family: an Illustration of the Adaptive Family Economy', *The World We Have Gained: Histories of Population and Social Structure*, Oxford, 1986, pp. 261–94.
5. G. Alter, 'Work and Income in the Family Economy: Belgium, 1853–1891', *Journal of Interdisciplinary History*, 1984, 2, pp. 255–76.

cant differences emerge when the material is analysed by occupation. Mid-nineteenth-century inquiries, like one done by Dr Fossion in Liège, show that height varied between coal miners and ironworkers, for instance.[6] Of course, interpretation is not easy for many factors intervened: nutrition, hardships in childhood and so on.

Finally, when we talk of wages, we should keep in mind the psychological aspect and cultural background. In the popular culture of the nineteenth century, people were more aware of fluctuations in nominal wages than fluctuations in real wages. They were used to evaluating their welfare according to the amount of money, of coins, they kept in hand, more than by the quantity of goods they could buy. This psychological effect served to exaggerate the actual fluctuation as nominal wages rose or fell. The major strike which took place in Wallonia in March 1886 provides a good example of the popular perception of the gap between the actual level of welfare and the one people had in mind. Of course, they were in a bad situation, but they considered themselves to be poorer than they actually were! N. L. Tranter has recently remarked upon this psychological factor in the case of nineteenth-century England.[7] We can also mention the results of an inquiry carried out by the *Institut français d'opinion publique* into fluctuations in the cost of living between 1949 and 1963.[8]

6. Fossion, 'Rapport sur la condition des ouvriers et le travail des enfants', *Annales du conseil de salubrité publique de la province de Liège*, 1844, I, pp. 75–202.
7. N. L. Tranter, *Population and Society, 1750–1940: Contrasts in Population Growth*, London, 1985.
8. A. Sauvy, *La machine et le chômage. Le progrès technique et l'emploi*, Paris, 1980, pp. 47–9.

M. J. DAUNTON

5.2 Income Flows, the Family Economy and Survival Strategies

Professor Zamagni argues in her paper that in order to make a real leap forward in comparing real industrial wages in various countries, the only viable solution is an international research project using common methods. Her paper attempts to provide an agenda for such a project, and I would not wish to dissent from her excellent account of the various methodological problems which arise. What I would suggest is that her agenda of common methods might be extended in three ways.

The first way in which the research might be extended relates to Zamagni's comment that 'it might be of interest to compare the earnings of workers in the same industry' in different countries. This seems to be a useful way of proceeding: the wages of, say, a hewer in a coal mine in South Wales might be compared with the Ruhr; or a Lancashire cotton spinner with his counterpart in New England. In fact, the result might not provide a good guide to variations in standards of living between countries, unless the wage statistics are firmly placed within the context of the social history of work and of the family.

It is helpful to turn to what Zamagni calls the 'basic needs' approach, that is, whether average wages allowed the purchase of recommended food allowances. Of course, such an approach was pioneered by Rowntree with his concept of the 'poverty line' — the minimum necessary expenditure required to maintain physical efficiency. He found that 9.9 per cent of the population of York fell below this level, which he defined as primary poverty; a further 17.9 per cent were in secondary poverty, receiving above the minimum level of income but spending part of it on items which did not fall into Rowntree's schedule. The analysis so far is static, a snapshot of poverty at one date, and Rowntree argues that it must be turned into a moving picture through the use of the 'poverty cycle'. Families moved into and out of poverty and comfort over their life, so that poverty was not confined to the same 9.9 per cent of the population. An individual over his life was likely to pass through five phases: in childhood, when his parents' budget was strained by the need to support children, he would experience

143

poverty; then, as he and his brothers and sisters went to work and supplemented the family income, he would move into a phase of relative
prosperity; this would continue until he married and had his own children,
when he would fall back into poverty; prosperity would return when the
children went to work and supplemented the family income; finally, when
the children left home and his own health started to fail, poverty would
return.[1]

There is nothing startling or original about this account of the poverty
cycle, but I would suggest that it may be used to modify the simple
comparison between adult wages in the same industry in different countries
which Zamagni proposes. It might be crucial to know at what age the adult
wage was attained, and indeed whether there was any certainty that it
would be attained, for these considerations might modify the shape of the
poverty cycle as described by Rowntree. We need to escape from a static
view of industrial wages by a comparison of adult wages at one point in
time, and to analyse how they relate to income flows over the duration of a
family. In order to show how this might happen, I shall take one leading
industrial district — Lancashire — and make a comparison between the
adult wage rate in two different occupations: adult cotton spinners and adult
hewers in the coal industry.

A static comparison of adult wages in these two occupations in
Lancashire would suggest that hewers were better paid: adult spinners in
Oldham in 1906 earned 41s 8d for a 5½-day week, and hewers in 1914
earned 8s 7d for a shift or 47s 2½d over 5½ days. A static comparison
would favour the hewer, but a comparison of income flows over the family
cycle would suggest that important considerations have been neglected. In
the coal industry, promotion along the road from the juvenile haulage grade
to face work was a certain process, and there was no disparity between the
numbers in the juvenile and adult grades. At the face, the hewer himself
paid a time wage to an assistant or 'filler', who straddled the line between
face and haulage work, juvenile and adult grades. The wage was not greatly
below the hewer, at 7s 8d a shift in 1914 or 42s 2d over 5½ days, which
was slightly more than received by an adult spinner. Promotion usually
took place at around the age of 20, before marriage; the further step to
hewer took place around the age of 27. Children therefore arrived at a time
of peak earnings, which in the case of mining would fall away with failing
strength and demotion to surface work.

In the case of cotton, promotion from the juvenile or subordinate grades
to the adult grade of spinner was not certain, and was likely to be long
delayed. Each cotton spinner or minder was assisted by two other workers:

1. B. S. Rowntree, *Poverty: A Study of Town Life*, London, 1901.

the little piecer — a juvenile grade receiving 14s 0d a week in Oldham in 1906; and the big piecer — partly a juvenile and partly a junior adult grade receiving 19s 7d a week. There was a permanent oversupply of would-be minders, with between three and five awaiting each vacancy, so that some piecers were forced into the casual labour market and never attained the income of 41s 8d a week. There was a marked disparity between juvenile and adult grades, and even when a big piecer *did* become a minder, promotion might be delayed until he was 30 or above, after marriage. Children would therefore be born before the husband attained the full adult wage rate, which would lead to poverty at this stage of the family cycle; promotion might coincide with the point at which the family started to move out of the phase of poverty as children went to work; and this affluence was likely to continue much longer for a minder in the cotton industry than for a hewer, since the work was less arduous and the high wage could be held into old age. These two industries in the same area therefore had different income flows over the family cycle, which are obscured by a simple comparison between adult wage rates.[2]

Neither can it be assumed that the relationship between adult wages and the family cycle was constant for the same industrial sector in different areas or countries. This is to fall into the trap of technological determinism: in fact, the social structure of the work-force and the nature of labour relations could produce divergent results even when the technology was identical.

The wide discrepancy in income between the minder and the two piecers in the Lancashire cotton industry was not technically necessary, and it was argued by some contemporaries that it would be preferable to adopt the so-called joiner and minder system which would allow the same total remuneration to be differently allocated: two adult joiners might be paid the same moderate wage earlier in life, with the assistance of one juvenile.[3] The minder-piecer distinction did not, therefore, arise from the demands of the machinery, and in the case of New Hampshire the same machines were used with a uniform grade of operators (often female), with a team of male supervisors and mechanics to repair and adjust the machinery.

The Lancashire system was embedded in a particular social structure rather than relying upon the dictates of the machines. The position of the minders rested in part upon their success in keeping control of the process when it became fully mechanised; this position they retained through the

2. *Enquiry into Earnings and Hours*, I, *Textile Trades in 1906*, Board of Trade, London, 1909, pp. 107–8; J. W. F. Rowe, *Wages in the Coal Industry*, London, 1923, pp. 61–2.
3. S. J. Chapman, 'Some Policies of the Cotton-spinners' Trade Unions', *Economic Journal*, X, 1900, pp. 467–73; J. L. White, *The Limits of Trade Union Militancy: The Lancashire Textile Workers, 1910–14*, Westport, Conn., 1978, pp. 36–7.

146 Real Wages in 19th and 20th Century Europe

strength of their union, from which the piecers were excluded. The union entered into agreements with the employers which created institutional rigidities, so that even if the employers did want to introduce the joiner system, the costs would be high in terms of industrial conflict. Change in the social system of work would also require a major alteration in the nature of the firm, for the minders paid and controlled the piecers. The minders received a lump-sum according to the output on their spindles, and they then paid the piecers a day wage. Any increase in the speed of the machinery would therefore tend to benefit the minder, and the employer would rely upon him to ensure that the subordinate labour worked harder.

The Lancashire cotton spinner was being paid, in part, for the control of subordinate labour, forming part of the management structure of the firm. A change in the structure of employment would oblige the employers to formulate new methods of labour control, and they had little incentive to undertake this task. In New Hampshire, where the pre-mechanised industry was less important, and where unions and the institutional rigidities of collective bargaining were less significant, the employers adopted a system of direct management rather than of 'internal subcontracting'. The spinners were therefore not paid for managerial tasks.[4]

These remarks suggest that a comparison between adult wages in the same industrial sector in different countries might be misleading. We might find that a Lancashire cotton spinner was paid more than a German cotton spinner; this might be at the expense of low wages for piecers in Lancashire, whereas wages in Germany were more moderate but more evenly distributed. The age at which the adult wage was attained might affect the shape of the poverty cycle: if it came after marriage and the arrival of children, it might lead to high infant mortality and a low level of diet in childhood. There is also the question of just what was being paid for. In Lancashire, it paid for control over subordinate labour which elsewhere might be left to a separate grade of supervisory workers. What this amounts to is that historians should not consider wages in isolation, but should pay attention to the social history of work and how it relates to the social history of the family.

The second way in which Zamagni's agenda might be extended relates specifically to the social history of the family. Her discussion is based predominantly upon a comparison between industrial wages of adult males rather than of family income. Yet, as she notes of Italian studies, one male

4. W. Lazonick, 'Industrial Relations and Technical Change: the Case of the Self-acting Mule', *Cambridge Journal of Economics*, 3, 1979; 'Production Relations, Labour Productivity, and Choice of Technique: British and U.S. Cotton Spinning', *Journal of Economic History*, 41, 1981.

wage was not enough to support a wife and two children on a basic dietary intake: two or more wages or no children were needed in order 'to cross the threshold of dire misery'. In assessing the standard of living, 'family incomes and dependency ratios appear crucial'. An important consideration in international comparisons is that the contribution of family members to the household budget differed between countries. Zamagni uses the studies carried out by the British Board of Trade before the First World War in order to indicate wage levels. Thus in her Table 5.1, if Britain is 100, the wage rate for a German fitter was 85 and a French fitter 76. However, the Board of Trade also showed that there was a divergence in household size between countries. At a weekly family income of 30s–35s, there were 5.2 members per household in Britain, 4.5 in Germany and 3.9 in France. In other words, the size of the German household was 87 per cent that of the British, and the French 75 per cent.[5] The discrepancy in wage rates disappears when household size is taken into account.

Furthermore, weekly family incomes were produced differently. French male wages were lower than in Britain and Germany, but there were fewer children, which therefore allowed the wife to contribute to the family income. And despite the fact that there were fewer children in French households than in German, they made a greater contribution to the family income because they could work full-time from the age of 14, whereas in Germany they had to attend continuation schools to the age of 16. The Board of Trade indicated that, at a weekly family income of 30s–35s, the husband contributed 91.2 per cent in Germany and 79.5 per cent in France. The wife contributed 6.1 per cent in Germany and 13.8 per cent in France, and the children contributed 2.7 per cent in Germany and 6.7 per cent in France. A comparison between male wage rates might therefore be misleading. Although male industrial wages were lower in France than in Germany or Britain, the greater contribution of wives and children to family income meant that the proportion of families with an income of 40s and above was higher in France (35 per cent) than in Britain (31 per cent) or Germany (15 per cent).[6]

The third area which might be added to the agenda for international comparison relates to what may be termed 'flexible survival strategies'. I have suggested that family income varied over the 'poverty cycle', and there were also shorter-term variations arising from seasonal influences, the trade cycle, or the chances of ill-health. Families had to devise means to equalise

5. *Report of an Enquiry by the Board of Trade into Working-Class Rents, Housing and Retail Prices Together with the Rates of Wages in Certain Occupations in the Principal Industrial Towns of France*, Board of Trade, London, 1909, p. xxxv.
6. Ibid., pp. xxxv–xxxvi.

the flow of income between times of poverty and relative affluence. These strategies were not costless, and should be considered in assessing real wages. At the most simple level, the price series used to convert money wages into real wages might be affected, for the further down the social scale the more likely it was that families would purchase small amounts of goods at a relatively high price and low quality. They might rely upon very expensive forms of credit, or they would use goods as a form of 'reverse saving' which could be pawned as necessary. Families might also attempt to purchase some protection against the worst insecurities of life, through insurance against the contingencies of death, ill-health or unemployment. In Britain, insurance against these three events formed a rising scale of income from the poorest to the labour aristocrats, with only the very highly paid workers able to move beyond contingency insurance to cash accumulation through savings banks or building societies.

It might be wondered how other countries differed in this respect. In the United States, for example, there were scarcely no friendly societies such as those which provided insurance in Britain against ill-health. Instead, there were large numbers of building and loan societies which allowed the accumulation of money for house ownership. Is this to be seen as a cultural difference or as a response to different income levels, and how did it effect the standard of living of families? The adjustment to the problems of social insecurity might in any case not rest entirely upon the working-class family income, for there might be a contribution from charity, the employer or the state which could vary between countries. Again, taxation policies might differ between countries, with a varying emphasis upon direct or indirect taxation which might affect international differences in wage levels. In general, it does seem puzzling to consider the industrial wages of those who were living on the margin without also considering the stratagems which allowed for survival, and which could be a major cost not caught by traditional cost of living measures.[7]

7. P. Johnson, *Saving and Spending: The Working-Class Economy in Britain, 1870–1939*, Oxford, 1985; M. J. Daunton, 'Home Loans versus Council Houses: the Formation of American and British Housing Policy, 1900–20', *Housing Studies*, 3, 1988, 233–40, makes some comparisons with American responses.

C. SCHROEVEN and P. SOLAR

6. The Construction of Historical Price Indices, with an Illustration from Interwar Belgium[1]

Introduction

The study of real wages is concerned with determining whether workers were better or worse off at one time or place rather than at another. Since the reality of the real wage is to be found in the goods and services that workers can command as the reward for their labour, the most direct approach to this problem would be to look at their consumption. Unfortunately, it is rarely possible for the historian to document with much precision or comprehensiveness changes in the consumption of individuals or groups. Instead, the problem of the standard of living must generally be approached in a less direct manner: by calculating the real wages as nominal or money wages divided by an index of prices. The result is an implicit index of the change in consumption.[2]

---

1. The authors wish to thank Professor H. Van der Wee and the members of the Workshop on Quantitative Economic History for their help in preparing the estimates on which the second part of the paper is based, and for their many and useful comments on earlier drafts. Special thanks are due to Jan Blomme, for supplying information on the consumption of agricultural products and their prices; Guido Pepermans, for help with the construction and computation of the indices; and Rony and Gerry Smet, for help in the translation and preparation of the text.
2. The relationship between these two approaches becomes quite clear when the problem is stated formally. Assuming that all the nominal wage (W) in any period is spent, then the wage in period 0 is $W_0 = \Sigma (P_{0i} * Q_{0i})$ where P_{0i} is the price of the commodity in the period 0, and Q_{0i} is the quantity consumed. The ratio of the wage in the period 1 to that in period 0 may thus be expressed as

$$\frac{W_1}{W_0} = \frac{\Sigma (P_{1i} * Q_{1i})}{\Sigma (P_{0i} * Q_{0i})} = \frac{\Sigma (P_{1i} * Q_{1i})}{\Sigma (P_{1i} * Q_{0i})} * \frac{\Sigma (P_{1i} * Q_{0i})}{\Sigma (P_{0i} * Q_{0i})}$$

The first term in the expression at the right is an index of quantities consumed, weighted at the prices of period 1. This measure of the change in consumption is thus equivalent to the ratio of nominal wages divided by the second term in

149

Both the direct and indirect approaches to analysing changes in the standard of living face a common conceptual problem: that of adding up apples and oranges. Neither the quantities consumed nor the prices of different goods move in the same direction or change at the same rate. If comparisons of aggregate consumption or overall price change are to be made across time or space, it is necessary to impose some weighting on the movements shown by individual items.[3] The problems in choosing these weights tend to dominate the theoretical discussion of index numbers, at least among economists.

But here the focus will be on the problems of constructing *historical* price indices. For the historian the difficulties begin earlier, with the collection and criticism of the price series that will make up the index. The limits of the historical evidence must be acknowledged, both in the construction and in the interpretation of indices.

This paper first makes a brief overflight of the problems involved in the construction of historical price indices. It begins with the collection of individual price series, then takes up the questions of which prices should be included in an index and how they should be weighted.

The second part of the paper illustrates some of these problems as they arise in the reconstruction of price movements in Belgium during the interwar period. The nature and defects of the existing indices for consumer prices are discussed, then a consumption deflator for food, beverages, and tobacco is described and compared to these indices. This consumption deflator forms a part of an ongoing project whose object is the reconstruction of the Belgian national accounts for the nineteenth and first half of the twentieth centuries.[4]

---

the right-hand expression, which is an index of prices, weighted at the quantities consumed in period 0. This quotient is nothing other than an index of the real wage. This equivalence between the real wage and an index of consumption depends on the assumption that all current income is spent. If there are savings, then the real wage describes possible consumption out of current wage income. It is likely that in the short term the existence of savings will mean that real wages would display greater fluctuations than actual consumption.

3. The partition of the change in nominal wages shown in the preceding note involves consumption in quantities weighted at the prices of period 1 and prices weighted at the quantities consumed of period 0. For each comparison (of prices or quantities) the weights are fixed, but note that they are not drawn from the same period. An alternative partition would weight the quantities at the prices of period 0 and the prices at the quantities of period 1.

4. The first results of this project concern the interwar period and are described in several working papers of the Centrum voor Economische Studiën, Katholieke Universiteit Leuven.

Problems in the Construction of Historical Price Indices

Which Price   Several problems arise in choosing the price to represent a particular element in consumption. The first set of problems arises from the fact that goods are far from homogeneous. This is obviously true of clothing, household furnishings, and especially housing. But basic agricultural products, such as wheat and butter, also come in a variety of qualities, whose prices can easily differ by 10 to 20 per cent or more. The historian must then choose from the great variety of goods. It is desirable that the items chosen be consumed by the population of interest, have well-defined qualities, and can serve to represent a class of more or less similar items.

Goods are not only heterogeneous at any one time, but their characteristics change over time, making it difficult to come up with long and consistent price series. The problem is not only that goods become better (or worse), though quality improvements are very important. Changes in style or fashion may also alter the set of goods for which prices are available. It may thus be necessary to splice together several short runs of consistent observations. A related problem is that the nature of the goods bought by particular individuals or institutions may change. Many price series for clothing and household goods during the nineteenth century and earlier are based on the average values of items purchased by institutions.[5] These may well reflect the financial health of the institution and the standards it aspires to maintain as well as the characteristics of the goods.

A second set of problems stems from the fact that identical goods can sell for different prices. The classic case is the difference between wholesale and retail prices. Goods in bulk bought in centralised markets are generally cheaper; the convenience of buying small quantities closer to home costs more. Unfortunately for the historian interested in the prices paid by households, long runs of prices are much more likely to be found in the records of wholesale markets and large firms. The implications of using wholesale prices for the short term are reasonably well known: wholesale prices tend to show greater cyclical fluctuations and to change more quickly than retail prices. For the long term, however, there is a serious lack of quantitative studies that deal with trends in the retail margin.[6]

Retail prices may themselves display a large dispersion within what may seem to be the same market. Not all retailers' costs are identical, nor is competition so perfect that profit margins are constrained to the same level.

---

5. For example, the prices collected by Lord Beveridge and his group (*Prices and Wages in England*, vol. 1, London, 1939).
6. H. Barger, *Distribution's Place in the American Economy since 1869*, Princeton, 1950.

Such price dispersions are an argument for averaging retail prices from a number of outlets.

Practical problems may also arise in dealing with the wholesale prices of fairly well-defined items. For agricultural goods, for example, newspapers and other sources often record not single prices, but the range of prices at which transactions took place. In some cases this range may be quite large. More worrying is the fact that the width of the range may change over time, which may be the result of changes in the nature of the goods, in nature of the market, or in the practice of reporting.

One Price from Many: Problems of Time and Space   What frequency of observations? Cost of living indices have usually been constructed on an annual basis, though some twentieth-century indices are monthly. This means that a price representing the year's experience must be reached. Prices often vary a great deal within a year's time. The greater the variation, for any particular item, the more frequently its price ought to be observed. Rents, for example, tend to change very infrequently. On the other hand, rent changes, when they occur, may be large and, if clustered, might be missed by taking a single observation per year. Other prices — notably those of agricultural products — change quite frequently. Fortunately, much of their variability is seasonal. If this seasonality is quite regular over time (something that ought to be examined), then a few well-chosen observations may suffice to capture quite accurately the trends in these prices.

Prices from Where? Two broad strategies may be discerned in geographical coverage of price indices, although in practice many indices show features of both. One is to construct a highly specific index, with prices drawn only from a limited area. Such an index is directly applicable to nominal wage data from the same place. It may also be applied to wages in other areas if a convincing argument can be made that prices there moved in a similar way. The other strategy is to base the index on prices that are averages across a number of markets. A broad index of this sort is applicable over the larger area, but requires much more data and is thus more commonly seen in the twentieth century. If interregional price trends are similar, then such a broad index has the advantage over a specific index of reducing the impact of sampling variation on the final index. By contrast, if regional prices move in different ways, then the broad index has the advantage of being applicable everywhere (which makes it suitable for deflating an equally broad collection of wage data), and the disadvantage of being applicable nowhere in particular (which limits its value for the study of individual labour markets). What is needed, in tandem with the development of cost of living indices, are more studies of the differences in regional price levels and of the way in which regional prices change over time.[7]

Which Goods?   The discussion to this point has concerned the construction of individual price series. Now we turn to the problems involved in representing the overall pattern of price change. The first is to specify the set of goods that is of interest. In the first instance, this depends on the use to which the price index is to be put. Is it intended to deflate the wages of common labourers, artisans, managers, or all workers? The range of goods should correspond to those consumed by the group in question.

Budget inquiries are the major source used to discern the patterns of consumption. While of great usefulness, they tend to have a number of weaknesses, particularly those done before the First World War. One is that they refer in most cases to low-income groups in the population. As such, the variety of the goods consumed is often quite limited. This variety may be further truncated by the biases of the investigators or the respondents. The consumption of alcoholic beverages, in particular, often tends to be unusually low and is occasionally absent altogether.[8] Finally, budget studies usually cover relatively short periods and may miss infrequent, but large, expenditures. These weaknesses suggest that this source should be used with caution and checked against estimates for aggregate consumer expenditure (where they exist), and against other, less quantitative, descriptions of consumer behaviour.

Budget studies also tend to summarise expenditure in fairly broad categories, so the problem still remains of designating particular goods to represent them. Which sorts of meat, clothing, or housing were consumed by a particular group? If prices for these sorts are not available, will those for other sorts be suitable proxies?

Two other problems in choosing the set of goods may be mentioned briefly. The first groups together the treatment of two phenomena common until this century: payment in kind and home production. In both cases the consumer does not intervene in the goods market. Payment in kind could be logically, though perhaps not practically, dealt with either by constructing a cost of living index that pertained only to the disposition of the cash wage, or by valuing the payment in kind, incorporating it in the wage, and its price in the index. As for household production of food and clothing, it is a ticklish problem to cross the line that separates the household from the market. One solution would be to include in the price index

---

7. For example, see the work done by N. F. R. Crafts on the variations in prices paid by Poor Law Unions in Britain in the nineteenth century.
8. J. G. Williamson, *Did British Capitalism Breed Inequality?*, London, 1985, pp. 207–23.

only the purchased inputs to household production (the rent of land, raw materials). Another problem in choosing the set of goods is that over the long term, new goods enter the consumption of a particular group. Some replace existing items; others serve new functions. To make comparisons it is necessary to keep the set of goods fixed, but this risks a distortion of price experience. This problem has no easy solution.

Which Weights?   Two distinct problems arise in turning a set of price series into a summary measure of the change in prices. As a general principle, the individual series ought to be weighted in a way that reflects the importance of various goods in consumption. The first problem is to specify clearly the population to which the index applies, and to come up with a quantitative estimate of its pattern of consumption. The other problem is a more technical one: supposing that there are changes in the way the group in question spends its income, which of its consumption patterns ought to be used to weight the price series?

In practice, most historical cost of living indices refer to a population lying toward the bottom of the income distribution. This is in part because this group has a particular historical interest (at its crudest, how have the poor fared under capitalism?) and in part because it provided the subjects of the budget inquiries from which estimates for the distribution of consumer expenditure can be drawn. The extent to which this group represents wage-earners as a whole, or even a large share of this class, is not clear, although the resulting cost of living indices are widely applied.

In some cases other populations have served as the reference for cost of living indices. Consumption deflators, such as the one described in greater detail below, pertain to all households, whether those of wage-earners or not. Other indices purport to cover the working class as a whole.[9] Such indices are important for analysis at a highly aggregative level. When composed to more restrictive measures of the cost of living, they may also serve to highlight how the price experience of low income groups differed from that of other workers. Another strategy, though rarely pursued, is the construction of indices corresponding to different levels of income.[10] This is a more explicit way of discerning the impact of relative price changes on different groups in society.

9. See, for example, the contrast between the weights for all working-class households used in C. H. Feinstein, *What Really Happened to Real Wages? Trends in Money Wages and the Cost of Living in the United Kingdom, 1880–1913* (typescript, Harvard University, 1987) and the weights for the same period in J. G. Williamson, *Did British Capitalism Breed Inequality?*
10. For example, T. R. Gourvish, 'The Cost of Living in Glasgow in the Early Nineteenth Century,' *Economic History Review*, 1972, pp. 65–80.

The second problem involved in combining a set of price series into a summary measure is that consumption patterns — even for a well-specified group — change. In a comparison between prices at two dates, then, alternative weights will, in principle, be available. Neither period's consumption may stand out *a priori* as the appropriate standard, in which case there is an inherent imprecision in the measurement of the overall change in prices between the two. The economic theory of price indices is concerned with setting this problem in the framework of the theory of consumer behaviour. From it come proposals for weighting other than the choice of one or the other period's consumption pattern, but these are generally impractical for historical work. When extended to more than two periods, the problem of choosing between alternative weights leads to the well-known differences between the Laspeyres and Paasche formulas for index numbers.[11]

The historian can rarely claim much precision for the weights to be used in a cost of living index. Most budget inquiries are based on small and possibly biased samples of ill-defined populations. Only very rarely are inquiries undertaken at different dates comparable in terms of their methods and results. In this sense it might be wiser for the historian to regard budget inquiries are merely indicative of the broad features of consumption. Since modern computing facilities make it easy to recalculate an index, many variants for the weighting may be tried. In this way it would be possible to obtain an idea both of the magnitude of the errors that could enter through incorrect weighting and of the imprecision that may result from changes in consumption patterns.

Sources of Error The possibilities for error in the construction of cost of living indices are abundant. Those involved in the weighting of the various price series often get the most attention, but this may be because they are the most easy to find. It has long been recognised, as well, that errors from this source will be small unless there are large relative price changes involving items with preponderant influence on the index.[12] Far greater distortions may lie hidden in the restricted scope of an index or in the defects of the price series upon which it is based. The almost general neglect of services and the weaknesses of housing price series are cases in point. But effective criticism of these elements generally calls for new evidence, and that means the tedious, often unrewarding, but utterly essential, job of resurrecting the prices of the past.

11. R. G. D. Allen, *Index Numbers in Theory and Practice*, Chicago, 1975.
12. Ibid., pp. 42–3.

The Existing Price Indices for Interwar Belgium

At present there are two cost of living indices for Belgium that cover the whole 1920–1939 period. These are the 'official' and the 'alternative' retail price indices. The first was constructed and published monthly during the interwar period by the Belgian Ministry of Economic Affairs.[13] The 'alternative' was developed by P. Scholliers in his 1984 doctoral dissertation. We will first describe and criticise these existing indices.

The Official Cost of Living Index[14]   The social and economic climate after the First World War made apparent the need for a reliable measure of the cost of living. In industry there was pressure after the war to adjust wages to the real cost of living and later to force an automatic link between the wages and the cost of living index. The Belgian government began research on the composition of a retail price index in the course of 1919. The index itself commenced in January 1920. It was published monthly in the *Revue du travail* by the Ministry of Industry, Labour and Social Security (later the Ministry of Economic Affairs and the Self-Employed).

Agents of the Ministry of Labour recorded the prices of fifty-six commodities in fifty-nine communities, between the tenth and the twentieth day of every month. The fifty-six commodities were composed of foodstuffs (thirty-four goods), clothing and footwear (twelve goods), heating and lighting (four commodities) and six remaining articles (cf. Appendix 6.1).

The fifty-nine communities were spread over the whole country. They included the most important communities in each district (generally its

13. Apart from the retail price index the Ministry of Economic Affairs also edited a cost of living index for the period 1923–39 and a 'stabilisation' index for 1928–39.

14. For this survey we consulted: P. Scholliers, 'De koopkracht tijdens het interbellum (lonen, prijzen, prijsindex, loonindexering)', Doctoral dissertation, V.U.B., 1984, vol. II, pp. 9–100; P. Scholliers, *Loonindexering en sociale vrede: Koopkracht en klassenstrijd in België tijdens het interbellum*, V.U.B., 1985, pp. 121–41; J. Arendt, 'L'Evolution des prix en Belgique', *Confédération des syndicats chrétiens de Belgique: XIIe Congrès Hasselt 15-16 août 1936, Compte rendu général*, pp. 34–51; K. Dubois, 'Wat onze indexen inhouden?', *De Gids op Maatschappelijk Gebied*, 1926, pp. 352–63; A. Wibail, 'Evolution comparée des index-numbers des prix de détail et coût de la vie', *Revue du travail*, 1938, pp. 1209–28; E. Paternotte, 'Des méthodes suivies pour l'élaboration des index-numbers publiées en Belgique', *Revue du travail*, 1933, pp. 819–33; A. Julin, 'La réforme de l'index des prix de détail', *Revue du travail*, 1939, pp. 701–30; B.N.B., 'Statistiques économiques belges 1919–28', *Bulletin d'information et de documentation*, Special Number, April 1929, p. 87; B.N.B. 'Belgische economische statistieken 1929–40', *Tijdschrift voor documentatie en voorlichting*, Special Number, pp. 259–63.

capital). Some rural communities that had regular markets were also included. In these communities, then, 15,000 prices were noted each month, in department stores as well as in cooperative wholesale societies and retail and luxury goods shops. Establishments or markets that existed in 1914 were preferred, so that data could be collected on pre-war prices. Moreover, shops were sought which sold the same commodities regularly and had a 'stable' character.

The Ministry of Labour gathered the monthly prices and constructed the retail price index, with April 1914 as base period. The calculation of the national index involved three steps. At the local level a simple average was taken of the price relatives, i.e. $(\Sigma(P_1/P_0)/56)$, where P_1 is the current price and P_0 the price of the commodity in April 1914. Then another simple average was computed for each province from the local indices. Finally, the national index was calculated as the arithmetical average of the nine provincial indices. This method of calculation was used from 1920 to 1938.

The resulting official cost of living index was not without critics. There were heated debates about the index number between the two World Wars. In his doctoral dissertation, Scholliers has dealt extensively with the deficiencies of the index, so we will only indicate briefly some points of concern.

Although the government wanted an index of currently used commodities, the choice of goods was not informed by detailed inquiry into the consumption patterns of the Belgian population. For this reason, the range of goods was out of balance in some respects (food and clothing were generally over-represented). Some currently used commodities were excluded while other, less desired commodities, were included. One contemporary stated: 'Certainly, some commodities, for instance cocoa, tea, are not really a matter of "daily usage" especially for less well-off families. Some of them may be deleted'.[15]

The communities where prices were recorded were spread over the country, but some regions were over-represented. Urban areas were particularly heavily weighted.

The major deficiency of the official index is the way in which it was calculated. The base period to which the commodity prices were related was just the one month of April 1914. By keeping the same pre-war base period for more than twenty years, changes in consumption patterns and quality changes were overlooked. More importantly, the index was a simple arithmetical average of the price relatives. Less important commodities (like tea) and vital commodities (like potatoes) all had a weight of 1/56. Moreover, the provincial and national indices were again simple averages, with no weighting by population or income.

15. K. Dubois, 'Wat onze indexen inhouden?', p. 361.

It was also alleged that the index was subject to manipulation by interested parties. As one contemporary noted: 'It must be stressed that certain acts by the Government and by commercial groups have a considerable influence upon the index number.'[16]

As the result of contemporary criticism, some changes were made in the composition and calculation of the retail price index in 1939. Thirteen new commodities were added, and many obsolete items were left out (cf. Appendix 6.1). Prices were recorded in sixty-two communities instead of fifty-nine. Six new communities were added, while two rural centers from the province of Liège were left out, and Herstal was incorporated with Liège. The main reform concerned the calculation of the index. The average prices during the period between 1936 and 1938 served as a new, broader base. Geographic weighting was introduced in calculating the index. The local indices were weighed according to the relative importance of their population in total provincial population. For the national index the importance of each province in the total population served as the weight. But the official index was not recalculated for the period up to 1938, so these reforms are largely irrelevant to an assessment of its usefulness for the interwar period.

An Alternative Cost of Living Measure: the Brussels Retail Price Index of Dr Scholliers.[17]   As part of his doctoral dissertation Scholliers put together an alternative to the official retail price index number. He first constructed a price index for Brussels, based primarily upon the price-lists of the Brussels' cooperative wholesale society 'L'Union Economique'. Prices were published for September from 1919 till 1933 and for October thereafter. Prices of other commodities and services were obtained from the archives of institutions and from the *Revue du travail*. In all, the Scholliers index takes into account 118 commodities, the choice of which was guided by the budget inquiry of 1928–29.[18] The commodities may be summarised as follows: foodstuffs [sixty-five items], clothing and footwear [nineteen], heating and lighting [five], housing [eight], hygiene [eight], wash [three] and miscellaneous [ten] (cf. Appendix 6.1).

The Brussels price index was calculated according to a weighted arithmetical average $\Sigma(_W (P_1/P_o))/\Sigma_W$. The weights, which were changed several times within the period, were the percentage shares of expenditure on the

16. J. Arendt, 'L' Evolution des prix en Belgique', p. 36.
17. P. Scholliers, 'De koopkracht tijdens het interbellum . . .', vol. II, pp. 108–35.
    P. Scholliers, *Loonindexering en sociale vrede,* pp. 156–64.
18. A. Julin, 'Résultats principaux d'une enquête sur les budgets d'ouvriers et d'employés en Belgique', *Bulletin de l'institut international de statistique,* 1934, pp. 519–59.

relevant items in the budget inquiries of 1921, 1928–9, 1932 and 1936.[19] Indices were calculated for four different periods, with bases in 1914, 1925, 1930 and 1935, then spliced together at the base years.

A comparison between the official retail price index for Brussels (reference base 1914) and the alternative Brussels index calculated by Scholliers (reference base 1914) reveals that the two indices give similar results until 1930. The official index then shows a greater fall in the cost of living during the 1930s. Between 1930 and 1939 Scholliers's index was on average 11.8 per cent higher.

Scholliers's index has an extensive and current range of goods and weighting according to the pattern of consumption. But it does have some deficiencies. First, it is essentially an index for Brussels, which accounted for only 11 per cent of the Belgian population.[20] We attempted to check its representativeness in two ways. First, we compared the official index for Brussels with the official national index. The two indices move in much the same way. Second, we compared Brussels prices for several commodities with their prices in other markets. This showed that price movements varied considerably across the country, but we could not detect systematic differences. It may be that such differences would wash out over a properly weighed national index, but it could also be the case that the similarity of the official indices for Brussels and the nation is fortuitous.

A second deficiency of Scholliers's index is that it refers only to prices listed in the months of September (till 1933) and October (after 1933). This introduces two problems. First, because the base year prices are averages over an entire year, the price relatives may, as the result of regular seasonal price fluctuations, be systematically too high or too low. We compared the price quotations of some commodities listed in September or October to their average annual prices over the period from 1920 to 1939.[21] The price of household bread in September and October was on average 2.4 per cent higher than its annual price, the price of potatoes 5.4 per cent lower, full-cream milk 1.2 per cent lower, and eggs 15.2 per cent higher. Second, the reliance on prices for only one month may make the year-to-year movements in the index subject to slight changes in seasonality mixed with

19. 'Une enquête sur la nature et le coût de l'alimentation des classes laborieuses', *Revue du travail*, 1922, pp. 690–6; G. Jacquemijns, *Enquête sur les conditions de vie des chômeurs assurés*, Liège, 1932–4, 5 vols; J. Arendt, 'Les conditions d'existence des travailleurs et des entreprises en Belgique en 1935–1936', *Confédération des syndicats chrétiens de Belgique. XIIe Congrès Hasselt 15–16 août 1936*, pp. 3–34.
20. 10.9 per cent in 1920 and 11.0 per cent in 1930. Source: NIS, *Algemene Volks- en Woningtelling op 1 Maart 1981*, vol. I: *Bevolkingscijfers*, Brussels, 1983, pp. 80–1.
21. For this calculation we utilised the monthly price quotations and the average annual prices, which were used by the Ministry of Economic Affairs for the construction of the retail price index.

a large element of sampling variance. The relationship between the
September or October price and the annual average for the commodities
just mentioned was far from stable.

The range of goods underlying the Brussels price index was based on the
budget inquiry of 1928–9. The number and the regional dispersion of households, the length of the inquiry, the detailed recording of the different goods all
speak for the usefulness of this source. We have to be aware, however, that the
budget inquiry paid attention only to the consumption patterns of white- and
blue-collar families. Groups such as farmers, executives, small businessmen
and their families were not within the inquiry's scope. Scholliers also splices
together indices based on weights from different budget inquiries. The
populations covered by these sources are not strictly comparable. The
budget inquiries of 1921 and 1928–9 deal with the consumption patterns of
white- and blue-collar families, whereas the 1932 inquiry deals mainly with
families with an unemployed head of the household, and the inquiry of 1936
does not define its population clearly. Finally certain fresh foods, like fish,
fruit and vegetables, were not in the range of goods of either the official or
the Brussels price index. Yet, according to the budget inquiry of 1928–9,
these products had a substantial share in the food category.

Construction of an Implicit Deflator for Food, Beverages and Tobacco

Methodology of the Consumption Deflator   The difference between a cost of
living index and a consumption deflator is not so much on the theoretical
level as in the range of products and the population involved. The deflator is
in principle based on information representing all goods and services
consumed in a country during a specified period. A price index number, by
contrast, deals with a range of goods defined by the consumption of a
particular group. In a deflator the population contains all households and
non-profit institutions — in other words the entire private sector as defined
within the framework of national accounts. Price indices, in general, refer
only to private households and often to only a part of the population.[22] In
addition, cost of living indices tend to be Laspeyres indices, in which the
weights remain those of the base period, while the consumption deflator is
generally of the Paasche form, which involves weighting by the current
period's quantities. The Paasche form is used for prices so as to correspond
to the usual Laspeyres form for consumption indices.

22. OECD *Consumer Price Indices: Sources and Methods and Historical Statistics*, Special
     Issue, March 1984, p. 78.

The aim of this section is to calculate a Paasche price index for the private consumption of food, beverages and tobacco. The current state of work in the Belgian national accounts for the interwar period does not allow us to cover a wider range of consumption goods. Nevertheless, food, beverages and tobacco accounted for a large share of consumption between the wars, so that comparison to the corresponding components of the official and Scholliers's indices ought to be enlightening.

A Paasche index has the following general form:

$$\frac{\Sigma P_t}{\Sigma P_o} \cdot \frac{Q_t}{Q_t} \ \text{or} \ \frac{\text{current consumption in current prices}}{\text{current consumption in prices of the base year}}$$

The data for the numerator and denominator can easily be obtained from our material for the national accounts.

For the interwar period, we have followed as closely as possible the current methodology of the National Institute for Statistics (NIS), so as to foster comparability with the postwar national accounts. The NIS has three basic rules for estimating consumption:

1. Seek separate data on prices and quantities. Then calculate series in constant prices by multiplying the amount during the current year by the price of the base year.

2. When separate data concerning prices and amounts are not available, either: (a) divide the available series in current prices by a suitable price index, or (b) multiply the value in the reference base year by a suitable quantity index.

3. If none of the previous rules can be applied, and the item is of small importance, then the series in constant prices equals that in current prices.

The consumption deflator is obtained by dividing the total private consumption in current prices by the total private consumption in constant prices.

Sources of the Price and Quantity Data   The sources of the data underlying our estimates for consumers' expenditure on food, beverages and tobacco are laid out schematically in Appendix 6.2. For a more detailed discussion see our paper 'Consumers' Expenditure on Food, Beverages and Tobacco in Interwar Belgium'.[23]

Most price data come from the Ministry of Economic Affairs and are based on the prices underlying the retail price index. Despite the fact that no geographical weighting was used by the Ministry, a check using other data

23. C. Schroeven, *Consumers' Expenditure on Food, Beverages and Tobacco in Interwar Belgium*, Discussion paper presented at the NFWO contact group 'Economic growth and industrial revolution in Belgium (19th and 20th century)', at Leuven, April 27th, 1987.

Table 6.1 Relation Between the Belgian Ministry of Economic Affairs' Prices and the Prices of the Budget Inquiry, 1928–29

Commodity	Price According to the Budget Inquiry (1928–29) BF	Average Annual Price M.E.A. (1928–29) BF	Share of Family Expenditure
Butter	30.51	31.24	2.92
Margarine	13.41	11.54	0.75
Lard	15.16	15.97	0.44
Beef Dripping	10.59	10.13	0.46
Full-cream Milk	1.98	1.94	24.21
Bread	2.33	2.31	30.85
Potatoes	0.90	0.90	35.44
Rice	4.74	4.75	0.40
Sugar	4.23	4.33	2.52
Coffee	24.83	23.07	1.11
Chicory	4.46	4.06	0.92
Total			100.00

showed that the average annual prices were representative of the national price level. We compared several commodity prices with the corresponding prices in the budget inquiry of 1928–9. This inquiry examined the expenditure patterns of white-collar and blue-collar families, and had a broad occupational and regional coverage. For those items for which we use the Ministry's annual prices and which were also part of the budget inquiry, we calculated both a weighted average of the budget inquiry prices for 1928–9, with weighting according to occupational distribution, and a corresponding unweighted average of the Ministry's monthly prices.[24] Then we calculated a weighted average of the price differences, while taking into account the relative share of the examined goods within the whole budget. This inquiry reveals that the prices according to the Ministry of Economic Affairs are on average 99.2 per cent of the budget inquiry's prices (cf. Table 6.1).

For foodstuffs (the prices of which were not available to the Ministry of Economic Affairs), we used import or production prices, augmented by a retail margin. For other commodities (especially meats), we have average annual prices from the 1928–9 budget inquiry. These were used to set the level for series based on the prices of similar commodities.

For wine and strong drink we made use of the price-lists of a distinguished and representative company: Simkens from Borsbeek (near Antwerp). These price-lists permitted us to calculate directly the selling prices of domestically produced items and to fix the profit margins to be applied to

24. The budget inquiry of 1928–9 began in April 1928 and ended in March 1929.

the import prices of alcoholic beverages produced abroad. The representativeness of these figures was judged as follows: from the price lists of the Simkens company for 1948–50 we estimated both the wholesale and retail margins for wines and other beverages. We compared these margins with the wholesale and retail margins given by the NIS for the same period. The differences were small.

For agricultural products we took into account consumption by producers, i.e. that part of the production which is consumed by the farmers themselves. This part was valued at farm prices, which can be found, for the most part, in official publications like the Statistical Yearbook and *Het Belgisch Staatsblad.*[25] These monthly or annual prices were weighted seasonally and regionally.

Calculation of the Deflator   We possess the annual figures for the quantities consumed and for average annual prices concerning most of consumption of food, beverages and tobacco, on average 92.5 per cent of the total in current prices. These data enable us to calculate both Paasche and Laspeyres indices. We first calculated the (consumption) deflator for food, beverages and tobacco according to the Paasche formula. As reference base we chose the three-year period 1936–8 used by the Ministry of Economic Affairs after the reform of 1939. These are three relatively stable years following the devaluation of the Belgian franc in March 1935. The 1936–8 period has often been used as reference point in works dealing with the interwar period.[26]

For each item the first step was to calculate current consumption in current prices and in base year prices. This method could not be used for all goods; these exceptions are discussed below.

For fruit and vegetables we had neither the annually consumed amount nor the average annual price. We were forced to resort to import and export prices. In general import prices were preferred, as better reflecting the prices faced by Belgian consumers. Only if a very substantial part of the Belgian production was intended for export (asparagus, grapes and chicory) were export prices regarded as the more representative.

The price index for fruit was constructed as follows: for fruit grown in greenhouses and in open air average prices from 1920 to 1939 were known. For both groups we calculated prices relative to the base period (1936–8),

25. J. Blomme, 'De economische ontwikkeling van de Belgische landbouw, 1880–1980', doctoral dissertation, Leuven, 1988, pp. 12–13, 20, 22–4, 26–7, 30, 33.
26. For instance, 'De algemene indexcijfers van de nijverheidsproductie en de voornaamste indexcijfers van de nijverheidsproductie', *Belgische Economische Statistieken 1941–1950*, vol. II, pp. 231–2.

then weighted each by the total value of its production annually. Consumption of fruit in constant prices was obtained by dividing consumption in current prices by the constructed price index.

For vegetables we operated in an analogous manner. Separate price indices were calculated for vegetables grown in open air, both for trade or for consumption by producers, and for vegetables grown in greenhouses. With the price index for vegetables cultivated for consumption by producers we deflate the consumption by producers of vegetables in current prices. In order to come up with a rough price index for vegetables intended for trade, both remaining price indices were weighted by the total value of the production for each group per year. We obtained the sale of vegetables in constant prices by dividing consumption in current prices by the rough price index for vegetables intended for trade.

Other categories for which the general method could not be applied were remaining foods, mineral water and lemonade, and fruit juices. Consumption in current prices of these goods was assumed to have been a specific percentage of the consumption in current prices of a related group of products. To obtain consumption in constant prices, consumption of remaining foods (in current prices) was deflated by the deflator for total food consumption; the consumption in current prices of mineral water and lemonade by the deflator for beverages; and fruit juices by the rough deflator for the category wines and other beverages. The deflator for food, beverages and tobacco as a whole resulted from the division of the total expenditure in current prices for all these products by the total expenditure in constant prices.

We also calculated a Laspeyres index from the same material, so that our results could be compared to Scholliers's index for retail prices. The weights used were the share of each item in the total consumption in current prices of foods (excluding remaining foods) during the base period 1936–8. The prices of goods in the remaining foods category were assumed to move with this weighted average. For beverages and tobacco the same formula and the same manner of weighting were used. The prices of fruit juices, mineral water and lemonade were assumed to move with those of the included items. The overall Laspeyres index for food, beverages and tobacco was arrived at by weighting the indices for the three categories by their shares in total consumption in current prices during the years 1936–8.

The deflator calculated according to the Paasche formula hardly differs from the one calculated with the Laspeyres formula. When they do differ, the Laspeyres index is always a little bit greater than the Paasche.[27] This

27. The Laspeyres index is on average 1.1 per cent higher than the Paasche index (coefficient of variation = 1.1 per cent) (cf. Appendix 6.3).

deviation is inherent to the formulae used. The Laspeyres index always maintains the same weights, whereas the Paasche index takes into account changes in the consumed quantities. Consequently, since prices and quantities tend to move in opposite directions, the Laspeyres index is greater than the Paasche.[28] The difference in the indices are, in any case, rather small.

Discussion of the Results

Comparison of the Consumption Deflator with the Official Retail Price Index and Scholliers's Alternative Index In order to compare the deflator for food, beverages and tobacco with the existing price indices for the interwar period, we must extract their relevant components and put them in terms of the same reference years, namely 1936–8. The Ministry of Economic Affairs put only its national prices at our disposal, which made it impossible to follow their procedure of building from local to provincial to national level in constructing an index for food, beverages and tobacco. As a check on the implications of bypassing these calculations, we constructed an index for all items using the national average annual prices. The differences between this index and the official national index were very small. Thus an index for food, beverages and tobacco based on average annual prices ought to approximate closely to an index constructed from the local data according to the Ministry's procedure. It is such an index that is used here. The second cost of living index with which the consumption deflator is to be compared is that put together by Scholliers, who kindly provided us with his index for foodstuffs, with 1925 as base. We have simply changed the reference period of this index to 1936–8.[29]

A comparison of the indices leads to the following results: Scholliers's index lies, with a few exceptions, always lower than our Laspeyres index,[30] while the official index is almost always higher[31] (cf. Appendix 6.3 and Figure 6.1). The indices tend to diverge from each other during the late 1920s and come together again during the early 1930s. Scholliers's index also shows greater fluctuations than the other two indices.

28. R. G. D. Allen, *Index Numbers in Theory and Practice*, Chicago, 1975, p. 64.
29. The justification for this method is to be found in R. G. D. Allen, ibid., pp. 27–30.
30. The Laspeyres index averages 1.6 per cent higher than Scholliers's index for foodstuffs (coefficient of variation = 3.3 per cent).
31. The Laspeyres index averages 3.3 per cent lower than the official index for food, beverages and tobacco (coefficient of variation = 3.1 per cent). The official index averages 5.1 per cent higher than Scholliers's index (coefficient of variation = 4.6 per cent).

Figure 6.1 Price Indices for Food, Beverages and Tobacco in Belgium, 1920–40.
Base Period 1936–38

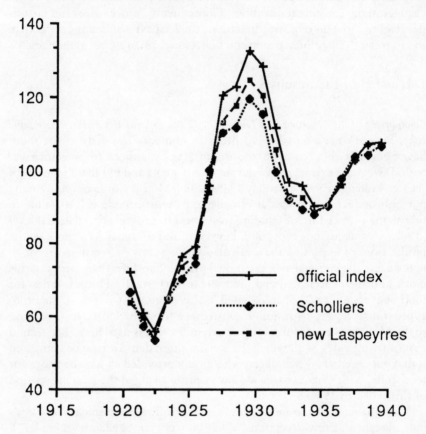

The year-to-year movements of the indices differ markedly in 1926. The consumption of food, beverages and tobacco, as deflated by Scholliers's index, shows a marked depression, whereas our index shows only a very modest decline. This result seems to be an example of the sampling error that may arise from the use of only one month's prices per year. The monthly prices in 1925–7 of a number of important foodstuffs show that there was a substantial price rise during the autumn of 1926, which was due to an expected and actual devaluation of the Belgian franc in October of the same year. Thus, an index based on prices in September produces a larger jump between 1925 and 1926 than would have been the case if the index had been based on average annual prices. We also investigated whether other differences between our index and Scholliers's might be due to his use of only one month's prices. We calculated two indices with the same weights,

Figure 6.2 Index based on Average Annual Prices versus Index based on
September–October Prices

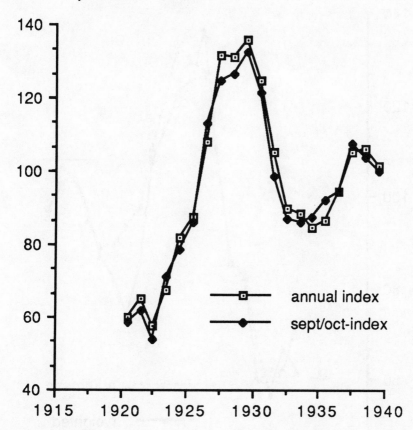

one used September or October prices for twenty commodities; the other
average annual prices.[32] In all, 60 per cent of the private expenditure on
food, beverages and tobacco was included. The weights were taken from
the 1928–9 budget inquiry. The index based on the average annual prices is
very similar to the consumption deflator we constructed, whereas that
based on September or October prices resembles Scholliers's index (cf.
Figure 6.2). The speed of the rise between 1925–6 can be seen to depend on
the choice of prices. The level of the annual index between 1927 and 1933
always is higher than the monthly one. This suggests that Scholliers's use of
monthly prices explains much of the difference between his index and ours.

32. It concerns the monthly prices which the Ministry of Economic Affairs took
    down for the construction of the official index.

Figure 6.3 Price Indices for Twelve Commodities 1920–40. Base Period 1936–38

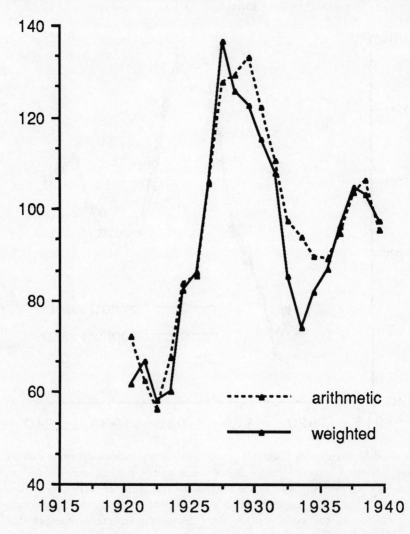

The consumption of food in constant prices, as calculated using the official index, almost always lies below our deflator. We believe that this difference in level results from the lack of weighting in the construction of the official index. The range of foods happened to be extensive and can be regarded as quite representative (thirty-six of the fifty-six index commodities were foodstuffs). Moreover, we have noted above that the recorded prices, in spite of possible manipulation, represent a realistic picture of the price level in the country. The cause for the deviant course remains only to be found in the manner of calculation. Neither the relative importance of the products nor geographical factors were taken into account.

To demonstrate the influence of the lack of weighting, we constructed weighted and unweighted indices for a group of twelve foodstuffs for which Ministry prices were available.[33] This is a limited check, for only 37.5 per cent of total consumption of foodstuffs in current prices is involved, but the results are suggestive. The unweighted index for these twelve products is on average 4.7 per cent higher than the weighed index (minimum 7.0 per cent lower, maximum 26.8 per cent higher). The differences are especially large from the end of the 1920s into the second half of the 1930s. Applied to the course of consumption, the weighted index produces a sharper rise in consumption at the end of the 1920s and a more marked drop during the 1930s.

We lack the necessary data for the application of a geographical weighting to this price index. Scholliers has calculated a geographically weighted version of the official national index number for fifty-six products.[34] In the early 1920s, the differences between the unweighted and weighted index numbers were small; from 1926 onwards the weighted index number averaged 2.38 per cent higher than the unweighted.

The price indices for the interwar period are not markedly different. Nevertheless, when used to deflate consumption their differences turn out to be significant (cf. Figure 6.4). Scholliers's index implies that there was a strong increase in the consumption of food, beverages and tobacco in the second part of the 1920s and that the impact of the depression was very heavy. The official index shows less of an increase at the end of the 1920s and the surprising result that the depression had very little impact on consumption. The consumption deflator, based on the material from the national accounts, shows an evolution between the two. We believe this to be more realistic, in part because consumers' expenditure on basic items like food, beverages and tobacco ought not to display big leaps from one year to another.

It is likely that when other consumption goods are taken into account the movements and levels of the different indices will show greater differences. We think that Scholliers's index will probably be closer to the truth, because it includes a large number of products and is weighted.

33. It concerns the quantity data which we calculated in the framework of the national accounts. We had both the prices of the Ministry and detailed amounts only for these twelve products. For this reason the spot-check could not be more extensive (cf. Figure 6.3).
34. P. Scholliers, 'De koopkracht tijdens het interbellum', p. 131.

Figure 6.4 Consumers' Expenditure on Food, Beverages and Tobacco at Constant Prices, 1920–40. Base Period 1936–38 (1000 BF)

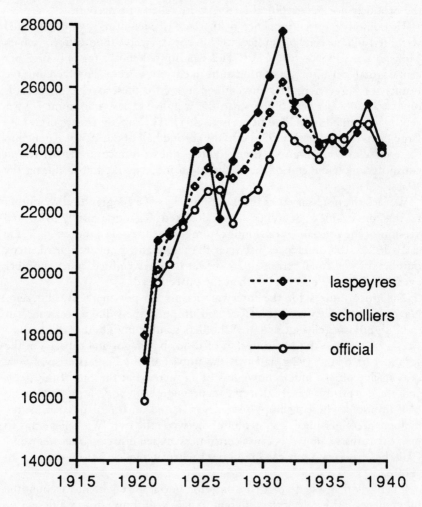

Appendix 6.1 Product Coverage of Official and Alternative Cost of Living
Indices

Official	*Scholliers*
Foodstuffs: household bread, potatoes, full-cream milk, skimmed milk (from 1920 till 1932), eggs, farm butter, factory butter, margarine, coffee, chicory, tea, rice, lump sugar, beans, olive oil, peanut oil, vinegar, salt, sardines, kippered herrings, beef dripping, entrecôte, minced meat, meat for soup, pork chops, home-produced bacon, American bacon (from 1921 till 1935), lard, black pudding, liver pâté, household beer in barrels, cocoa, chocolate, macaroni (Added in 1939: Dutch cheese, tinned salmon, two qualities of tinned peas, apple dough, table beer in bottles, veal ragout and cooked ham) (Deleted in 1939: skimmed milk (since 1932), kippered herrings, olive oil, table beer in barrels, American bacon (since 1935), black pudding, liver pâté, tea)	*Foodstuffs:* bread, flour, raisin bread — margarine, butter — animal dripping, lard — eggs — milk, canned milk — Gruyère cheese, Gouda cheese — liver pâté, black pudding, corned beef, bacon, Ardennes' ham, ham, sausage, pork, beef, fresh sausages, dried peas, tinned tomatoes, tinned mushrooms, tinned soup, tinned peas, tinned French beans, tinned spinach, tinned asparagus, dried beans — potatoes, tinned salmon, tinned sardines, herring, tinned pickled herring, raisins, prunes, tinned pineapple — malt, chicory, coffee — beer — jam, gingercake, biscuits, cookies, cocoa, chocolate — vinegar — meat extract, nutmeg, pepper, tinned gherkins, salt, mustard, ketchup, flavouring — macaroni, vermicelli — rice — syrup, sugar — olive oil, peanut oil
Clothing: white cotton shirt, white shirt in mixed linen, collar, working socks, ordinary socks, bowler hat, working cap, smart cap, waistcoat, men's shoes, clogs, resoling of men's shoes (Added in 1939: working trousers, wool and unbleached cotton) (Deleted in 1939: white shirt in mixed linen, ordinary socks and working cap)	*Clothing:* suit — cap, trilby hat — slippers, children's shoes, women's shoes, shoe polish, shoe repair — trousers made to measure, ready-to-wear trousers, tie, collar, tights, socks, knickers, pants, shirt, wool, umbrella
Heating and lighting: coal, gas electricity and candles (Added in 1939: nutcoal (20/30)) (Deleted in 1939: row coal and candles)	*Heating and lighting:* coal — gas, electricity, candles, matches
Remaining articles: pipe tobacco, matches, scrubbing brush, floor-cloth, brown soap, Sunlight soap (Added in 1939: starch)	*Housing:* rent — dishcloth, coffeepot, coffee grinder, breadknife, floor cloth, soft soap, broom
	Hygiene: solid white soap, medicines, comb, razor, toothpaste, toothbrush, shaving soap, eau de Cologne

Appendix 6.2 Sources of Data Underlying Estimates of Consumers' Expenditure on Food, Beverages and Tobacco in Interwar Belgium

Expenditure Item	Prices	Quantities
I. 1. *Food*		
1. Bread and cereals		
1.a. Bread and related products (household bread, special varieties of bread, sandwiches)	Average annual price of bread (Ministry of Economic Affairs)	Production of bread cereals (Jan Blomme)[a]
1.c. Rice	Average annual price of rice (Ministry of Economic Affairs)	Net imports (Foreign Trade Statistics)[b]
2. Meat and meat products (different kinds of fresh, frozen, canned and salted meat)	Level: weighed average price according to the budget inquiry of 1928–9; fluctuations: price quotations of the M.E.A. for various kinds of meat	Production data (Statistical Yearbook)[c]; (Blomme)
3. Fish (fresh and cured fish)	Average import price, increased by the distribution margin	Statistical Yearbook — annually published sea-fishery statistics and net imports
4. Milk, cheese, eggs		
4.a. Fresh and preserved milk (full-cream milk, skimmed milk, butter milk, yogurt and cream)	1) Average annual price (M.E.A.) 2) Level: weighed average price according to the budget inquiry of 1928–9; fluctuations: average annual price of milk 3) price data from the Flandria dairy	Data on milk production (Blomme)
4.b. Cheese	Level: weighed average annual price according to the budget	Percentage of the total milk production

	inquiry of 1928–9; fluctuations: average annual import price	
4.c. Eggs	Average annual price (M.E.A.)	Consumed quantity (Blomme)
5. Oils and fats		
5.a. Butter (farm and factory butter)	Average annual price (M.E.A.)	Production data (Blomme) net imports
5.b. Margarine	Average annual price (M.E.A.)	Belgian production and net imports were published in the Statistical Yearbook
6. Potatoes, fruit, vegetables		
6.a. Potatoes	Average annual price (M.E.A.)	Consumption data (Blomme)
6.b. Fruit	Part of the production in total value multiplied by a coefficient of commercialisation	
6.c. Vegetables	Part of the production in total value multiplied by a coefficient of commercialisation	
7. Coffee, tea, chicory	Average annual price (coffee and chicory) Tea: level: weighed average price according to the budget inquiry of 1928–9; fluctuations: average annual import price	Net imports (tea and coffee) Belgian production (Blomme), increased by net imports (chicory)
8. Sugar, jam, confectionery		

continued

Appendix 6.2 continued

Expenditure Item	Prices	Quantities
8.a. Sugar	Average annual price (M.E.A.)	Quantity intended for consumption published in the Statistical Yearbook
9. Remaining foods (pastry and biscuits, chocolate, jam . . .)	8.72 per cent of the value of the consumption on the other foods	
I.2. *Beverages*		
1. Mineral water and lemonade	6.66 per cent of the value of the consumption on other beverages	
2. Beer	Price data from the Confederacy of Belgian Brewers; average annual price of household beer (M.E.A.)	Quantity for consumption published in the Statistical Yearbook
3. Alcohol	Price-lists of the Simkens Company; import prices	Imports (Foreign Trade Stat.) home production (Statistical Yearbook)
4. Wines and other beverages	Price-lists of the Simkens Company; import prices	Imports (Foreign Trade Stat.) home production (Statistical Yearbook)
I.3. *Tobacco Products*	Official revenue statistics (Statistical Service of Customs and Excise-duties); Fedetab statistics (Confederacy of Tobacco Industries)	Official revenue statistics (Statistical Service of Customs and Excise-duties); Fedetab statistics (Confederacy of Tobacco Industries)

(a) Dr Jan Blomme has calculated the Belgian interwar agricultural production and the farm prices in his doctoral dissertation, 'De economische ontwikkeling'.

(b) From 1920 till 1931: *Tableau du Commerce Extérieur de la Belgique et du Grand-Duché de Luxembourg*, Brussels. From 1932 onwards: *Bulletin mensuel du Commerce Extérieur de l'Union Belgo-Luxembourgeoise avec les pays étrangers*, Brussels, NIS.

(c) NIS, *Statistisch Jaarboek van België en Belgisch-Kongo*, Brussels, 1920–40.

Appendix 6.3 Price Indices for Interwar Belgium: Food, Beverages and Tobacco

Year	Official Index	Scholliers Index	New Deflator (Paasche)	Laspeyres
1920	70.23	64.85	61.33	61.88
1921	59.09	55.29	57.46	57.85
1922	54.04	51.46	50.00	51.63
1923	63.24	62.77	60.56	62.68
1924	74.19	68.19	69.71	71.69
1925	77.20	72.62	74.34	74.54
1926	94.09	98.10	91.41	92.23
1927	118.67	108.37	110.59	111.06
1928	121.08	109.64	114.17	115.85
1929	130.81	117.57	120.66	122.88
1930	126.28	113.49	116.83	118.69
1931	109.74	97.81	102.50	103.91
1932	94.86	90.11	89.55	91.14
1933	93.78	87.65	89.98	90.54
1934	88.15	86.15	86.14	86.56
1935	88.20	88.31	88.48	88.48
1936	94.23	95.86	94.20	93.97
1937	100.70	101.87	101.11	100.91
1938	105.13	102.28	105.54	105.27
1939	105.57	104.49	104.64	105.01

D. J. VAN DER VEEN

6.1 The Sophistication of Real-Wage Series

After reading the preceding paper, I was confronted with a serious problem: how to make comments on such a very thorough investigation. A famous definition of history is 'discussion without end'. However, if there is one field where the discussion is ending because we are running out of questions it must be the construction of historical price indices in interwar Belgium. I want to compliment the authors on their research which, as far as I know, has no match in the Netherlands.

I would like to discuss, however, the selection of articles for the price indices in connection with a question concerning the usefulness of budget inquiries. One of the weaknesses of this source in their view is that 'the variety of the goods consumed is often quite limited' (p. 153). Although this must be irritating to researchers determined to make the right selection of goods for their indices, this 'weakness' might be a strong point at the same time. One conclusion that can be drawn from a systematic analysis of several budget inquiries is that there is a strong connection between spending power and the number of articles purchased. This connecton is well known, especially in the field of dietary patterns (e.g. the work of John Burnett and Derek Oddy).[1] Is there a relation between this observation and the topic we are discussing, the construction of historical price indices? I think there is, because it would mean that various price series are needed for various social groups, even within the working classes (using a plural seems very appropriate here). Of course, there is a possibility of disagreement about this suggestion; as we are talking about interwar Belgium, the variety of food patterns within the working classes should not be overestimated. It appears to me that this is true only for staple foods and not for items which can be considered more or less as luxuries. Some research, undertaken by the Dutch government during the crisis of the 1930s, provides evidence

1. J. Burnett, *Plenty and Want*, London, 1966, p. 29. D. J. Oddy, 'A Nutritional Analysis of Historical Evidence: the Working Class Diet 1880–1914', in D. J. Oddy and D. S. Miller, *The Making of the Modern British Diet*, London, 1976, pp. 214–32.

176

pointing in this direction.[2] Besides, since the interwar years contain a period of boom and a severe economic crisis as well, we are faced with an additional problem: there is evidence that during the years of crisis, social differences even within the working classes increased. In connection with the suggestion of the existence of a relation between prosperity and variety of food and spending patterns, this would mean that during the crisis even more price series are needed, or at least that the weights assigned to various articles should be adjusted.

Secondly, I would like to go deeper into the paper's suggestions about the study of alcohol consumption. I agree that working-class budgets tend to underestimate the use of alcoholic beverages. But what should be used as an alternative source? Figures on per capita consumption may be better, but before we can arrive at definite conclusions, at least more research should be done into social differences in alcohol consumption. This is a very difficult subject indeed. Research into the consumption of alcohol in the Netherlands suggests a decline of consumption beginning about 1870 until well into the 1950s. Various causes can be given for this: better food, fewer working hours and, last but not least, cultural processes. From the end of the nineteenth century working-class families tended to imitate middle-class lifestyles and values, which meant a rising pressure on working-class families to mitigate drinking habits. Even during the 1930s alcohol consumption in the Netherlands declined. Is a comparable situation discernible in interwar Belgium and, if so, would Schroeven and Solar feel forced to change the weight assigned to alcohol in their price series?

From the comments given here, one might get the impression that I am critical about the idea of real wages and the construction of price series altogether, and prefer the analysis of working-class budgets in solving the question put in the first lines of the paper's general introduction. As a matter of fact, I am not, but I would suggest a different relationship between the study of real wages and the analysis of working-class household accounts. From Schroeven and Solar's paper I got the impression that in their view working-class budgets function mainly to get a list of the purchased goods and services and, preferably, the weights to assign to them. Next, the authors construct price indices and perhaps later real-wage series. These two sets of data seem in their view to have more sophistication than budgetary analyses, and especially these last two sets of data should give the

2. J. F. Reith and A. Gorter, 'De Nederlandse voedingsenquetes', *Voeding*, 3 (9e jaargang, 1948), pp. 81–106. D. J. van der Veen, 'Standard of Living and Nutritional Standards of Working-class Families in the Netherlands, c. 1850–1940', paper for colloquium 'The Standard of Living in Western Europe', Amsterdam/Leiden, 15–17 September 1983.

answer to the standard of living question. I would suggest a different strategy.

To begin with, the construction of real-wage series is very important. But at some point, perhaps when series more or less corroborate one another, it seems useful to put a provisional end to this type of research. The set of data compiled then might serve as a starting point for further investigation, in the end aiming at the sophistication of the real-wage series. In the study of standard of living I would suggest a division between the situation workers had to cope with (real-wage series could be a reflection of this situation) and the way working-class families faced this situation. The latter might be studied from working-class budgets, which give insight into the flexible survival strategies employed by the families under review. From the study of household accounts new questions can be raised which, when answered, will improve the construction of real-wage series.

I will only raise a few questions here. First, while food-prices might raise problems, other categories of prices are even more difficult to study. In particular, housing costs are difficult to study, to say nothing of the difficulties found in assessing qualities to the amounts found in sources. Can this problem be solved? I am not sure. For the Dutch situation, working-class budgets give some information and larger collections in particular even provide us with a sort of pattern. The problem, however, is far from solved.[3] We should be aware of this problem, because a real-wage series might be compared with a chain, which implies that its significance is as strong as its weakest link. Secondly, there is a problem in the field of wages. Suppose we find evidence that part of the improvement in working-class families' living conditions is used to withdraw women and children from the labour market. As far as the Netherlands are concerned, this situation in my view is not as hypothetical as I put it here. But how should we take this aspect into account when constructing real-wage series?

To sum up, I am quite impressed by the authors' price series. I would suggest, however, a different relationship between the construction of real-wage series and the analysis of household accounts. I think both approaches can corroborate one another and, what is more, cannot do without one another. I have severe doubts as to whether the standard of living question raised in the general introduction can be solved, if at all, solely by the study of real wages.

---

3. D. J. van der Veen, 'Bestedingen aan huur door arbeidersgezinnen aan het begin van de 20e eeuw', in P. M. M. Klep et al. (eds), *Wonen in het verleden 17e–20e eeuw, economie, politiek, volkshuisvesting, cultuur en bibliografie*, Amsterdam, 1987, pp. 39–48.

J. L. VAN ZANDEN

6.2 One Cost of Living Index?

The first part of Schroeven and Solar's paper is a valuable attempt to summarise the main sources of error found in the construction of historical cost of living indices. The points I would like to add are related to the assumption, implicit in this kind of research, that products and consumers are more or less homogeneous and that the market mechanism works well. When these conditions are met, the construction of *one* cost of living index is appropriate. When price controls, black markets, dual economic structures and other distortions are present, the concept of *one* cost of living index may lose its value.

The authors acknowledge that large differences in income levels and in patterns of consumption between social classes may make it necessary either to select an income group for which an index is constructed, or to construct separate indices for different income groups. Of course, it is clear these exercises only become relevant when large differences in income level occur in combination with rapid changes in *relative* prices. A number of recent studies on the development of income-specific cost of living indices of groups of households in the Netherlands, Sweden and the United Kingdom concluded that the differences between the various indices were small and almost insignificant.[1] One has to turn to 'dual' economies — Poland in the seventeenth and eighteenth century[2] or Indonesia in the 1930s — to find more meaningful examples of the construction of income-specific cost of living indices. In Table 6.2 the comparison of the indices of European and Indonesian government officials and of 'average Indonesians' in a period of very rapid changes in relative prices shows that under these extreme circumstances, large differences in the development of the cost of living may occur. Apart from such extreme examples, in the greater part of our work it seems safe to restrict research to the construction of one 'working-class' index.

1. These studies are summarised in B. M. Balk, 'Huishouden-specifieke prijsindex-cijfers 1980–82', *CBS Statistisch Magazine*, 4, 1982, 2, pp. 5–17.
2. W. Kula, *Théorie économique du système féodal*, Paris, 1970, pp. 92–7, gives another example.

Table 6.2 Indices of the Cost of Living in Indonesia, September 1936
          (1929 = 100)

Income group Government officials	Average per capita income in 1929	Index
European (high income)	2580	58.9
European (low income)	1164	56.3
Indonesian (high income)	540	51.8
Indonesian (low income)	192	47.3
Average Indonesian	60	41.0

Source: *Changing Economy in Indonesia*, V, National Income, p. 80.

The most important sources of error which Schroeven and Solar over-look in their paper are the problems that arise from government policies to keep down prices through price controls and rationing. During both World Wars such policies were enacted on a large scale, and after 1945 rationing was only slowly abolished. The point is that every effective policy to control prices and every 'effective' rationing system is accompanied by a black market, where prices are much higher than the official (maximum) prices. The role of the black market becomes crucial, especially when the quantities of food that are distributed are insufficient to cover the daily needs of the population. G. T. Trienekens, for instance, estimated that 20–25 per cent of the food consumption of the population of the Netherlands in 1942–3 and 1943–4 was withheld from the rationing system and sold/bought in the black market.[3] It is well known that in other countries, Belgium for instance, the black market was even more impor-tant.

The coexistence of two markets, an official one and a black one, makes it very difficult to generalise about movements in prices and the cost of living. As far as I know, the official indices only make use of the official maximum prices and are therefore often almost useless. Data on black-market prices are scarce and of dubious quality. Moreover, it is very hard to find out what share of the budget was spent on black-market goods.

To offer some idea of the bias that may occur when black markets are ignored, an alternative cost of living index for the Netherlands in 1942 and 1943 was calculated, based on extremely conservative estimates on the degree of dependence on the black market (Table 6.3). It turns out that the actual cost of living, estimated in this way, increased much faster than the official index; real wages were almost halved between 1938–9 and 1943. This finding illustrates that the official indices of the years during, and

3. G. M. T. Trienekens, *Tussen ons volk en de honger*, Utrecht, 1985, p. 361.

Table 6.3 Cost of Living Indices of Working-class Families in the Netherlands, 1942–43 (1938–39 = 100).

	1942	1943
Official index	143.4	148.7
Estimated relative level black market prices (official prices = 100)	500	700
Corrected index[a]	190.4	221.9
Nominal wages	115.9	127.1

[a] Based on the estimate that 22 per cent of the food consumption is bought on the black market.
Source: B. Pruijt, *De prijsbeheersingspolitiek*, Leiden, 1948.

directly after, both World Wars are extremely unreliable; new research has to be done before anything can be said on the movement of the cost of living in these periods.

7. Historical and Institutional Determinants of Long-Term Variation of Real Wages

In the capitalist mode of production, labour power has become a commodity, and therefore has a price. This is a statement of fact, a recognition of what goes on in real life, not a value judgment on the intrinsic nature of labour. Far from implying any disparagement of labour, it implies a moral condemnation of capitalism, of market economy, because they reduce labour power to the status of a commodity.

Like the prices of all commodities, the price of the commodity 'labour power' (i.e. wages: we speak of 'real wages' in the sense of eliminating the influence of money fluctuations on wages) oscillates around its value as a function of the law of supply and demand. Its value can roughly be defined as the reproduction costs of labour power at the given average productivity of labour: the amount of social labour necessary to reproduce that commodity, to enable the worker — and in a larger sense the working class — to restart working with the given intensity of effort each day, week, month, year, etc. These reproduction costs of labour power fluctuate with the average productivity of labour in agriculture and with the wage goods (goods and services) sector of industry.

Stable real wages can therefore imply a decline in the value of labour power *ceteris paribus*, a declining share of *productive* labour in a growing national income, once there is a lasting increase in that average productivity of labour. As the secular trend is obviously one of such a lasting increase, stable real wages would indeed imply such a declining average share, which can be statistically 'dissolved' or 'hidden' by operating with the category 'wage share' in the national income, adding wages of productive and wages of unproductive labour in an indiscriminate way.

But the long-term trends of wages are not a mirror reflection of the long-term fluctuations of the commodity labour power's value. The law of supply and demand weighs upon wages not only in a short-term way, within the framework of the business cycle (demand for labour power increasing strongly in phases of boom and overheating, and declining in phases of crisis and stagnation). It also operates in the long term, sometimes even on a secular basis, in relation with the historically given dimension of the *reserve army of labour*, of the excess supply of labour power. Five basic historical situations and/or trends must be examined in a separate way, in that context, although there are obvious interconnections between them:

(a) The population situation at the outset, i.e. at the inception of the capitalist mode of production. Thinly populated or 'empty' countries or, what amounts to the same, countries with large unappropriated reserves of land on which potential wage-earners can settle as free independent farmers as an alternative to working for capitalist employers, will therefore enjoy from the start a higher wage level than densely populated countries with a large pool of unemployed or underemployed urban and especially rural labour. Witness the wage level from the beginning of the nineteenth century in the USA and Australia versus Western (not to say Eastern and Southern) Europe. Witness the wage level from the nineteenth century on in Argentina and Uruguay versus Mexico. Witness the significant long-term wage differentials between Siberia and European Russia.

(b) The long-term (say, within a time framework of several decades) relation between the rate of growth of the economy (of accumulation of capital) on the one hand, and, on the other hand, the rate of growth of the supply of labour that has no independent means of subsistence. This second movement has in its turn to be decomposed into the demographic movement, and the movement of transforming traditional peasants and handicraftsmen into dispossessed proletarians not immediately gainfully employed, i.e. the creation of a huge labour surplus in town and countryside. If the economy's rate of growth is higher than the supply of labour's rate of growth, the long-term tendency of real wages will be upward. If the economy's rate of growth is lower than that of the supply of labour, the long-term trend of real wages will be downward (except for the wages of scarce, highly skilled labour). The second tendency was predominant in Europe from the fifteenth century until the middle of the nineteenth century, if not later in the less-industrialised capitalist countries. It was predominant in the so-called 'third world' throughout the nineteenth and most of the twentieth centuries. The first tendency started to assert itself in the second half of the nineteenth century, first in England, then in France, certain parts of Germany, Belgium, Bohemia, Northern Italy, parts of Austria and Spain, etc.

(c) Once a capitalist country is widely industrialised, the relation between the economy's rate of growth and the productivity of labour's rate of growth strongly influences the fluctuations of the reserve army of labour, and thereby the fluctuations of real wages. When the first equals or outdistances the second, the tendency is towards full employment. When the second outdistances the first for a longer period — a depressive long wave

— structural unemployment grows. Under capitalist conditions, a relatively high rate of growth of productivity of labour is always essentially labour-saving, i.e. substitutes fixed capital (machinery) for living labour. That is why there is this implication of the correlation between the average rate of capital accumulation and the average rate of growth of productivity of the labour.

(d) Large long-term international migration of labour as a partial correction of the situations and movements described in (a) and (b). Capitalism has been characterised by huge shifts in the world population through large-scale migration, a factor that has not yet been sufficiently integrated into economic analysis and theory. The basic law (trend) is that surplus labour emigrates towards areas with a relative scarcity of labour compared to available capital, and not the other way around, (although the second trend coexists with the first as a minor phenomenon). The largest international migration movements are those from Europe towards North America since the 1840s, towards Argentina, Brazil and Australia since the end of the nineteenth century; from Puerto Rico, Mexico and Central America towards the USA; towards the Pacific Ocean countries (and Australia) from China; towards Western Europe from East Germany, Southern Europe and Northern Africa; towards Israel from Europe (including the USSR) and the Arab countries; from Egypt, Palestine, Pakistan and Sri Lanka to the richest OPEC countries (Saudi Arabia, Kuwait, the Gulf Emirates); and from Lebanon to South America and Western Africa, in the twentieth century.

But these movements are not continuous and come in waves (they are in fact tied to the 'long waves of capitalist development'). In that respect, 'positive' and 'negative' effects upon the long-term trends of real wages are undeniable. This can be studied in specific cases like those of Canada, Australia, New Zealand and Hong Kong, where the relative abundance of immigration, or its sudden 'drying up', has clear effects upon wage trends.[1] But it is also obvious that there is no automatic regulation here, no mechanical 'overdetermination' by 'long waves', but an interplay of spontaneous economic forces and of institutional interventions: government immigration policies/legislation; the relative weight of employers/lobbies and trade-union intervention upon them; the pressure of racism and xenophobia in public opinion, including that inside the labour movement, etc.

(e) The relation of gainfully occupied women as against women tied to

---

1. The most striking recent examples are those of the German Federal Republic, where wages remained relatively low as long as a constant stream of refugees from the East entered the labour market, and Hong Kong where the same phenomenon occurred, as long as there was a massive influx of refugees from mainland China. As soon as these streams were stopped, sustained and rapid economic growth led to a steep rise of wages.

domestic labour pure and simple, and the degree to which an increase of the first is partially or totally neutralised by lowering the average retirement age of male labour, and by extending effective scholarisation of youth.[2]

A 'secular' increase in women's employment has a positive effect on wages in general, i.e. leads to a rise of the value of the commodity labour power. Domestic labour under capitalism is unpayed labour. But it constitutes an essential contribution to the reproduction of labour power, providing the unpaid services of cooking, washing, laundering, heating, child-rearing, etc. When housewives become more and more employed outside the family, as a result of the burden of a 'double work day' imposed on them, their physical and psychological disposition to provide these services declines. Hence the appearance of commodities and services to replace that unpaid labour, at least in part. Hence the need for wages to include the purchasing price of these goods and services.

In other words: the supply of potent labour on the labour market is not a straight function of the purely demographic trend, but has to be seen in the light of its interaction with the trends which have been outlined in (e). The combination of all these five factors will go a long way to explain why the relations of supply and demand *historically* make for different trends (or degrees of increase) of real wages, say in Britain or Belgium at the beginning and at the end of the nineteenth century; in northern (and later central) Italy around 1870 and 1910; in the industrialised parts of Poland in 1890 and 1910, and then again (in the reverse) in the 1920s and 1930s, etc.

The reproduction costs of any commodity are an objective real social *datum*, not an abstract entity or concept. The value of the commodity 'labour power' is likewise neither individual nor subjective nor 'ideal', but can be read concretely from data in each country with a minimum of capitalist (wage labour/capital) relations of production and of distribution. But there is a difference between the commodity 'labour power' and all other commodities. Whereas the constitutive elements of the social reproduction costs of other commodities are generally given by purely technological coefficients — the relative inputs of fixed capital, raw materials and living labour which enter their output at a prevailing technique of production — no such stability exists regarding the social reproduction costs of labour power.

2. We do not examine here the specific problem of highly skilled labour's wages, as significantly deviant from average wage trends. This is obviously tied to the problem of skill formation through the education system, involving not only the overall level of expenditure on education, but also the relative flexibility of the education system to the changing needs of highly skilled labour, as a result of successive technological revolutions.

Here two different elements enter the equation: the physiological minimum below which real wages (real workers' consumption) cannot fall without destroying labour power, i.e. making continuation of production impossible,[3] and a variable element which Marx called the 'moral-historical' component of wages.

We have to understand that component, and the variety of real wages it implies both in time and space, in a threefold sense. First, a given level of socially recognised needs exists in every precapitalist society, when capitalist relations of production start to unfold, i.e. when wage labour starts to develop into something more than a socially marginal phenomenon. That the small peasant and handicraftsman's level of historically determined and socially recognised average consumption will be the starting point from which the wage level will develop — especially the level of consumption in precapitalist towns.

Now, these levels vary strongly among different countries, not to say different continents. They were much lower among precapitalist handloom weavers in India than among precapitalist handloom weavers in China, Italy or Flanders, for various historical reasons.[4] They were much lower in eighteenth-century Mexico and Peru than in eighteenth-century English-speaking North America. This fact undoubtedly has an influence on the level of real wages at the inception of the capitalist mode of production, and at the inception of the industrial revolution. Of course, these initial levels of real wages can be lowered or increased at subsequent stages, even radically so. But they are historical co-determinants of the wage level, which it would be unscientific to negate.

Second, the historically transmitted pattern of consumption and of wage

---

3. This can be expressed in physical terms, i.e. inputs in calories compared with capacity to produce energy. When a growing imbalance occurs (as e.g. during the Second World War in most of the countries of continental Europe), workers will start to lose weight. Their capacity for physical effort will decline. The rate of sickness and accidents will rapidly increase, in addition to obvious psychological side-effects. Similar phenomena can be observed at present in the poorer countries of the Third World, where real wages have dropped dramatically.

4. This question has not yet been sufficiently studied by economic historians. One of the keys to answering it lies probably in the degree of combination between agriculture and handicrafts, or (which is the same), in the degree of autonomy of the crafts and the relative strength of their economic organisation in independent corporations. The general rule seems to be that the higher the integration of agriculture and the crafts, the lower the average income of the precapitalist producers. Handicraftsmen occupied full time as such must have a money income which enables them to buy food. This is not the case when the handicraftsman is a part-time peasant providing his family with the minimum food, or when he has land at his disposal on which the members of his family can supplement the meagre income from the sale of the products of his craft.

differentials is a strong subjective (moral) component of the willingness of wage labour to assure the given intensity of work required by employers both for objective reasons (resulting from the used technology/machinery) and for reasons of intended profit maximisation. Long before wages have fallen to absolute physiological subsistance levels, the intensity of work, care taken of equipment and attention given to the quality of production will decline dramatically if real wages are drastically lowered.[5] Except under conditions of extreme poverty and of huge unemployment, the willingness to work, e.g. on night-shifts or during religious holidays, will depend upon extra payments. Normally, workers are not ready for such efforts just at the given average wage-rates.

Thirdly, real wages are linked to socially recognised (accepted) levels of consumption of wage labour. But this average package of goods and services which the average wage is supposed to buy is not stable throughout time, nor equal in all countries. New goods and services can be integrated into it, i.e. new needs can be transformed from luxury needs, only to be satisfied for the upper-middle class and the ruling class, into popular needs for which every average blue- and white-collar worker demands satisfaction. In an analogous way, goods and services which were parts of the socially recognised consumption pattern of wage labour can be expelled from that pattern.

There is no automatic correlation between either economic growth, level of industrialisation or level of productivity on the one hand, and, on the other hand, the integration of new needs into the workers' consumption pattern, the integration of the price of a series of new goods and services into the workers' real wages. Much literature has been devoted to the phenomenon of so-called 'fordism', i.e. the connection of new labour processes and economies of scale in mass production in the USA in the 1920s and 1930s, and the growth of real wages enabling workers to buy refrigerators, washing machines and automobiles in the 1930s and 1940s. The examples of Mexico, Brazil and South Korea, where in the 1960s and 1970s

---

5. The commodity labour power has a double-use value (function) for the capitalist entrepreneur. It is a means to *preserve* existing value (that of constant capital) as well as a means to *create* new value (including surplus value). The first function is often forgotten or underestimated by commentators and apologists, as well as critics of capitalism. The more the stock of fixed capital (machinery) which the workers put into motion, supervise or care for, increases in value, the more vulnerable it becomes to bad care, and the more the efficiency of the workforce in fulfilling the said first function becomes a key factor regarding the prosperity of the enterprise. Hence the need for an adequate wage level which does not undermine that function. 20 per cent more wages for 1,000 workers can cost a high-technology firm much less than a loss of 20 per cent of the value of advanced equipment, as a result of insufficient care.

the automobile industry grew to a level similar to that of the USA relative to these countries' population, without real wages enabling workers there to buy automobiles, confirm the absence of such automatical/mechanical correlations.

As Marx correctly indicated (we would say predicted, more than deduced from already largely realised trends), this integration of new needs into socially recognised workers' consumption patterns depends upon the *relationship of forces between capital and labour*. The right of labour to paid holidays was first socially recognised after the huge strike waves of 1936 in France, Belgium, Czechoslovakia, etc. Likewise, the reduction of the work week by one blow from forty-eight hours to forty hours was achieved after that strike wave, whereas it took the international labour movement thirty years to achieve the eight-hour day/forty-eight-hour week. It should be noted that some of these conquests were realised in countries with a huge level of unemployment, e.g. in the USA where that level was higher than it is today.

In the opposite sense, consumption standards established through major shifts (including political ones) of the class relationship of forces in favour of labour, can be reduced dramatically as a result of historical defeats and big political shifts at the expense of the working class. In France, the forty-hour week introduced after the victory of the 1936 general strike was abolished — together with a partial *de facto* retraction of paid holidays — after the defeat of the general strike of 1938. Similar developments occurred in Belgium, Spain and Czechoslovakia. Between 1919 and 1929, the German and Austrian working classes succeeded in including into their average levels of consumption many elements of social security and 'municipal socialism' (cynical commentators would say, as a price paid by the capitalist class for the social-democratic leadership of these working classes consciously maintaining the bourgeois state and the capitalist system during the revolutionary crisis of 1918–19). These elements were largely eliminated after the victory of fascism (and clerico-fascism) in 1933–4.

Likewise, in most Western European countries, the USA, Australia and New Zealand, the 1948–73 period witnessed a dramatic increase in social services paid by the state (and partially by the employers) and integrated into workers' real wages. The 1980s generally witnessed a reversal of that trend. Certainly, it is debatable whether this extension of state-paid social services really represents a substantial increase in real wages. Only the *net* wage can be considered constituting the reproduction costs of the commodity wage-labour. Taxes on wages and on wage goods are part of surplus-value, not part of variable capital. If the increase in these taxes pays for the increase in social services, there is no true increase in real wages, all other things remaining equal. (There is of course such an increase if there is simultaneously an increase in net wages.) But a *reduction* in the quantity and quality of social services like the one occurring in the West since the early 1980s, without a proportionate reduction in taxes paid by workers and taxes weighing upon wage goods, certainly represents a lowering of real wages, i.e. an elimination of constituent components from the wage goods package.

A synthesis of all the elements enumerated up till now would lead to the following conclusion: the long-term evolution of real wages is a result of the combined correlation of a series of partially autonomous variables weighing upon the long-term demand and supply of wage labour *hic et nunc*, inflected by the current objective relationship of forces between Capital and Labour.

It is important to stress that the relevant element in the formula 'supply and demand of wage labour' is just that: *wage labour*, and not industrial labour, and even less 'manual industrial labour'. Independent from whether or not a unified labour market exists, independent from segmented labour markets' importance in explaining wage differentials and objective obstacles to the unification of the labour movement, the reserve army of labour is always an objective, historically produced reality weighing upon the long-term evolution of real wages. That is why the fluctuations (especially the increase) in the number of wage-earners engaged in the public sector (including state administration, in the service sector, etc.), have a bearing upon real-wage dynamics. That is why it is wrong and misleading to reduce the proletariat, i.e. the wage-earning class, to productive workers, i.e. workers producing surplus-value. This is even wrong for determining the mass and the rate of surplus-value, for these depend also upon the wage level, and the wage level in turn is influenced by the *general* level of employment, i.e. the fluctuations of the reserve army of labour.

But in order to avoid excessively mechanistic economic determinism, at this point one has to integrate into the analysis an additional determinant of the long-term fluctuation of real wages: the relative level of militancy and class-consciousness of the working class, and the relative influence and strength of its most conscious vanguard layers.[6] When that level is relatively

6. In spite of the relative decline in union strength, unionised workers in the United States still enjoy wages on average superior to 30 per cent of those of nonunionised ones. Likewise, in Japan there is a clear two-tier system of wages: in factories which employ less than 100 salaried persons (generally the more 'archaic' sector of the economy), unionisation is very low, and wages are below 50 per cent of those in the large, modern, high-technology plants, where 95 per cent of unionised labour is located. Contrary to popular belief in the West two-thirds of Japanese labour works in the first category of firms, not in the second one.

high at the beginning of a depression (of a depressive 'long wave' of capitalist development), real wages will decline much less than when that level is relatively low, *irrespective* of a given (similar or identical) level of unemployment. Many instances can be quoted to confirm that conclusion. One has only to compare the rapid fall of wages in the early 1930s in Britain to what occurred in the early 1980s; the fall of real wages in Italy in the 1920 depression to the relative rigidity of real wages in the depression of the 1980s; the steep decline of real wages in Argentina in the 1980s, compared to the strong resistance of real wages in Brazil during the same period, etc.

Likewise, when there is a conjunctural turning point from the lowest level of a crisis in the normal business cycle, even a partial, limited upsurge of working-class militancy can lead to impetuous mass struggles and to a strong increase in real wages after a relatively short interval, in spite of the permanence of high levels of unemployment. This occurred in the USA, France, Spain and Czechoslovakia from 1934 on. Where that level of militancy is absent, such an increase in real wages does not occur, or occurs only in a marginal way, even if the level of unemployment declines (Britain, Italy and Japan in the late 1930s).

So, obviously, these fluctuations of real wages are not a direct function of the correlation of supply and demand of wage labour, deflected by the objective relationship of forces between capital and labour. They are also a function of all these objective correlations deflected by the 'subjective factor of history', the given level of class militancy and of class consciousness. This relative level of class militancy and class consciousness in a given historical situation is not a direct reflection of the existing economic situation or prevalent trend of development. It is much more a function of the accumulated strength and weaknesses of the labour movement *during the previous historical stage*, of the historical results (victories, defeats) of a whole period of working-class struggles.

What weighed upon real wages in Britain in the 1930s was the cumulative effect of the defeat of the general strike of 1926 and of the collapse of the Labour government of 1931. What weighed upon real wages in Germany, Italy (after 1937 Spain) and Japan in the thirties was the destruction of working-class organisations and, the victories of fascism (and military dictatorship in Japan). What stimulated an upsurge of real wages in the USA, France, Czechoslovakia, Belgium (to a lesser extent) and Spain (1935–7), was the tumultuous victorious strike wave in these countries, the strong antifascist surge, the growth of working-class parties and the increased influence of radical vanguard militants in the factories and the unions. The seeds of all these developments had already been sown in the previous period, in the midst of the depression.

A comparison between the fluctuations of real wages in the early 1930s

and the early 1980s underlines the same point: while levels of unemployment are sometimes similar if not equal to those of the first slump, nowhere
in the industrialised countries (the third world countries are another story!)
was there a decline of either nominal or real net wages (disposable income)
in the 1980s compared to that of fifty years ago. The difference can be
explained by the different *subjective* correlation of forces between capital and
labour, the accumulated strength of working-class organisations in the
1950–80 period (which unemployment, in and of itself, has eroded but not
broken), the absence of fascism, the greater instability (weakness) of the
capitalist order on the world scale, etc.

The deliberate policies (political/social plans, economic strategy, etc.) of
the bourgeoisie must certainly be integrated into this picture of the subjective correlation of forces between the basic classes of bourgeois society. The
shift to the Reagan-Thatcher type of regime implies a deliberate attempt to
weaken the trade unions, to reduce their weight (and the weight of organised labor) in society, with all its consequences in the field of the so-called
welfare state. It implies a long-term strategy of creating a 'dual society', i.e.
dividing wage labour between a protected and an unprotected sector. The
second sector would have substantially lower real wages than the first one,
which would tend both to lower the 'official' wage level in the longer run
and to bring down the *average social* wage in the shorter run. This impact of
deliberate bourgeois policies upon real wages' long-term dynamics can be
also seen in semi-industrialised countries, when one compares, e.g. their
development in Singapore to their development in South Korea in the early
1980s. Economic resources and possibilities overdetermine these choices,
but the choices are there. The 'subjective factor in history' does have a
relative autonomy.

There is undoubtedly a deeper objective causality (determinism) between
long waves of economic development and the *relatively autonomous long
cycles of class struggles*. Each long depression stimulates a frantic search by
capital for technological revolutions, which generally imply revolutionary
modifications in work organisation at factory and firm level. The working
class, including its vanguard elements, are generally experienced in con-
fronting capital and management in the framework of the production
processes (organisation of the work process) of the *previous* phase. Militant
industrial unions (as different from crafts unions), conquering rudimentary
forms of workers' control of the rhythm of the conveyor belt etc., were the
obvious answer to industrial taylorism in mass-production factories. As
there is an inevitable time-lag between the accumulation of such experiences
and the introduction of new production methods and work processes in the
factories, technological revolutions generally lead to initial periods of
weakened working-class militancy, disorientation and confusion, when

confronted with employers' and state offensives. To this must be added the increased ideological influence of the employers, when there is no credible overall answer to that offensive. The fear of unemployment adds its weight to these processes.

But this correlation between objective and subjective class relationships of forces is only relative for two reasons. First, new technologies are introduced in a long depression only to an experimental, limited, even marginal extent. In spite of 'optical illusions', their overall weight in the production process — and therefore their initially negative impact upon working-class militancy — is much more limited than it appears at first sight. Second, the degree of *potential* (possible) working-class resistance is much less a straight function of shifts in production techniques and work processes than of relative strength and imaginative responses of union and vanguard militants at plant level. Where that response is given, the dis-orientation of larger numbers of workers will only be temporary. Strong resistance movements are unavoidable. The rigidity of real wages will then be much higher than both employers and moderate labour leaders expected.

7.1 Historical Change in the Institutional Determinants of Wages

Professor Mandel's paper is particularly interesting because of the way it moves through time and across countries to pick up examples of different types of pressures upon real wages. But I do not agree with the theory of wage determination which underlies the paper. My comments will thus comprise two parts: a criticism of the wage theory underlying Mandel's arguments, and some reflections on the change in institutional determinants of wages from the 1930's onwards.

Criticism of the Wage Theory Underlying Mandel's paper

I have tried to represent the Marxist wage theory by a diagram (Figure 7.1). This diagram comprises, from right to left, five points which I will deal with one by one. My aim is to denounce the circular nature of the argument.

Professor Mandel argues as follows. Labour power is a commodity. As with all commodities, the price of labour power — the wage — fluctuates around the value of labour power. Fluctuations are determined by the law of supply and demand; if labour supply is higher than the demand, wages will fall below the value of labour power; inversely, if the demand is higher than the supply, wages will rise (point 1 of Figure 7.1). Supply and demand determine the fluctuations, the basic trend being given by the value of labour power. What determines this value? It is the value of the average bundle of consumer goods. As shown in point 2 of Figure 7.1, the value of labour power is measured by the quantity of work required to produce the consumer goods.

Now, let us move up the diagram. Point 3 shows that an increased productivity decreases the amount of work necessary to produce the bundle, and thus reduces the value of labour power. The value of labour power goes down as productivity goes up.

Up to now what can we conclude? If the bundle of consumer goods does not change, and if labour productivity rises, we should observe a steady

194

Figure 7.1 Marxist Wage Theory

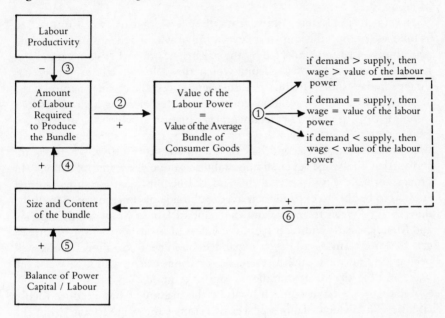

decrease of wages through time. At this stage, the only way to explain a stability or an increase of wages in the long term would be a permanent excess of demand on the labour market. This is shown by the upper arrow of point 1 on Figure 7.1. Of course, Mandel does not claim that this is the historical explanation of the tendency for stable or increasing real wages. On the contrary, he reminds us of the existence of a reserve army of labour, of the most frequent excess supply of labour. This excess supply of labour should bring wages below the value of labour power, along the downward arrow of point 1. The fall in wages should thus be even greater than the fall in the value of labour power! If we follow the logic of the argument, the question thus becomes: why don't we observe a permanent lowering of wages?

We must look for the reply in points 4 and 5 of Figure 7.1. The answer given by Mandel is that the value of labour power does not go down over time because the average bundle of consumer goods is not constant. This is point 4 on the diagram.

What does the expansion in the bundle depend on? Mandel tells us (p. 188) that 'there is no automatic correlation between either economic growth, level of industrialisation or level of productivity on the one hand, and, on the other hand, the integration of new needs into the workers' consumption pattern . . .' The expansion of the bundle of consumer goods depends on the balance of power between capital and labour. This is point 5 of Figure 7.1.

The conclusion Mandel draws from these five points may be summarised as follows (p. 190): the long-term evolution of wages depends upon demand and supply of labour, inflected by the balance of power between capital and labour. This conclusion — from which the value of labour power has disappeared — short-circuits, and thus denounces, the circular nature of the argument. Figure 7.1 implicitly contains a dotted arrow which closes it.

This is my argument. Let us imagine a situation in which the demand for labour increases faster than the supply. This was the case in several European countries in the second half of the nineteenth century. The diagram shows that the wage level should stabilise above the value of labour. In other words, the workers at the end of the nineteenth century earned enough to be able to expand their average bundle of consumer goods. If the difference between the wage and the value of labour holds a long time — and Mandel clearly indicates from the outset of his paper that the difference can be long term — the new expanded bundle of consumer goods will become the norm. If such is the case, we cannot deny a link between the wage and the size of the bundle of consumer goods.

But then, we have come full circle; the argument has become totally circular. The value of labour power determines the wage (point 1) but the wage in turn determines the value of labour power (point 6). If so, let us forget this diagram, and retain simply Mandel's conclusions, from which the value of the labour power has vanished: the long-term evolution of real wages depends on demand and supply of labour, inflected by the balance of power between capital and labour.

This statement (which I willingly agree with, and which the majority will also accept, I assume), has no need of the value theory. Then, the most useful thing would be to understand how the balance of power affects the determinants of wages. This would certainly lead us to the institutional determinants of wages — institutional determinants which are present in the title of Mandel's paper, but do not really appear in the paper itself. I will briefly discuss this question in the second part of my comments.

Reflections on the Change in Wage Determinants from the 1930s Onwards

Commenting on the influence of the balance of power between capital and labour on the evolution of wages, Mandel quotes the example of the 1930s. In the US, in France, in Belgium, the increase in real wages at the end of the crisis — in spite of a high level of unemployment — seemed to be connected with the upsurge of workers' organisations which had been so long inactive.

I would like to develop this example, and suggest that what happened in the 1930s was something more than a momentary rise in wages gained by a more militant working class. In my opinion there was a modification *in the very mechanisms of wage formation*. By developing this example, I will argue in favour of the following thesis:

Through history, we can observe successive periods corresponding to distinct modes of wage formation. These distinct modes are related to the changes in the balance of power. How? The evolution of the balance of power gives rise to institutions (e.g. collective bargaining) which affect wage determination. The 1930s were to mark the rupture between two great historical periods, and the origin of a new mode of wage formation, which has prevailed until the present crisis.

What kind of social changes happened in the 1930s which led to a remodelling of the wage determinant? It seems to be the new relationship between trade unions, the employers and the state. In the United States, Sweden, France and Belgium, a social compromise was established at the end of the 1930s, a compromise which was to have a determining influence on the long-term wages evolution, since it was to last practically until the present crisis.

What was the origin of this compromise, and what were the consequences? To put it simply, we can say that the compromise originated from three types of evolution:

The first one was *the very rapid development of the trade union movement* just after the First World War. In Belgium, for example, union membership increased four-fold between 1913 and 1920. This fact gave strength to the workers to claim higher wages.

The new element was not only the rise of the trade unions, the novelty also lay in the second tendency that must be underlined, namely *state intervention in the organisation of social relations*. The state intervened in worker/employer conflicts; it obliged the parties to negotiate. And social opponents accepted negotiation (in the 1920s, they were not yet called social partners . . .). They came to negotiate in representative negotiating committees *(commissions paritaires)*. These committees multiplied during the 1920s and became an essential institution in the framework of wage negotiation. As from 1926, their decisions affected about half the workers in Belgian industry.

It was through these committees that the practice of linking wages to the cost of living index spread; it was through the intervention of these negotiating committees that, later, in the 1950s, real-wage increases were linked to rises in productivity. This trend, which first appeared in the 1920s, developed in the 1930s and finally became explicit after the Second World War.

Why? Probably because of the third trend I want to mention: *the introduc-*

tion of mass production technology in the consumer industries. The logic of my argument is the same as that of Henry Ford's famous 'five dollars a day': By increasing workers' wages, Ford created — either directly or indirectly — new markets for mass-produced cars. From the 1930s onwards (and especially after the Second World War), employers' representatives realised that increased wages widened markets, and were necessary for mass production introduced by new production techniques.

The compromise which came to birth in the 1930s included advantages for both partners. Workers received higher wages; in exchange they were asked to submit to the discipline of the new production techniques. Social compromise was born around the idea of economic growth. This appeared clearly in Belgium under the Van Zeeland government. A new institution influencing wage determination appeared in 1936: the National Labour Conference. From then on, representatives of the workers and of the employers were called social *partners*.

The pact was sealed. It was to be renewed and even enforced after the war, by the *Declaration Commune sur la Productivité* (Common Declaration on Productivity) signed in 1954 by the representatives of the main groups of workers and employers. After this social agreement, finalised after decades of preparation, the wage determinants now had little in common with those prevailing in the nineteenth century. (I prefer to talk about nominal wage determinants, and then draw useful conclusions concerning real wages.)

In the nineteenth century, it was unemployment which seemed to have a preponderant influence on nominal wages. After the First World War, the variations in nominal wages began to correspond to changes in the cost of living. Indexation of wages was far from perfect, but unemployment was certainly no longer the only explicative variable of wage fluctuation.

This change in wage determination has been shown by French and US data. It also clearly appears, in an original way, through the Belgian data of the interwar period. The change in wage determinants first appeared in those industries where the proportion of unionised workers was high. During this period, if you divide industry into two sectors (non-sheltered and sheltered), the first one being highly unionised, you note that nominal wages followed the tendency of the cost of living in the unionised sector (Figure 7.2), but not in the non-unionised sector. In the latter, wages were still much more sensitive to the level of employment.

This change in wage determination was the first effect of the institutions created in the 1920s and 1930s. Later, after the Second World War, when negotiating committees became common, the nominal wage was the consequence not only of the cost of living, but also of increases in productivity. By the intermediary of institutions, wages were directly linked to the cost of living and productivity increases were partly reflected in real-wage

Figure 7.2 Belgium 1920–40. Nominal Wage in the Non-sheltered Sector and Cost of Living. Annual Rate of Growth (in per cent).

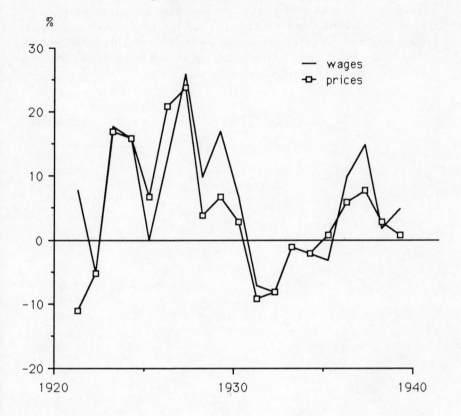

Source: I. Cassiers, *Croissance, crise et régulation en économie ouverte: la Belgique entre les deux guerres*, Brussels, 1989.

increases. These new wage determinants which have gradually become an integral part of the economic scene following conflicts and compromises, relegate the influence of supply and demand on the labour market. Wages were far less influenced by unemployment in the 1960s than at the end of the nineteenth century.

As a conclusion, I would say that the evolution of the balance of power and the institutions born out of it, have had three major effects:

(1) A decrease of the influence of unemployment upon wages

(2) A progressive link of nominal wages to the cost of living — partial link at first, almost perfect link from the 1950s onwards

(3) The appearance of a positive influence of labour productivity upon
    wages.

These new determinants of wages have no reason to be everlasting. They
depend on the viability of the institutions and, seemingly, on the economic
growth which supported the social agreement. What will happen tomorrow
to economic growth and to social institutions is not so clear, and neither is
the future trend of real wages.

J. VUCHELEN

7.2 Labour Unions, International Competition and the Social Reproduction Cost of Labour

The analysis of the long-term level and variation of real wages as performed by Professor Mandel deserves our attention, not only for the particular insights he offers, but also because it is something of a neglected area of research. Economists concerned with current economic, financial and social problems seem to have given a negative answer to the question, 'Has an historical and institutional analysis of (real) wages anything to offer for our current problems?' In fact, they are right to the extent that in the short run these historical background phenomena can be neglected. This leads to the standard econometric approach where variations in wages are explained by current economic variables. However, this approach has to be questioned. Although the medium and long run are a succession of short runs, it is not straightforward to generalise the short-run approach as also being applicable to the medium run.

The integration of the short- and longer-term approaches does create a difficulty that one also encounters in Mandel's paper. His attention (e.g. to the influence of the labour unions), although correct in the short run, does not seem relevant from a long-term perspective. In fact labour markets, as other markets, function more efficiently in the long run compared to the short run. As a result, all interference can only be temporary and does not produce lasting results on the wage rate. They only produce short-term 'bubbles'. (To avoid misunderstandings, this argument is not applicable to situations where labour unions break the monopoly power of entrepreneurs because that action results in a better-functioning labour market; labour unions then increase the efficiency of labour markets).

Furthermore, it can be questioned whether such interference does have a positive total effect on the workers. By 'total' I not only mean on the wage rate but also on employment. Is it not true that labour unions are especially interested in the welfare of their members, and that this could be different from the welfare of the working population — or even the total population? This can be illustrated by the recent Belgian experience: in the period 1975–81, real wages were too high and affected negatively the competitive

201

position of Belgian industries. The unions (and other groups who claimed to defend the position of workers and lower social groups) could prevent a quick and sharp intervention by the government. However, this intervention was only postponed, not prevented; in the meantime, unemployment increased.

This brings us to another point that is not very clear in Mandel's paper: the role of international competition. It does seem to me that over the last century, external constraint has become more and more stringent. In other words, the relative freedom industrialised countries possessed in the past gradually crumbled away. Of course, this process did not affect all sectors of the economy to the same extent, but it is certainly an explanatory factor in the evolution of real wages.

The effects of the competitive position of a sector or an economy in the medium and longer run are appearing through the international mobility of factors of production, and especially of capital, since it is fair to say that important emigration flows are over. However, I feel that in the future we will observe another kind of migration: highly skilled workers will be moving in search for higher real net of tax wages. This will have a multiplicative effect on employment and so a depressive effect on wages. This could then result in a vicious employment circle: high tax rates lead to emigration of highly skilled workers which, due to complementary effects, results in lower employment; this requires (as a result of the unemployment compensation to be paid by the government) higher tax rates, etc. This analysis illustrates, furthermore, that for workers (i.e. the supply side of the labour market), real net of tax wages are important. One can argue — and this is probably the view taken by Mandel since he is not considering income taxation — that in the past this has not been a major explanatory element. This can be questioned and will change in the future.

Returning to the international mobility of capital and labour, it is correct to say that wages were higher in thinly populated areas or countries. Although this is not fundamentally disputed by the following argument, one has to take into account that those who emigrated to these areas are not a good sample of the population. They were relatively young and not highly skilled workers who nevertheless showed, by definition, some dynamism. That they emigrated is probably explained more by the lack of job prospects in their country rather than by the high wages they could get by emigrating. The role played by wages seems to be minor.

A last point on this is that Mandel argues 'surplus labour emigrates towards areas with a relative scarcity of labour compared to available capital, and not the other way around . . .' This has been true in the past up to, I would say, the 1960s. But then capital started to become more mobile compared to labour. The mobile factor is therefore not constant through time. This mobility can furthermore change quite rapidly, as is illustrated by the Belgian experience: in the 1960s, foreign investment, especially by US firms, accounted for a high share of total investment. In the 1970s, however, partly as a result of the rise in wages, capital moved to less developed countries. Today this trend has changed again, partly as a result of the increased technology of production which requires, contrary to what was the case in the last century, a relative high level of skill.

One of the interesting features of Mandel's paper is the discussion of the social reproduction cost of labour. He mentions three elements (socially recognised needs when the industrialisation process started, historically transmitted patterns of consumption and wage differentials, and socially recognised levels of consumption). I would like to add — and this seems to me a rather important explanatory variable — intervention by the government. I see three different types of intervention:
1) Progressive taxation, implying that poorly paid workers got tax reliefs
2) The development of social security, especially unemployment benefits
3) The imposition of minimum-wage laws
The total effect of these regulations is to introduce a floor below which wages could not fall. The question is, again, whether this is, in the end, beneficial to the workers. This role of the government is one of the weak parts of the paper. One partial answer could be that this effect is rather limited given the very long period that Mandel covers. Another answer could be that the forces between capital and labour, as Mandel states, are also present on the governmental level so that, in the end, adding this institutional dimension to the analysis would not change much. I believe, however, that the inclusion of the government into the picture Mandel draws would at least make it clearer.

Another element whose role is not clear to me, but which certainly has some explanatory value, is the role of the self-employed. Is it not true that at certain periods they function as a reserve for contractual employment, reducing in this way the downward pressure on wages? At the same time, however, they function as one of the conservative forces in the economy. The total effect of these self-employed on wage variation in the long run is not clear to me, but neglecting it could be a mistake.

Concluding, I would like to say that Mandel's paper draws a broad picture of the explanatory variables in the evolution of real wages. The interrelationships are, however, not always very clear and complete. Since the aim of his paper was not to propose a complete theory about the long-term variation in real wages, but rather to illustrate the main determinants, I did not discuss his theoretical framework. He is correct in pointing out that this evolution is the result of a series of partially autonomous variables. However, I would add that in the short run these effects can be amplified or limited by endogenous economic phenomena such as a period of inflation or depression. The difficult task now is to go one step further in trying a quantitative evaluation.

D. J. VAN DER VEEN AND J. L. VAN ZANDEN

8. Real-Wage Trends and Consumption Patterns in the Netherlands, c. 1870–1940

Introduction

This article deals with developments in real wages in the Netherlands from about 1870 to 1940. Although the standard of living issue was raised a long time ago, real-wage series — in our view an important approach to standard of living questions — increasingly attract attention from economic historians. In recent years publication in this field of research has increased. The results have made possible some advance in the debate on the standard of living which is so dividing our colleagues from the Anglo-Saxon world. A prominent contributor on this debate, N. F. R. Crafts, noted 'Such has been the volume of literature that even the masterly surveys of the standard of living debate as those of Flinn and Taylor are now seriously out of date'.[1]

Historians from the Netherlands have, however, hardly contributed to this fruitful discussion. This is partly to be explained by the fact that standard of living questions never aroused much interest in the Netherlands. Current textbooks point to a gradual improvement of standards of living of Dutch workers from about 1850, and this view is hardly ever cast into doubt.[2] An often-quoted article on Dutch real-wage series supports this view.[3] As a consequence, investigations into real wages are exceptionally scarce in the Netherlands. Can this be explained, as R. T. Griffiths suggests, by a deep-seated lack of interest among Dutch historians for participating in international debates in the field of economic history?[4] In

---

1. See above, p. 75.
2. T. van Tijn, 'Het sociale leven in Nederland', in D. P. Blok et al. (eds), *Algemene geschiedenis der Nederlanden*, vol. 12, Haarlem, 1977, pp. 131–66 and vol. 13, Haarlem, 1978, pp. 77–100, 295–326.
3. J. van der Spek, 'Een eeuw lonen en prijzen, 1870–1970', *Sociale Maandstatistiek*, 1971, no. 8, pp. 418–26.
4. R. T. Griffiths, 'Economische ontwikkeling in industrieel Europa', in F. van Besouw et al. (eds), *Balans en perspectief, visies op de geschiedwetenschap in Nederland*, Groningen, 1987, pp. 147–66.

our view there is some support for a less harsh judgement.[5]

Be that as it may, in this article we want to publish some new evidence on the development of real wages in the Netherlands, seriously questioning existing views on the subject. Further, we want to compare these new data with evidence on trends in consumption patterns and workers' budgets.

Wages and Costs of Living in the Netherlands, 1880–1940

In recent years research into the labour market and the formation of wages became increasingly popular among Dutch historians. Their efforts were mainly confined to the years preceding 1850.[6] Research focused on the rigidity of the wage-level in Holland between 1635 and 1850. During these years nominal wages of Dutch workers hardly changed. An important question in this field of research is whether these comparatively high wages delayed Dutch industrialisation during the nineteenth century.

In comparison with the large number of articles concerning the years up to 1850, research into wage formation from 1850 to 1940 has seriously lagged. On the issue of nominal and real wages we have only one article at our disposal, written by J. van der Spek. In this article van der Spek presents highly inaccurate guesses of real wages during some years of the period 1870–1903. His guesses are obviously based on an extremely limited research into original sources.[7] Also J. A. de Jonge, in his book on Dutch industrialisation, presents some material on real wages more or less as an afterthought. He stressed that his guesses give only an inaccurate indication of developments of wages and costs of living.[8] With regard to this scanty evidence both authors refer to the lack of sources and research in this field. This argument is valid, however, only for the years prior to 1903. After the passing of the Accidents Insurance Act (*Ongevallenwet*) in 1901, government officials collected enough data on employment and wages in industry to give accurate estimates of the development of wage levels. Remarkably, historians have never used these sources and since the first tentative

---

5. K. Davids, J. Lucassen and J. L. van Zanden, *De Nederlandse geschiedenis als afwijking van het algemeen menselijk patroon*, Amsterdam, 1988.

6. J. de Vries, 'An Inquiry into the Behaviour of Wages in the Dutch Republic and the Southern Netherlands, 1580–1800', *Acta Historiae Neerlandicae*, X, 1978, pp. 79–97; L. Noordegraaf, *Daglonen in Alkmaar*, n.p., 1980; L. Noordegraaf, *Hollands Welvaren?*, Bergen, 1985; and J. M. M. de Meere, 'Daglonen in Belgie en Nederland in 1819 — een aanvulling', *Tijdschrift voor sociale geschiedenis*, VI, 1980, pp. 357–85.

7. J. van der Spek, 'Een eeuw lonen en prijzen'.

8. J. A. de Jonge, *De industrialisatie in Nederland tussen 1850 en 1914*, Amsterdam, 1968, pp. 502–9.

attempts of van der Spek and de Jonge hardly any progress has been made in research on the development of workers' wages.

There is hardly any need to elaborate on the usefulness of this type of research. During the years 1895–1930, scarcely interrupted by the First World War, Dutch industrialisation reached a decisive phase. From a country where agriculture and commerce dominated the economy, the Netherlands evolved into a modern industrial society. An investigation into the relation between industrialisation and the standard of living, a major theme in international literature on the subject, can only be undertaken on the basis of a thorough analysis of the development of real wages. Questions concerning the influence of the economic crises of the 1880s and the 1930s on standards of living of Dutch working-class families can only be answered on the basis of similar data.

In this article we try to draw up an inventory of available sources and studies enabling us to compute series of nominal and real wages and cost of living indexes during the years 1880–1940. However, figures and conclusions on the years 1880–1903 have a preliminary character; on the basis of results from current research on the development of workers' wages and salaries our conclusions will probably have to be revised in the future. Data on the years 1903–40 are fairly reliable, enabling us to give a more accurate analysis of wage levels during these years.

Nominal Wages   Concerning the 1880–1903 era we have at our disposal only two studies providing annual wage series covering developments in a limited number of firms. A study by E. J. Fischer on wage-formation in the textile industry during the Twenties provides average annual wages per worker in a number of representative factories in Hengelo.[9] On the basis of the three wage series presented by Fischer, (non-weighted) averages were calculated, resulting in a nominal wage index. Indexes under review concern an industrial town where wage levels were comparatively low. It is to be expected that when wages rose as a consequence of expansion of this branch of industry, increases would be comparatively high. Fortunately, a second study deals with Amsterdam, a city characterised by high wage levels. Archives from three enterprises situated in this city enabled J. L. van Zanden to compute average wage series.[10] These wages series, computed into one index using non-weighted averages from the three series under review, seem fairly representative for developments of nominal wages in Amsterdam industry.

9. E. J. Fischer, 'Economische theorie en historisch onderzoek', *Economisch en Sociaal-historisch Jaarboek*, 48, 1984, pp. 45–66.
10. J. L. van Zanden, *De industrialisatie in Amsterdam, 1825–1914*, Bergen, 1987, pp. 111–13, 131–4.

Figure 8.1 Nominal Wages in Amsterdam and Hengelo, 1880–1910 (indices 1901 = 100)

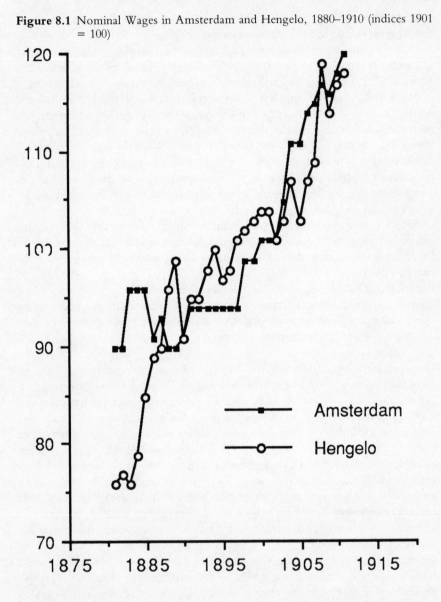

Figure 8.1 represents the wage series discussed above. From 1890 to 1910, wages in industry in Hengelo and Amsterdam rose at more or less the same pace. Both cities witnessed an increase in wage levels of about 20 per cent. However, pre–1890 data from both cities show less conformity. While wages in Amsterdam tended to stagnate, in Hengelo wages rose consider-

ably, especially in the years from 1882 to 1888. On the basis of information from qualitative sources on developments in wages during the 1880s — when large parts of the Dutch economy suffered from a severe crisis — data on Amsterdam seem to be more or less in conformity with developments in Dutch economy as a whole. Rises in nominal wages which appear from data on Hengelo must have been highly exceptional during these years.[11] As a consequence, in computing one index on wage developments, for the 1880s we made use of data only on Amsterdam; from 1890 to 1903 both series were used.

From 1903 we have available detailed information on average daily wages of Dutch (male and female) workers insured at the Rijksverzekeringsbank (National Insurance Bank) by virtue of the *Ongevallenwet*. Official figures under review until 1921 deal mainly with large parts of industry and a small part of commercial services. From 1921 almost all industry and commercial services are represented. Daily wages to be insured were set at a maximum of f.4 a day until 1919, when this amount was raised to f.8 a day.[12]

Cost of Living   From 1900 official CBS figures on costs of living are reliable enough to be useful. Except for the limitation that until 1936 data cover only Amsterdam, no serious fault can be found in these official figures.[13] For the second half of the nineteenth century van Zanden constructed price-index figures on the cost of living. Although this index is based on a limited number of price series, especially from 1870 it seems to reflect developments in the cost of living in a fairly reliable way.[14]

Real wages   Depicted in Figure 8.2 are the series of data on the cost of living and real wages in the Netherlands (i.e. Amsterdam) before the First World War (computed as discussed above). In these years, developments in real wages are more or less a reflection of price movements. Until 1896 trends in real-wage developments on the whole were moving upwards, with only a brief intermission between 1888 and 1892. More than 80 per cent of the increases in real wages between 1880 and 1896 are accounted for by falling prices. Rises in nominal wages were negligible during these years of crisis.

After 1896, when prices started to rise again, the increase in real wages actually came to an end. Between 1896 and 1913 real wages increased only by 4 per cent, as compared to an increase of 47 per cent in the years

11. See also the studies of van der Spek and de Jonge quoted in notes 3 and 8.
12. J. B. D. Derksen, 'Berekeningen over het nationale inkomen van Nederland voor de periode 1900–1920, *Maandschrift CBS*, 1941, pp. 86–7.
13. CBS, *Zestig Jaren Statistiek*.
14. Van Zanden, *De industrialisatie*, pp. 134–40.

Figure 8.2 Real Wages and Cost of Living, 1880–1913 (indices 1900 =100)

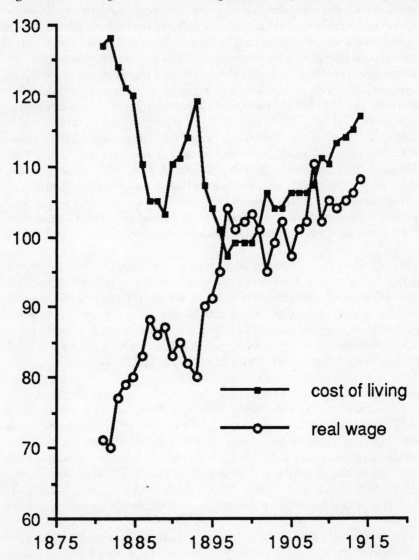

1880–96. During the former period, when Dutch industrialisation reached a decisive phase, a high level of economic growth was achieved and a modern trade-union movement came into existence, Dutch workers hardly profited from the rapid increase in labour productivity. It is even plausible that their share in national income was declining. The industrial breakthrough of the years 1895–1913 was not associated with a clear fall in workers' families' standards of living, but neither did it result in a clear upsurge.[15]

The First World War caused dramatic changes in prices and wages. During the first years of the war, including 1917, nominal wages hardly rose. Price levels nevertheless rose considerably, even according to official statistics, which were clearly underestimating the increase in prices, because they were based on the maximum official prices on articles fixed by the government. According to our estimates, between 1913 and 1916 real wages fell by more than 13 per cent and stabilised at this level in 1917. Falling real wages, combined with huge war profits by particular groups of entrepreneurs, contributed considerably to social unrest during these years. The trade-union movement increased its membership considerably during and immediately after the war — especially from 1916, when there was a marked rise in the number of successful strikes.

These developments and favourable conditions in the Dutch economy during these years meant that nominal wages rose substantially after 1917. Between 1917 and 1920 nominal wages almost doubled. As a consequence, real wages in 1918 were again at the pre-war level of 1913. In 1919 and 1920 real wages were 23 per cent higher than they had been in 1913. The post-war economic boom reached its highest level in 1920; after this year prices started to fall again, at a high rate in 1921 and much slower afterwards. As ever, nominal wages lagged behind these developments, and even rose in 1921, only later falling gradually. As a consequence, in 1921 real wages skyrocketed, and even in 1922 showed some improvement. This strong increase in real wages during the economic recession of 1920–3 may have contributed to the comparatively favourable evolution of the Dutch economy in these years.

On balance, real wages between 1913 and 1923 had risen by 55 per cent. This is reflected in the evolution of income distribution. After a strong rise in inequality between 1917 and 1920, between 1920 and 1923 a sudden shift took place which mainly benefited lower-income groups. As a consequence, social inequality in 1923 was considerably less pronounced than in 1913.[16] During the interwar years this pattern more or less stabilised. Changes in real wages show the same pattern. Compared to conspicuous upsurges between 1917 and 1920, real wages in the following decades remained remarkably stable. In fact, during the 1920s we see a repetition of the developments of 1895 and 1913 — rapid economic growth in combi-

15. The same happened in France, Germany and the U.K. See W. A. Lewis, *Growth and Fluctuations*, London, 1978, pp. 94–111.
16. J. M. M. de Meere, 'Long-term Trends in Income and Wealth Inequality in the Netherlands 1808–1940', *Historical Social Research*, 27, 1983, pp. 13–16.

Figure 8.3 Real Wages and Cost of Living, 1913–39 (indices 1913 = 100)

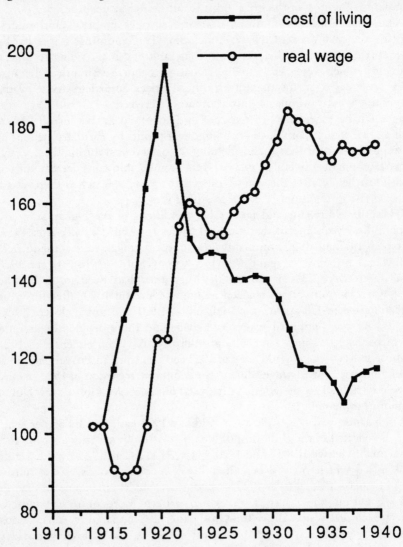

nation with hardly any rise in real wages. Between 1922 and 1929 real wages increased by 6 per cent but real per capita incomes during the same years rose fivefold, by 30 per cent.[17]

17. CBS, *Macro-economische ontwikkelingen, 1921–1939 en 1969–1985*, 's Gravenhage, 1987.

The economic crisis beginning in 1929 first became apparent in the price level. The cost of living between 1929 and 1932 fell by 16 per cent — as a comparison, between 1920 and 1923 it fell by more than 25 per cent — while nominal wages started to fall considerably only after 1931. As a consequence, real wages increased somewhat between 1929 and 1931 and fell slightly between 1931 and 1935. Full-time industry workers were therefore able to consider the 1930s more favourably than the 1920s. Working-class purchasing power as a whole showed a less favourable picture, because of rapidly rising unemployment. Nevertheless, investigations by A. van Schaik bring us to the conclusion that workers' real incomes (including social benefits) during the 1930s did not fall below the levels of 1929, when conditions were not unfavourable. After an initial rise between 1929 and 1931, real wages fell considerably between 1931 and 1934. All the same, these declines were not able to wipe out improvements in previous years. According to van Schaik, after 1935 conditions improved.[18]

To sum up, it is conspicuous that there is no connection between developments in real wages and conditions in the Dutch economy. Four different situations arose:

(1) *Economic growth in combination with stable or declining real wage levels.* This situation occurred between 1896 and 1913 (stable real wages), 1913–17 (falling real wages) and 1922–9 (slightly increasing real-wage levels).
(2) *Economic growth in combination with evidently rising real wage levels.* This 'normal condition' only presented itself during the highly atypical years of 1917–20.
(3) *Economic stagnation in combination with rising real-wage levels.* The periods 1880–96, 1920–2 and 1929–31 fit into this pattern.
(4) *Economic stagnation in combination with falling real-wage levels.* 1931–5.[19]

This conclusion, that economic growth does not necessarily cause increases in real wages, should be explained by developments in prices. Inflation was closely linked to economic growth, although the causal relations between both variables are not easy to establish. Because negotiations on wage levels — if there were negotiations at all — were always carried out in nominal terms, increases in nominal wages were always undermined by inflation. The absence of a clear connection between developments in real wages and economic growth is, in our view, a remarkable conclusion.

18. A. van Schaik, *Crisis en protectie onder Colijn*, Amsterdam, 1986, pp. 184–210.
19. Developments after 1935 — economic recovery in combination with stable real wages — are not easy to classify in this scheme.

Real Wages and Consumption Patterns

The value of real-wage series is sometimes cast into doubt when discussing the development of workers' families' standard of living. The main points of criticism of this approach are roughly as follows: since wages and total family incomes are not the same, real wages only reflect a part of the reality.[20] Historians who subscribe to this criticism often suggest that conclusions on standards of living should be based upon analyses of consumption. Besides, argue critics, real wages give no information on working hours and unemployment. In this section we intend to go briefly into these criticisms, focusing on the following question: is it possible to discuss the broad pattern of rising real wages discussed above, utilising information found in various sources on consumption? If both approaches come up with more or less the same conclusions, information from both groups of sources would not contradict but corroborate each other.

Various approaches are used in studying the consumption and expenditure of working-class families. In this field of research repeated use has been made of figures on per capita consumption of specific food articles and stimulants. Table 8.1 shows the main trends in consumption of some articles. These articles have been chosen on the basis of the following criteria: first, data had to be reasonably reliable and second, the articles concerned had to form an important part of dietary patterns of working-class families. The use of these data to arrive at conclusions about standards of living has been severely criticised. Several authors have stated that such data do not permit far-reaching conclusions concerning the standard of living. H. J. Teuteberg concluded that they only have a limited use.[21] J. Burnett in his stimulating book *Plenty and Want* also stated his doubts concerning the use of the data: 'Statistics of per capita consumption at best establish a framework: they describe the average, and the average consumer no more existed in early Victorian England than he does today. To discover more about the food of the past, we must turn to real people, their earnings and expenses and where possible their actual budgets and household accounts'.[22] Contemporaries showed a difference of opinion about the value of this source as well. In the speech from the Dutch throne in 1897, the prosperity of the people was concluded to have risen. A socialist member of Parliament, van der Zwaag, furiously opposed this passage. The region that

---

20. A. J. Taylor, Editor's Introduction, in A. J. Taylor (ed.), *The Standard of Living in Britain in the Industrial Revolution*, London, 1975, pp. xxiv–xxx.
21. H. J. Teuteberg and G. Wiegelmann, *Der Wandel der Nahrungsgewohnheiten unter dem Einfluß der Industrialisierung*, Göttingen, 1972, p. 45.
22. J. Burnett, *Plenty and Want*, London, 1966, p. 29.

elected him to the Second Chamber was faced with serious unemployment and, as a consequence, the inhabitants were obviously impoverished. The Minister of Finance, Mr Pierson, chairman of the cabinet, disagreed with him and stated that in his view he focused too much on the gloomy side of things without keeping to the point. In Pierson's view, standards of living certainly were rising, as could be seen from the rise of consumption of food and stimulants. This plea met with stiff opposition. Dr P. Brooshooft, an influential liberal publisher, gathered some household accounts to show that workers fared far worse than Pierson suggested.[23]

On the other hand, D. J. Oddy concluded that per capita consumption of some food articles and stimulants coincided approximately with the amounts computed from family budget surveys.[24] In the Netherlands the statistics concerned were carefully compiled; where possible the amounts of seed for sowing, industrial use, cattle-fodder, etc. were estimated and subtracted from the total consumption. H. Baudet and especially H. van der Meulen (who is an expert on these statistics) pointed to the fact that these data are fairly reliable, especially in comparison with other figures.[25] Considering the foregoing it seems sensible to use these data and compare them with other sources. In Table 8.1 some data on per capita consumption are summarised.

Interpreting Table 8.1 is far from easy, since at first glance various series hardly show identical developments. This raises the following question: what conclusions can be assigned to a rise or decline in consumption? Although the answer seems obvious, in our view the matter is not that simple for two reasons. First, figures on per capita consumption deal with the population as a whole, and therefore do not discriminate between regions or social classes. Growth in one region or social group can easily be compensated for by decline in another social group or region. T. van Tijn has tried to solve this problem by presupposing that families with a non-working-class background had food enough at their disposal and therefore that rises in consumption mainly benefited workers' families. As a consequence, he believes that rises in per capita consumption of food and

23. P. Brooshooft, *Officieele en feitelijke waarheid*, Bijdrage tot de kennis van onze arbeidstoestanden, The Hague, 1897 (Official and factual truth. Contribution to the knowledge on working class conditions).

24. D. J. Oddy, 'A Nutritional Analysis of Historical Evidence: the Working Class Diet 1880–1914', in D. J. Oddy and D. S. Miller, *The Making of the Modern British Diet*, London, 1976, pp. 214–32.

25. H. Baudet and H. van der Meulen, *Consumer Behaviour and Economic Growth in the Modern Economy*, London, 1982, passim.

Table 8.1 Average Annual Per Capita Use of Some Food Articles and
Stimulants[26]

Years	Wheat kg.	Potatoes kg.	Coffee kg.	Sugar kg.	
1852–56	34	177	4.4	2.7	(1851–53)
1857–61	47	210	4.2		
1862–66	53	276	3.8	4.5	(1862)
1867–71	60	240	4.6		
1872–76	69	286	7.7	5.2	(1872)
1877–81	84	229	6.7		
1882–86	93	305	8.4	7.5	(1886)
1887–91	101	238	5.9	8.8	(1892)
1892–96	104	321	6.7	9.9	
1897–01	103	310	7.8	12.0	
1902–06	107	268	7.0	13.5	
1907–11	107	239	6.7	14.8	
1912–16	124	226	5.7	16.6	
1917	66	395	2.9	20.9	
1918	33	432	1.6	25.7	
1919–20	97	302	4.5	23.1	
1921–25	117	263	5.0	25.0	
1926–30	129	251	4.7	27.5	
1931–35	132	236	4.6	27.2	
1936–39	121	151	4.3	26.7	

stimulants are a valuable indicator of working-class standards of living.[27]

Although this solution might charm us by its simplicity, in our view conclusions arrived at without any investigation into the correctness of this presumption are not on firm ground. There is indeed ample proof that, as J. M. M. de Meere has shown, social inequality in the Netherlands was not constant (it increased until 1880, declining gradually thereafter) and that differences in regional developments at least complicate the interpretation of per capita figures on consumption:[28] during the Agricultural Crisis of the

26. *Onderzoek naar het verbruik van sommige voedings- en genotmiddelen*, 's Graven-hage, 1895 (deals with the years 1852–91), continued under the same title, with figures on the years 1892–1918, in *Maandschrift van het Centraal Bureau voor de Statistiek*, jrg. 15 (1920), nr. 1, bijlage 1. Figures from the interwar years are to be found in *Jaarcijfers van het Centraal Bureau voor de Statistiek over 1939*, (Annual figures of the Central Statistical Office on 1939), The Hague, 1940. Figures on rye are omitted from Table 8.1 since they were only available for the years 1852–6 and 1887–91. Figures on annual consumption of rye (for the years mentioned, 75.6 and 80.5, respectively) do not considerably enhance our view on consumption.

27. T. van Tijn, 'Het sociale leven', p. 307.

28. J. M. M. de Meere, 'Long-term Trends in Income and Wealth Inequality in the Netherlands 1808–1940'.

1880s and the beginning of the 1890s urban workers (as van der Zwaag has already stated) benefited from falling food-prices, while workers in rural areas were severely hit by unemployment and probably wage cuts.[29]

Besides — and this brings us to a second complication in interpreting figures on per capita consumption — what conclusion should be assigned to a rise or fall in consumption of particular articles? The answer to this question seems obvious, but if we look at long-term developments and do not stop (as most authors do) about 1900 or the beginning of the First World War, then interpretation of the figures becomes complicated. Annual per capita consumption of wheat gradually rose, stabilised about 1887–91, rose again, stabilised again with a brief interruption during the First World War and fell again during the 1930s. Were standards of living of the Dutch population as a whole falling during the 1930s?

Consumption of potatoes is also significant. It rose until 1890–1900, and thereafter it fell with a short interruption produced by a spectacular upsurge during the First World War. Again, were standards of living falling during the interwar years? This seems highly improbable. Maybe information based on analysing household accounts can be of some help here. From these working-class families' budgets it appears that workers' families had a clear 'survival strategy': when real wages rose workers initially tried to get enough food on the basis of their traditional, monotonous food pattern. Only later, when real wages rose further, or when the improvement was thought to be lasting, were food patterns refined and as a consequence focused to a smaller extent on staples. In Great Britain a pattern like this was described by John Burnett, and in our view it also existed in the Netherlands.[30] This implies that initial rises in potato (and maybe wheat) consumption by workers as well as later reductions were signs of prosperity. At last people had food enough, and a certain saturation point was reached.

This brings us to a third complication in interpreting per capita figures on consumption of food and stimulants: we should not only be able to arrive at figures on per capita consumption of various social groups in various regions, but also we should be informed about the extent to which one food article is substituted by another. To complicate matters even further, a well-known sign of prosperity is the substitution of potatoes by wheaten

29. T. van Tijn, 'Het sociale leven', pp. 81–4, and J. M. M. de Meere, *Economische ontwikkeling en levensstandaard in Nederland gedurende de eerste helft van de negentiende eeuw*, The Hague, 1982, pp. 77–114, esp. pp. 98–111.
30. J. Burnett, *Plenty and Want*, and D. J. van der Veen, 'Standards of Living and Nutritional Analysis of Working-class Families in the Netherlands, c. 1850–1940', paper for colloquium on the standard of living in Western Europe, Amsterdam, Leiden, 22–4 September 1983.

bread.[31] As a consequence, figures on consumption of articles which can be considered more or less as luxury have a particular significance. In this respect, Table 8.1 is of little help. Developments in consumption of coffee hardly offer any clue. Figures show a gradual increase in consumption, although rises are especially conspicuous until 1896, a datum which could corroborate our real-wage series discussed above. The decline in coffee consumption after 1900 is not easy to explain (with the exception of 1917 and 1918, when falling standards of living and supply problems would account for the decline), especially when in interwar years coffee consumption reached the same level as in the 1850s. To a lesser degree, the same problems arise in interpreting figures on sugar consumption.

Here we see a more or less uninterrupted rise in annual per capita consumption, even during the last years of the First World War. Neither do figures on sugar consumption seem to be of much help on the issue under review. In their excellent book on changing food patterns in Germany, H. Teuteberg and G. Wiegelmann have shown that figures on meat consumption are especially significant.[32] Alas, figures on Dutch meat consumption are either too unreliable or too scattered to provide any clues.[33]

Should we conclude from these critical remarks that figures on per capita consumption have no significance at all? This conclusion would go too far. Rises in per capita consumption of wheat, initial growth and later stagnation, seem to corroborate the developments in real wages discussed in the previous section. Besides, the fact that potato consumption continued to rise until a relatively late date seems to confirm that standards of living were hardly rising during Dutch industrialisation. It seems sensible, though, in investigating changes in standards of living not to isolate studies of per capita consumption from other sources. As suggested above, information in particular on social inequality, regional differences and substitution should not be ignored.

Since dietary surveys do not offer sufficient insight into changes in workers' standards of living, we will now turn to another source, house-

---

31. Things can be complicated even more. In these years in the Netherlands we see a substitution of rye bread by wheaten bread. On this issue see J. J. Voskuil, 'De weg naar luilekkerland', *Bijdragen en mededelingen tot de geschiedenis der Nederlanden*, 98, no. 3, 1983, pp. 460–83, and B. Altena and D. J. van der Veen, 'Een onbekende enquete naar broodconsumptie in Nederland in 1890', *Tijdschrift voor sociale geschiedenis*, XII, no. 2, May 1986, pp. 135–52.
32. H. Teuteberg and G. Wiegelmann, *Der Wandel der Nahrungsgewohnheiten . . .*, pp. 94–133.
33. J. L. van Zanden, *De economische ontwikkeling van de Nederlandse landbouw in de negentiende eeuw*, Wageningen, 1985, p. 106. He calculated the following figures on per capita consumption of meat (in kg.) 1810 – 35.7, 1850 – 27.3, 1880 – 33.0, 1910 – 43.3.

hold accounts of working-class families. Opinions on the value of this source may differ. It is not always easy to prove their reliability and representativeness. In connection with research presented in this article, it would lead us too far to go extensively into this subject. We believe this source is especially valuable for at least two reasons: first, it is the only source that presents information on wage and income acquisition and spending patterns in combination with each other. Besides, household accounts might offer clues to prices of goods normally absent in prices series, such as housing costs. To improve reliability of data in Table 8.2, only groups of workers' budgets are used which were found to be reliable enough.[34]

In interpreting Table 8.2 the following indicators are used (because of the method of compilation on the accuracy of ancillary information on wages): expenditures on food (absolutely and as a percentage mainly of total income), amounts spent on various items (since they more or less reflect parts of income that can be spent at will), and food and clothing. Finally, some attention will be paid to housing costs, since they are often omitted from price series.

What conclusions can be reached on the basis of this table? Until the First World War, household accounts show a continuous improvement. However, the pace at which standards of living rose differed. Unfortunately, the limited number of years from which budget data are available do not permit us to shade the pace of improvement to the extent found possible in the study of real wages. Some remarks can nevertheless be made which lead us to the conclusion that these figures do match with conclusions arrived at from the real-wage series.

Household accounts from 1880 were found to be more reliable than those from 1886.[35] If the latter, for the time being, is omitted from Table 8.2, improvements from 1854 (or even 1880) to 1889–90 are quite spectacular. Living standards rose and workers' families were able to adjust spending patterns. Improvements must not be exaggerated, however, for food patterns hardly changed. It seems that improvements in real wages were to

34. J. F. Reith and A. Gorter, 'De Nederlandse voedingsenquetes', *Voeding*, 3, 1948, pp. 81–106. This is a very valuable summary of all but a few dietary surveys from 1916 up to 1948. Since only small groups were the object of investigation, figures cannot be considered representative for year-to-year developments. Calorie intake per adult varied from 2,569 (unemployed workers in Rotterdam, 1935) to 3,745 Kcal. (workers in Westzaan, 1930). Most inquiries come up with a figure of about 3,000 Kcal a day.
35. Household accounts from 1886 were found to be highly atypical because from five workers under review, three ran a shop. This explains comparatively high expenses on housing.

Table 8.2 Spending Patterns of Dutch Working-class Families in Large Cities, 1854–1935 (weekly amounts).[37]

Years	Number of budgets	Total exp. fl.	Food %	Expenditures on Housing %	Shoes & Cloth. %	Various %	Index costs of living 1900 = 100
1854	8	10.0	67.0	19.1	5.0	8.8	125
1880	9	12.54	57.3	24.0	10.3	8.3	126
1886	5	12.14	40.0	34.3	1.5	24.2	104
1889–90	7	12.40	41.6	31.3	11.9	15.2	110
1910–11	32	18.35	47.0	23.4	10.1	19.3	112
1917	43	21.27	51.3	22.1	7.4	19.1	136
1918	36	24.84	55.5	20.2	9.4	14.8	162
1923–24	21	<34.60	46.3	21.2	7.8	24.7	145
	66	<46.15	40.4	19.1	9.1	31.4	
1930	9	>34.60					
1934–35*	78	<46.15	36.2	15.4	13.3	35.1	133
	15	19.30	41.1	40.8	4.9	13.3	113
	24	21.72	36.3	32.1	5.6	25.9	
	3	31.70	35.5	25.4	7.2	32.0	
	4	23.65	40.8	34.9	5.9	18.4	
		33.92	31.3	28.7	7.7	32.3	

*From 1934–35 the following five categories are depicted in this table (in order of appearance): workers, unemployed, receiving social benefits; workers, earning f. 26.90 at a maximum; workers, earning between f. 26.90 and f. 36.55; officials, earning f. 26.90 at a maximum; officials, earning between f. 26.90 and f. 36.55.

a large extent wiped out by rising housing costs. The latter is not surprising, since pressure was put on the housing market by large-scale migration from rural areas into the large cities.[36] On the other hand, workers' families were able to spend smaller parts of income on food without making diets worse, that is, even more monotonous. Improvements between 1889–90 and 1910–11 seem considerable, but attention should be paid to two conspicuous points. First, it seems probable that the data overestimate improvements, since workers' families from 1910–11 were certainly more privileged than those from 1889–90 who were drawn to a greater extent from broken families. Second, if we look at the improvements between 1890 and 1910 food patterns in particular seem to have ameliorated, while spending patterns remained more or less the same.

From the figures in Table 8.2[37] we can conclude that working-class families' standards of living fell during the last two years of the First World War: total expenditures rose, but not enough to make up for rising prices. In addition, spending patterns changed in a way that suggests worsening conditions. A larger part of income was spent on food, and even by doing this, working-class families were not able to prevent their diets from deteriorating.[38] Finally, it should be noted that income also underwent a

---

36. D. J. van der Veen, 'Bestedingen aan huur door arbeidersgezinnen aan het begin van de 20e eeuw', in P. M. M. Klep et al. (eds), *Wonen in het verleden*, Amsterdam, 1987, pp. 39–48, esp. pp. 39 and 45.

37. Sources in order of appearance: 1854, 'Huishoudelijke budjets van gezinnen van werklieden te Amsterdam, behorende bij een adres van den heer Paul van Vlissingen, aan de leden der Staten-Generaal 21 november 1854 ingediend', *Tijdschrift voor Staathuishoudkunde en Statistiek*, XIII, 1863; 1880, J. M. Welcker, *Heren en arbeiders*, Amsterdam, 1978, pp. 312–36; 1886, W. P. J. Bok, 'Budgets', *Bijdragen van het Statistisch Instituut*, III, 1886, pp. 22 ff.; 1889–90, J. H. Tours, 'Huishoudbudgetten', *Bijdragen van het Statistisch Instituut*, VIII, 1891, pp. 143–80; 1910–11, *Arbeidersbudgets, jaarbudgets van 70 arbeidersgezinnen in Nederland*, Amsterdam, 1912; 1917, *Arbeidersbudgets gedurende de crisis*, The Hague, 1917; 1918, *Arbeidersbudgets gedurende de crisis*, II, The Hague, 1919. Later information: *Marktanalytisch Handboek voor Nederland*, 's Gravenhage, 1937.

38. Nutrional values of workers' families' diets could be computed, since in the 1917 and 1918 budget inquiries not only amounts spent but quantities consumed were given as well. These figures point to a deterioration of conditions from 1917 to 1918 as well. The commission leading the inquiries reported that diets of families using the *Centrale Keuken* (or 'central kitchen' — a provision instituted by the municipality offering hot meals at low prices) gave no cause for alarm. Families not using this facility from 1917 to 1918 saw their daily protein intake decline from 74 to 72 grams a person. Caloric value of nutrition fell from over 3,000 to 2,834 daily. At the same time, it was observed that composition of diets was changing for the worse. While families under review in 1917 derived 9 per cent calories from potatoes, in 1918 this figure had risen to 18 per cent for

change that workers must have experienced as a setback: from Table 8.3 it is clear that workers were less able to cover expenses by regular wages of the male bread-winner alone. This cannot be explained by a different structure of families, since the families interviewed in 1918 were the same as those interviewed in 1917. This conclusion, that standards of living fell during the last years of the First World War, is remarkable. From 1917, real-wage series showed a considerable increase of income. The difference in conclusions, arrived at on the basis of both sets of data can possibly be explained by the time at which the 1918 budget inquiry was undertaken (from February 23 to March 22). Improvements might have taken place later during the year under review.

From 1918, as could be expected, standards of living rose considerably, to stagnate again in the 1930s. Spending patterns were obviously adapted to new conditions. For those out of work and receiving social benefits in 1934–5, standards of living fell, but as could be seen from the real-wage series, not below pre-1900 levels. If we compare the standard of living of privileged workers from 1910–11 and of workers out of work in 1934–5, differences do not seem to be large. Finally, the amounts of money spent on housing are quite high. Rises in housing costs must at least partially have wiped out rising nominal wages. It is not possible to find out whether higher expenses on these items meant better houses and more comfort.

When dealing with real wages in previous sections, we presumed that real wages were a good indicator on standards of living, as incomes were for a large part earned by the male bread-winner. From Table 8.3. it can be seen that this presumption was correct, since wages earned by wives and children were not an important source of income (incidental income was mainly earned by the male bread-winner, as well). Figures from this table seem to fit in with suggestions given above. Besides, they provide information on one interesting point: from Table 8.2 we concluded that standards of living fell between February 1917 and February 1918. Seemingly, workers tried to make both ends meet by resorting to acquisition of extra income in various ways.[39]

In sum, figures from household accounts confirm to a large extent the conclusions arrived at on the basis of real-wage series. Especially in combination with real-wage series, workers' budgets give better information on working-class conditions than figures on per capita consumption of food

---

families using the *Centrale Keuken* and even 27 per cent for families persisting in preparing their own hot meals. Source: *Arbeidersbudgets gedurende de crisis*, II, pp. 102 and 123.

39. Extra income for a small part is rent from boarders, but mainly overwork, extra work done at home on piece-rate.

Table 8.3 Income Acquisition by Dutch Working-class Families, 1910, 1911, 1917, 1918 (Average Weekly Amounts)

	1910–11		1917		1918	
	f	%	f	%	f	%
Man	13.98	82.9	19.15	90.0	21.30	80.8
Woman	0.54	3.2	0.37	1.7	0.61	2.3
Children	1.16	6.9	0.54	2.4	1.14	4.3
Various	1.18	7.0	1.22	5.7	3.31	12.6
Total	16.86		21.27		26.36	

Source: Household accounts[40]

and stimulants. In comparison with real-wage series, household accounts on one hand have a serious defect, that they do not inform us properly on year-to-year changes, since we do not possess sufficient groups of budgets. On the other hand, however, household accounts confirm real-wage series in important ways. First, budgets inform us better on expenses on housing than real-wage series. Second, information on problems of family income is, in our view, valuable. Finally, while real-wage series provide us with a framework of year-to-year figures with a high level of sophistication, household accounts tell us how workers reacted to developments analysed on the basis of the former source.

Conclusion

Finally, we wish to consider briefly the results which have emerged. First, it seems obvious that there is a large degree of conformity between conclusions drawn on the basis of real wages and those arrived at by analysing household accounts. On this 'rule' we only found one exception — developments in workers' conditions from 1917 to 1918 — but as was suggested above, this difference might be accounted for by seasonal influences. While household accounts were compiled in February and March, rises in real wages can have taken place later during the year.

Second, we concluded that during two periods of rapid economic growth (1896–1913 and 1922–9), real wages hardly improved. This seems to be a correction of the commonly accepted view that from 1896 industrialisation in the Netherlands coincided with considerable improvements of workers' standards of living.[41]

40. For sources, see note 37.
41. R. T. Griffiths, *Achter, achterlijk of anders*, pp. 8–9; T. van Tijn, 'Het sociale leven'.

Table 8.4 Estimates of Nominal Hourly Wages of Male Workers in Industry of Several Countries[42] (cents)

	1913	1930	1939
Netherlands	22	58	50
Belgium	26	44	41
Germany	40	54	63
United Kingdom	70	146	121
France	31	52	50
United States	69	147	163

Table 8.5 Spending Patterns of Working-class Families in Various Countries and Cities in Europe, c. 1910[43]

City or country	Number of families	Expenditures on		
		food %	housing %	clothing %	various %
Amsterdam	23	47.2	16.1	12.4	24.3
Netherlands	70	50.2	14.3	11.5	24.0
Germany a	184	53.2	17.2	9.4	20.4
b	320	51.5	12.3	12.7	23.5
Copenhagen	76	46.0	14.4	9.8	29.8
Norway	62	47.6	15.0	12.2	25.2
Stockholm	34	46.1	19.2	8.7	26.0
Sweden	381	52.5	12.4	11.9	23.2
Vienna	38	60.2	14.4	6.0	19.4

Finally, an international comparison of real wages and standards of living might offer new insights and, since we can only undertake this exercise in a more or less accidental way, provide a starting-point for further investigation. From Table 8.4 we can conclude that in 1820 the Netherlands was a high-wage economy, but that by 1913 wages were comparatively low in an international perspective. It would be interesting to find out when and how this development took place.

On the other hand, there are no indications that, in an international perspective, standards of living in the Netherlands were very low. Table 8.5 shows that, judged by their spending-patterns, Dutch workers (especially those in Amsterdam) were by no means worse off than workers in other countries.

42. P. Scholliers, *Loonindexering en sociale vrede*, p. 268 and figures presented in this article.
43. W. H. van der Goot, *De besteding van het inkomen*, 's Gravenhage, 1930, p. 69.

This would mean that costs of living in the Netherlands were comparatively low. At this moment we do not possess material to support this hypothesis. What would be needed to answer this question are figures on the Netherlands such as Zamagni presents on other countries.[44]

From Table 8.4 we might also conclude that during the interwar period wages in the Netherlands rose faster than in Belgium, Germany and France. These observations suggest that important structural changes took place, in the Netherlands, influencing the Dutch economy's capacity for international competition. These observations in our view justify further investigations.

Appendix 8.1 Real-Wage Series in the Netherlands

Before publishing real-wage series, we first wish to consider briefly the representativeness of data from the Rijksverzekeringsbank Statistics. They were used by the Centraal Bureau voor de Statistiek (CBS: Central Statistical Office) to give estimates on wage-incomes, which provide us with information on average daily wages of men, women and children *together* (information on the various groups cannot be separated) in certain branches of industry. Therefore, daily wages (as represented in this source) tend to be lower than average daily wages earned by men. On the other hand, various sources suggest that female- and child-labour were comparatively rare in Dutch industry. In addition, wage levels in commercial services were higher than in industry. Biases discussed above might more or less compensate for each other. CBS statistics from 1926–38 provide us with additional information on a more strictly defined group: hourly wages of male workers over twenty years of age performing manual labour in industry. On the basis of an eight-hour working day (the maximum fixed by law), daily wages of workers in 1926 were 6 per cent higher than corresponding figures based on returns from the *Ongevallenwet* discussed above. Between 1926 and 1938 this margin only varied between 2 per cent (1932) and 11 per cent (1938). The correlation coefficient of both series was r = .95 .9. In other words, developments in wages from the *Ongevallenstatistiek* (statistics of the returns on behalf of the Accidents Insurance Act) are representative for developments of wages in industry.[45]

The maximum of f. 4 daily, fixed by law until 1919 (or until 1916 in practice), was rarely surpassed. According to J. B. D. Derksen, legal restrictions only made their influence felt during the years 1917–19.[46]

44. See pp. 107–39.
45. Sources: CBS, *Zestig jaren statistiek in tijdreeksen*, The Hague, 1959; *Statistiek Ongevallenwet*, 1926–39.
46. J. B. D. Derksen, 'Berekeningen over het nationale inkomen van Nederland in de periode 1900–1920', *Maandschrift CBS*, 1941, p. 87.

Increases in wages during these years are systematically underestimated. When in 1919 the maximum of four guilders was raised, this deficiency was put to an end. To correct figures on wages for the years 1917–19, use has been made of a wage index, constructed by F. A. G. Keesing, which covers the years 1913–25. This index (based on CBS statistics on wages in various branches of industry such as mining, metallurgical industry, construction and public utility), shows in 1917 and 1920 an almost identical rise in wages as do figures from the *Ongevallenstatistiek*. This, again, underlines the reliability of sources used. On one point both series differ: rises in wages in 1918 in Keesing's index are higher than indicated by figures from the *Ongevallenstatistiek*.[47] Final figures for 1918 and 1919 are therefore corrected on the basis of Keesing's index, to make up for the *Ongevallenstatistiek's* underestimations.

47. F. A. G. Keesing, *De conjuncturele ontwikkeling van Nederland*, Utrecht/ Antwerp, 1947, p. 39. From 1926, CBS data are used on average gross wages earned by male manual workers of age in industry. Differences between gross and net wages during these years in the Netherlands were small: At the end of the period under review, in 1938, net wages were only 3 per cent under gross wages.

Table 8.6 Wages and Cost of Living in the Netherlands, 1880–1913
(indices 1900 = 100)

	nominal wage	cost of living	real wage
1880	88	126	70
	88	127	69
	94	123	76
	94	120	78
	94	119	79
1885	89	109	82
	91	104	87
	88	104	85
	88	102	86
	89	109	82
1890	92	110	84
	92	113	81
	94	118	79
	95	106	89
	93	103	90
1895	94	100	94
	99	96	103
	98	98	100
	99	98	101
	100	98	102
1900	100	100	100
	99	105	94
	101	103	98
	105	103	101
	101	105	96
1905	105	105	100
	106	105	101
	116	106	109
	111	110	101
	113	109	104
1910	115	112	103
	117	113	104
	120	114	105
	124	116	107

Table 8.7 Wages and Cost of Living in the Netherlands, 1913–39
(indices 1913 = 100)

	nominal wage	cost of living	real wage
1913	100	100	100
	100	100	100
1915	102	115	89
	111	128	87
	120	136	89
	162	162	100
	216	176	123
1920	239	194	123
	257	169	152
	235	149	158
	225	144	156
	218	145	150
1925	216	144	150
	215	138	156
	219	138	159
	223	139	161
	231	138	168
1930	231	133	174
	227	125	182
	207	116	179
	203	115	177
	195	115	170
1935	187	111	169
	183	106	173
	191	112	171
	195	114	171
1939	199	115	173

P. SCHOLLIERS and J. HANNES

9. Some Conclusions and Suggestions for Further Research

N. Crafts concludes his paper by saying that the 'past decade has been an exciting period in research on the standard of living debate in general and on real wages and inequality in particular'. Indeed, real wages are at the centre of attention of many researchers, who certainly do not all study the British living standard between 1750 and 1850. This success can be explained by the ease and simplicity offered by a row of figures, which are supposed to provide information on various complex economic and social developments.

The compressing of such information into one central indicator leads, alas, to numerous difficulties. The papers in this volume lay more emphasis on methodological and theoretical aspects than on new results of the study of real wages. Despite the fact that computations of real wages have been going on for about a century and that the data and the calculations have been constantly refined, few real-wage series have been presented here. This may surprise some readers, who are familiar with the frequently cited real-wage statistics by, for instance, J. Lhomme, A. Desai or E. H. Phelps Brown. Even when these series have been called upon in this volume, alternatives are at once suggested. Thus, V. Zamagni presents real-wage series for various countries, criticises them and considers three serious alternatives for making international comparisons. Also, P. Bairoch, although using real wages in a limited, well-defined sense, concludes his contribution with suggestions for exploring other possible indicators. D. Morsa is amongst those doubting the relevance of real wages with regard to the measurement of the standard of living. So, is there a crisis in the investigation of real wages? Obviously, questions raised by this kind of research are much more imperative than the possible answers!

Doubting the relevance of real wages certainly is not new. But it seems that a new phase has been entered in criticising and interpreting real-wage statistics, a phase that is closely linked to the state of research in overall social and economic history. The contribution by family history definitely cannot be overlooked when the standard of living is studied. D. Ebeling,

229

M. Daunton, R. Leboutte, D. Morsa, P. van den Eeckhout and R. Wall all emphasise the decisive importance of considering the family income (over the family life cycle) rather than the individual (male) wage. Moreover, L. D. Schwarz, R. Wall, M. Daunton, J. Lucassen and J. Vuchelen stress the importance of the non-monetary income of the family. It is clear that the study of real wages must take into account these aspects, which might well lead to completely new insights into the history of the standard of living. Still, such contributions seem difficult to incorporate into real-wage series, unless one is able to construct year-to-year incomes, including all wages and non-monetary incomes of well-defined families.

Alongside the contribution of family history, other fields of social history have much to add to the investigation of real wages. L. D. Schwarz, M. Daunton and I. Cassiers plead for considering the social history of work and of the wage, while R. Leboutte, D. Morsa, P. van den Eeckhout and V. Zamagni want to look at work frequency (short-time, overtime, unemployment). N. Crafts, D. van der Veen and J. L. van Zanden and C. Schroeven and P. Solar want to consider the results of the social history of food, housing, clothing, household budgets, etc. in order to refine the knowledge of the historical patterns of consumption (and, thus, the composition and calculation of price index figures) and in order to check the trends in real-wage series.

Also, new results in economic history offer possibilities for testing, correcting or reinterpreting series of real wages, as is done by N. Crafts, P. Bairoch and V. Zamagni. Finally, new theories place the study of real wages in new frameworks, which is done here by E. Mandel (the decisive role of the labour movement) and by I. Cassiers (the contribution of the *régulationnistes*). These theoretical concepts, as well as the other contributions to this volume, bear testimony to political or ideological disagreement which is, for instance, quite obvious in the contributions of E. Mandel and J. Vuchelen, and which is stressed in this volume by D. Morsa.

So, it seems more appropriate to talk about an enrichment of the study of real wages, rather than to point to a crisis, since the new approach undoubtedly means an improvement in the conceptualisation of real wages. However, these insights make the study of real wages more complex: the newly emerging difficulties join the 'traditional' ones. Real-wage statistics are as strong or as weak as the strength or the weakness of each component. Alas, shortcomings in one or another part of the computation still exist.

C. Schroeven and P. Solar, D. Ebeling and V. Zamagni consider price indices in general terms and stress the fact that more representative data on household budgets and more homogeneous goods and prices should be considered. However, one may ask to what extent such in-depth investigation is really necessary and to what extent new research is altering the picture. Perhaps the main efforts should be directed towards a better knowledge of the prices of housing and services.

The new approach to the history of real wages has greater implications for wage series than for price series (see above: family income, work frequency). Apart from this, the authors of this volume emphasise the difficulties in choosing a 'good' wage indicator. P. Bairoch advocates the use of the wage of unqualified urban labourers, especially with regard to international comparisons, although this indicator has some limitations. V. Zamagni, L. D. Schwarz, F. Daelemans, P. van den Eeckhout, N. Crafts, J. Lucassen, R. Leboutte and D. Morsa consider the construction of wage index figures, pointing to difficulties such as the representativeness of the series, their weighting, the source material, the relevance of national averages omitting regional differences, and the calculation of yearly wages, based on daily or weekly data. All these elements should be seriously reconsidered. V. Zamagni's suggestion of looking at the disaggregated wage series of specific categories of workers in various countries seems relevant, only when wage statistics 'are firmly placed within the context of the social history of work and of the family', as M. Daunton puts it. So, the authors cannot reach agreement on which wage series should be used: one wage held representative, an average of several wages and salaries, or separate wages of well-defined categories? When international comparisons are considered, the first and last solution are perhaps the most adequate, although rather limited. Particular attention to regional disparities should not only refine the national picture, but also should improve the quality of aggregated wages series.

The difficulties in the choice and methodology of the statistics are, to a certain extent, linked to the aims of the researchers. P. Bairoch and V. Zamagni are primarily interested in the measurement of the level and evolution of European economies, whereas other collaborators to this volume consider the problem of the standard of living. As to the former, the consideration of simple, disaggregated data (e.g. hourly wages of urban unqualified workers divided by wholesale corn prices), has a well-defined meaning, providing evidence on economic processes (such as the cost of labour or productivity). However, it goes without saying that such data are to be rejected when considering the living standard. This contrast between economic and social data is underlined here by D. Ebeling, D. Morsa and J. Lucassen.

Did the new approach to real wages lead to new findings? As already noted, the questions put by the authors of this volume are much more imperative than the answers: it seems too early to present totally new results. However, some collaborators present revised series of prices and wages. C. Schroeven and P. Solar, while considering methodological

Table 9.1 'Best guess' Real-wage Development, Yearly Growth (in %)

	Germany	France	Belgium	Great Britain	the Netherlands	Italy
1780–1820	–	–	–	+0.56	–	–
1820–1850	+0.00	–	–	+1.27	–	–
1850–1870	+0.23	+0.60	+1.28	+0.83	–	–
1870–1890	+0.58	+1.02	+0.72	+1.72	+1.67	+2.39
1890–1913	+1.37	+0.69	+0.87	+0.30	+1.01	+2.04
1913–1939	+0.12	+0.51	+0.14	+0.96	+2.05	+0.48
1939–1950	–0.42	–	–	+0.13	+0.00	+2.22
1950–1975	+4.53	+4.65	+5.06	+2.61	+5.28	+5.77
1975–1980	+3.95	+1.73	+1.47	+0.16	+1.23	+1.38

Sources: Germany: 1820–1913: Gömmel, 26–8; 1914–38: Lehouiller, 214; 1938–50: Grumbach and König, 150; 1950–80: Van der Wee, 167. France: 1850–1913: Lhomme, 46; 1914–38: Lehouiller, 214; 1938–54: Singer-Kérel, 540–1; 1950–80: Van der Wee, 167. Belgium: 1850–1913: Neirynck, 181–2 and Scholliers, 322; 1914–38: Lehouiller, 214; 1950–80: Van der Wee, 146. Great Britain: 1780–1850: Crafts (this volume); 1850–1914: Mitchell, 343–5; 1914–38: Lehouiller, 214; 1938–50: Key Statistics, Table E; 1950–80: Van der Wee, 167. The Netherlands: 1880–1940: Van der Veen and van Zanden (this volume); 1939–50: Van der Spek, 1144; 1950–80: Van der Wee, 167. Italy: 1870–1890: Geisser and Magrini, 837; 1890–1913: Zamagni (this volume); 1914–38: Lehouiller, 214; 1938–50: Annuario statistico, 1954, 476 and 490; 1950–80: Van der Wee, 167. (Full references: see the Bibliography.)

problems, present a completely new prices deflator for interwar Belgium; P. Bairoch compares prices and wages in eight countries for the years 1815–1929; V. Zamagni collects wages and prices for seven countries from 1890 to 1913, though only slight corrections were made with regard to the well-known series; N. Crafts adds a new chapter to the British standard of living debate by revising the recent work on real-wage indices, extending the series back to 1750; D. van der Veen and J. L. van Zanden present completely new series for the Netherlands in the nineteenth and twentieth centuries; I. Cassiers discusses a graph with data on prices and wages in interwar Belgium.

While we await the results of further research, it seems appropriate to consider — very briefly and without comments — the development of real wages in some countries such as they have been used until now, but incorporating some findings of the present volume (see Table 9.1).

The participants of the symposium abundantly express warnings with regard to the shortcomings of all series of real wages. Still, in spite of these warnings most participants go on believing in the usefulness of real wages: they advocate the disposal of definitive series, which stand beyond all criticism. Time-consuming investigations into price and wage develop-ments, continuously leading to reinterpretations, cannot go on for ever. Is it not somewhat surprising that there is still no common conclusion as for the *trend* in real wages in Great Britain during the industrial revolution? Problems involved with real-wage series would perhaps vanish from the moment well-defined data, responding to a minimum number of internationally accepted criteria, are taken into account.

So, what are the best possible ways to improve the reliability and comparability of series of real wages? V. Zamagni calls for a broad programme, saying that, 'if we are going to make a real leap forward, an international research project that would fill in existing gaps using common methods is the only truly viable solution'. Such a project not only requires an inventory of all gaps and then filling them in using identical methods, but also the reconsideration and uniformisation of all existing price and wage series! Can this kind of extensive work be done (even using data banks and computers extensively)? But also, is it really *worth* doing? We believe it is.

The following suggestions are not meant to outline the international project advocated above, but merely are made in order to provoke debate and new empirical work.

Wages

Average national wage series seem to be unrealistic. Huge inter- and intra-sectoral and regional *wage differentials* should be considered. This should lead to the publishing of wages by region, by town, by occupation and by trade. In addition to such detailed information, the number of people earning a given wage in a given period should be looked at, aiming at learning something like the 'normal' wage. In this respect, the mode and the median should be paid as much attention as the mean, since they both respond in a better way to social and economic reality.

One should prefer to publish both the *basic wage* and the *effective earnings*. Next to the hourly or daily wage, wages per week and per year should be looked for. This implies investigations into the work frequency and the working hours. In doing so, social and economic historians will be able to use data from the same series, but with different starting points.

Also, it is better to publish and use just those wages which are *absolutely reliable*, meaning that one must be perfectly aware of the source of the data, the skills required for the job, the form of the wage, the nature of the work, the working time, etc.

Together with the well-defined wage data, information with regard to the wage-earners and their families, together with the *family income*, should be taken into account. It becomes more and more obvious that the consideration of the sole male wage isn't sufficient anymore. Whether the standard of living is looked at, the cost of labour or any other issue, the family income must be studied for a correct view of the living standard or for explaining different wage levels. This is probably the most difficult task for further investigations into real wages.

Other social groups should be incorporated into the research: artisans, shopkeepers, and above all, white-collar workers. Civil servants seem to offer an interesting field of study, since the lower strata 'enjoyed' a social status which presumably lay not much above that of labourers. Civil servants' wages were supposed to be able to keep a modest family alive; these wages could be used as reference-wages (stressing the long-term development).

Prices

Effective retail prices should be considered rather than wholesale prices, meaning that retail prices of shops, cooperative stores and department stores should be preferred to institutional prices and certainly to wholesale prices, since the former prices undergo very specific short- and medium-term fluctuations. Available effective retail prices should be compared with the commonly used institutional prices and the wholesale prices in order to check the usefulness of the latter ones.

It is recommended to publish and use only those prices which are *absolutely reliable*: the source of the data, the quality of the goods and services, the weight and so on must be well known.

When reconstructing the consumers' basket in the past, one should strive for the collecting of an *optimum number* of goods and services, meaning that at least the important expenditure items are considered (these, of course, change in the course of time and from place to place). It should be checked whether 'average' consumers' baskets diverge highly from working-class consumption patterns.

When constructing price index numbers, the *weighting* of the prices is naturally preferable but as far as a sufficient number of prices is available, it is better not to use weights at all, rather than to use false or incomplete ones. Again, the problem of whether index numbers using 'average' weights diverge from index numbers using weights based on working-class consumption patterns deserves further attention.

In considering the selected prices and weights, *precise checkings* based on all kinds of criteria (consumption figures, trade, agricultural output, etc.) must be operated. Also, all price index numbers computed by official statistical bureau (mostly since the 1920s), should be subject to severe checkings.

When the above criteria with regard to both price and wage series are taken into account, international comparisons of the fluctuations of real wages should become perfectly attainable and significant.

Testings

Finally, after having reconstructed new price and wage series and checked existing series (perhaps altering their components and calculations), various *tests* could be incorporated in the study of real wages. Agricultural output, international trade, unemployment, social and economic policy, labour movement, household budgets, life expectancy, nutrition, stature, literacy, economic performance in general and other features should be considered, aiming at checking the credibility of the results. Only this incorporation of real wages into broad economic, social and political development will lead to a substantial step forward and to a decisive judgement of the relevance of real wages.

Select Bibliography of Wages, Prices and Real Wages in Europe in the 19th and 20th centuries, with Special Emphasis on Statistics and Methodological Problems

Abelin, P., *Essai sur la comparaison internationale des niveaux de vie ouvriers*, Paris, 1936

Aftalion, A., 'Le salaire réel et sa nouvelle orientation', *Revue d'économie politique*, 1912, 541–52

Anderson, S., 'Real wages, inflation and unemployment', *Cahiers du GAMA*, 1984, 61–90

Artus, P., 'Salaire réel et emploi', *Revue économique*, 1987, 625–59

Avondts, G., J. Hannes, R. Moonen, E. Scholliers, P. Scholliers and A. Tassin, *De Gentse textielarbeiders in de 19e en 20e eeuw* (Ghent textile workers), Brussels, 1976–9, 7 vols

Bairoch, P., 'Ecarts internationaux des niveaux de vie avant la révolution industrielle', *Annales ESC*, 1979, 145–71

Bauchet, P., 'Evolution des salaires réels et structure économique', *Revue économique*, 1952, 297–337

Baudhuin, F., 'Le mouvement des salaires en Belgique d'une guerre à l'autre, *Revue du travail*, 1944, 481–98

Beck, B., et al., 'Die Entwicklung der Reallöhne Schweizerischer Arbeiter, 1890–1920', W. Conze and U. Engelhardt (eds), *Arbeiterexistenz im 19. Jahrhundert*, Stuttgart, 1981, pp. 46–56

Beckerman, W., *Comparaison internationale du revenu réel*, Paris, 1966

Beenstock, N. and P. Warburton, 'Wages and Unemployment in Interwar Britain', *Explorations in Economic History*, 1986, 153–72

Bengtsson, T. and R. Ohlsson, 'Age Specific Mortality and Short-term Changes in the Standard of Living: Sweden, 1751–1859', *European Journal of Population*, 1985, 309–26

Beveridge, Lord, *Prices and Wages in England: from the 12th to the 19th Century*, London, 1965[2]

Bienaymé, G., *Le coût de la vie à Paris à diverses époques*, Nancy, 1896–1899, 2 vols

Bils, M., 'Real Wages over the Business Cycle: Evidence from Panel Data', *Journal of Political Economy*, 1985, 666–89

Boje, P., 'The Standard of Living in Denmark, 1750–1914', *The Scandinavian Economic History Review*, 1987, 171–9

Borgeaud, M., *Le salaire des ouvriers des mines de charbon en France depuis 1900*, Paris, 1938

Botham, F. and E. Hunt, 'Wages in Britain during the Industrial Revolution', *Economic History Review*, 1987, 380–99

Bowley, A. L., *Wages and Income in the United Kingdom since 1860*, Cambridge, 1937

—— and G. Wood, 'Statistics of Wages in the United Kingdom during the Last Hundred Years', *Journal Royal Statistical Society*, 1899–1906

Boyer, R., 'Les salaires en longue période', *Economie et Statistique*, 103, 1978, 27–57

Braun, R., 'Einleitende Bemerkungen zum Problem der historischen Lebensstandardforschung', W. Conze et al. (eds), *Arbeiter und Industrialisierungsprozess*, Stuttgart, 1979, pp. 128–35

Bry, G., *Wages in Germany*, Princeton, 1960

—— and C. Boschan, 'Secular Trends and Recent Changes in Real Wages and Wage Differentials in Three Western Countries, the United States, Great Britain and Germany', *Second International Conference of Economic History*, Paris, 1965, 175–201

Cassiers, I., 'Une statistique des salaires horaires dans l'industrie belge, 1919–1939', *Revue économique de Louvain*, 1980, 57–85

——, *Crise et régulation en économie ouverte: la Belgique entre les deux guerres*, Brussels, 1989

Chapman, A., *Wages and Salaries in the United Kingdom, 1920–1938*, Cambridge, 1953

Chapman, J. C., *Real Wages in Soviet Russia since 1928*, Cambridge, Mass., 1963

Chapman, S. J., *Work and Wages*, London, 1904–14, 3 vols

Combe, P., *Niveau de vie et progrès technique en France depuis 1860*, Paris, 1955

Les comparaisons internationales des salaires réels. Etude méthodologique, Geneva, 1956

'Comparative Real Wages in London and Certain Other Capital Cities Abroad', *Ministry of Labour Gazette*, July, 1923

Conze, W. and U. Engelhardt (eds), *Arbeiterexistenz im 19. Jahrhundert. Lebensstandard und Lebensgestaltung deutscher Arbeiter und Handwerker*, Stuttgart, 1981

Coppieters, B. and G. Hendrix, 'De koopkrachtevolutie van loontrekkenden in periodes van economische depressie: een vergelijking voor de jaren 1929–1939 en 1974–1984', *Revue belge d'histoire contemporaine*, 1986, 275–308

Courtin, R., 'La production et le pouvoir d'achat dans le cycle économique', *Revue d'économie politique*, 1935, 45–94

Crafts, N., 'English Workers' Real Wages during the Industrial Revolution; Some Remaining Problems', *Journal of Economic History*, 1985, 139–44

——, 'British Economic Growth, 1700–1850: Some Difficulties of Interpretation', *Explorations in Economic History*, 1987, 245–68

Debray, B., *Taux des salaires, salaires réels et coût de la main-d'oeuvre dans l'industrie française (1930–1938)*, Paris, 1939

Dehem, R., 'L'évolution des salaires en Belgique et en Grande Bretagne, 1919–1939', *Bulletin de l'institut des recherches économiques et sociales*, 1946, 78–119

Delaire, M., 'Les variations des salaires dans l'industrie du bâtiment à Paris depuis 1830', *La réforme sociale*, 1891, 431–45

De Maddalena, A., *Prezzi e mercedi a Milano del 1701 al 1860*, Milan, 1974, 2 vols

Denis, H., *Les phases de l'histoire des prix depuis 1850 et la corrélation des phénomènes économiques*, Brussels, 1913

Desai, A., *Real Wages in Germany, 1871–1913*, Oxford, 1968

Devons, E., 'Wage Rate Indexes by Industry, 1948–1965', *Economica*, 1968, 392–423

Dimsdale, N. H., 'Employment and Real Wages in the Interwar Period', *National Institute Economic Review*, 110, 1984, 94–103

Dunlop, J. G., 'The Movement of Real and Money Wage Rates', *Economic Journal*, 1938, 414–23

Edgeworth, F. Y. and A. L. Bowley, 'Methods of Representing Statistics of Wages and Other Groups Not Fulfilling the Normal Law of Errors', *Journal Royal Statistical Society*, 1902, 325–57

Elsas, M. J., *Umriss einer Geschichte der Preise und Löhne in Deutschland*, n.p., 1936–1949, 3 vols

Feinstein, C. H., 'Wages and the Paradox of the 1880s', *Explorations in Economic History*, 1989, 237–47

Fett, H. G., *Die Methoden regionalen Reallohnvergleiche in ihrer historischen Entwicklung*, Marburg, 1957

Flinn, M., 'Trends in Real Wages, 1750–1850', *Economic History Review*, 1974, 395–411

Fourastié, J., *Le grand espoir du XXe siècle*, Paris, 1949 (1958⁴, 'édition définitive')

——, *Pouvoir d'achat, prix et salaires*, Paris, 1977

—— and Cl. Fontaine, *Documents pour l'histoire et la théorie des prix*, Paris, 1958–60, 2 vols

Frenkel, J. A., 'Purchasing Power Parities: Doctrinal Perspective and Evidence from the 1920s', *Journal of International Economics*, 1978, 169–91

Gazeley, I., 'The Cost of Living for Urban Workers in Late Victorian and Edwardian Britain', *Economic History Review*, 1989, 207–21

Geisser, A. and E. Magrini, 'Contribuzione alla storia e statistica dei salari industriali nella seconda metà del secolo XIX', *La riforma sociale*, 1904, 753–906

Gerhard, H.-J. (ed.), *Löhne im vor- und frühindustriellen Deutschland*, Göttingen, 1984

Gerss, W., *Lohnstatistik in Deutschland*, Berlin, 1977

Gilboy, E. W., 'The Cost of Living and Real Wages in Eighteenth-century England', *Review of Economic Statistics*, 1936, 134–43

Gini, C., 'Sui confronti internazionali dei salari reali', *Rivista di politica economica*, 1927

Goemmel, R., *Realeinkommen in Deutschland. Ein internationaler Vergleich (1810–1913)*, Nuremberg, 1979

Gottschalk, M., 'Le pouvoir d'achat et la consommation des ouvriers belges à différentes époques', *Revue internationale du travail*, 1932, 823–41

Goulène, P., *Evolution des pouvoirs d'achat en France, 1830–1972*, Paris, 1974

Goux, C., 'Productivité, production et salaire "réel"', *Revue d'économie politique*, 1969, 946–53

Groeber, R., *Nominallohn und Reallohn*, Leipzig, 1932

Grumbach, F. and H. Koenig, 'Beschäftigung und Löhne der deutschen Industriewirtschaft, 1888–1954', *Weltwirtschaftlichen Archiv*, 79, 1957

Hachtmann, R., 'Lebenshaltungkosten und Reallöhne während des "Dritten Reiches"', *Vierteljahrschrift für Sozial- und Wirtschaftsgeschichte*, 1988, 32–73

Halbwachs, M., *La classe ouvrière et les niveaux de vie*, Paris, 1913

Hall, A., 'Wages, Earnings and Real Earnings in Teeside: A Re-assessment of the Ameliorist Interpretation of Living Standards in Britain, 1870–1914', *International Review of Social History*, 1981, 202–19

Hartwell, R., 'The Rising Standard of Living in England, 1800–1850', *Economic History Review*, 1961, 397–416

Henry, S., J. Payne and C. Trinder, 'Unemployment and Real Wages', *Oxford Economic Papers*, 1985, 330–8

Hobsbawm, E., 'The British Standard of Living, 1790–1850', *Economic History Review*, 1957, 47–61

—— and R. Hartwell, 'The Standard of Living during the Industrial Revolution: A Discussion', *Economic History Review*, 1963, 120–46

Hohorst, G. et al., *Sozialgeschichtliches Arbeitsbuch. Materialen zur Statistik des Kaiserreichs 1870–1914*, Munich, 1975

Holtfrerich, C.-L., *Die deutsche Inflation, 1914–1923*, Berlin-New York, 1980

——, 'Zu hohe Löhne in der Weimarer Republik?', *Geschichte und Gesell-*

schaft, 1984, 122–41

Huber, M., 'La comparaison internationale des salaires réels', *Bulletin de l'institut internationale de statistique*, XXIII, 1928, 693–718

Hunt, E., 'Industrialisation and Regional Inequality: Wages in Britain, 1760–1914', *Journal of Economic History*, 1986, 935–66

'International Wage Comparisons: a Report of Two International Conferences and a Critical Review of Available Statistical Data', *Social Science Research Council Bulletin*, 1932

Jackson, R., 'The Structure of Pay in Nineteenth-century Britain', *Economic History Review*, 1987, 561–70

Jeanneney, J., *Tableaux statistiques relatifs à l'économie française et l'économie mondiale*, Paris, 1957

Kaufhold, K., 'Forschungen zur deutschen Preis- und Lohngeschichte', H. Kellenbenz and H. Pohl (eds), *Historia socialis et oeconomica*, Stuttgart, 1987, 81–101

Keynes, J. M., 'Relative Movements of Real Wages and Output', *Economic Journal*, 1939, 49, 34–51

Kiesewetter, H., 'Regional Disparities in Wages. The Cotton Industry in 19th-century Germany', P. Bairoch and M. Levy-Leboyer (eds), *Disparities in Economic Development*, London, 1981, pp. 248–58

Klezl, F., 'La comparaison internationale des salaires réels', *Revue internationale du travail*, 1925, 500–18

Kravis, I. B. et al., *A System of International Comparisons of Gross Product and Purchasing Power*, Baltimore, 1975

Kuczynski, J., *Die Entwicklung der Lage der Arbeiterschaft in Europa und Amerika, 1870–1933*, Basel, 1934

——, *Löhne und Ernährungskosten in Deutschland 1820 bis 1937*, Libau, 1937

——, *Die Geschichte der Lage der Arbeiter unter dem Kapitalismus*, Berlin, 1960–72, 40 vols

Kuczynski, R., *Arbeitslohn und Arbeitszeit in Europa und Amerika, 1870–1913*, Berlin, 1913

——, *Die Entwicklung der gewerblichen Löhne seit der Begrundung des deutsches Reiches*, Berlin, 1909

Kunz, A., *Einkommensentwicklung und Sozialverhalten von Arbeiternehmergruppen in den Inflationszeit 1914 bis 1924*, G. Feldman (ed.), *Die deutsche Inflation*, Berlin-New York, 1982, 347–84

Labrousse, E., R. Romano and F. Dreyfuss, *Le prix du froment en France au temps de la monnaie stable (1726–1913)*, Paris, 1970

Lavirotte, P., *L'évolution des salaires en France depuis la guerre*, Paris, 1939

Lehouiller, F., 'Salaires hebdomadaires réels dans divers pays de 1914 à 1939', *Bulletin de la statistique générale de la France*, 1944, 207–47

Lhomme, J., *Les enseignements théoriques à retenir d'une étude sur les salaires dans la longue période*, Geneva, 1967

——, 'Le pouvoir d'achat de l'ouvrier français au cours d'un siècle, 1840–1940', *Mouvement social*, 1968, 41–70

Lindert, P. and J. Williamson, 'English Workers' Living Standards during the Industrial Revolution: a New Look', *Economic History Review*, 1983, 1–25

——, 'English Workers' Real Wages: Reply to Crafts', *Journal of Economic History*, 1985, 145–53

Loschky, D., 'Seven Centuries of Real Income per Wage Earner Reconsidered', *Economica*, 1980, 459–65

Madinier, P., *Les disparités géographiques des salaires en France*, Paris, 1959

Mahaim, E., 'Changes in Wages, and Real Wages in Belgium', *Journal Royal Statistical Society*, 1904, 430–8

March, L., *Mouvements des prix et des salaires pendant la guerre*, Paris, 1925

Maréchal, J.-P., *L'orientation du pouvoir d'achat*, Le Landeron, 1949

Marley, J. G. and H. Campion, 'Changes in Salaries in Great Britain, 1924–1939', *Journal Royal Statistical Society*, 1940, 524–32

Menges, G. and H. Kolbeck, *Löhne und Gehälter nach den beiden Weltkriegen*, Meisenheim, 1958

Minde, K. B. and J. Ramstad, 'The Development of Real Wages in Norway about 1790–1910', *Scandinavian Economic History Review*, 1986, 90–121

Mitchell, B. R., *Abstracts of British Historical Statistics*, Cambridge, 1976, 341 ff

Mokyr, J., 'Is There Still Life in the Pessimist Case? Consumption during the Industrial Revolution, 1790–1850', *Journal of Economic History*, 1988, 69–92

—— and N. Savin, 'Some Econometric Problems in the Standard of Living Controversy', *Journal of European Economic History*, 1978, 517–25

Morsa, D., 'Salaire et salariat dans les économies préindustrielles (XVI–XVIIIe siècle): quelques considérations critiques', *Revue belge de philologie et d'histoire*, 1987, 751–84

Mueller, H.-H., *Produktivkräfte in Deutschland, 1870 bis 1917/18*, Berlin, 1985

Mueller, J., *Nivellierung und Differenzierung der Arbeitseinkommen in Deutschland seit 1925*, Berlin, 1955

Neale, R. S., 'The Standard of Living, 1780–1844: a Regional Case Study', *Economic History Review*, 1966, 590–606

Neirynck, M., *De loonen in België sedert 1846*, Antwerp, 1944

Nolleau, H., 'Réflexions sur la notion de pouvoir d'achat', *Economie et politique*, 1971, 119–30

O' Brien, P. and S. Engerman, 'Changes in Income and Its Distribution during the Industrial Revolution', R. Floud and D. McCloskey (eds), *The*

Economic History of Britain since 1700, Cambridge, 1982, I, 164–81

Orsagh, T., 'Löhne in Deutschland. Neue Literatur und weitere Ergebnisse', *Zeitschrift für die gesamte Staatswissenschaft*, 1969, 476–83

Peeters, M., 'L'évolution des salaires en Belgique de 1831 à 1913', *Bulletin de l'institut de recherches économiques*, 1939, 389–420

Petzina, D. et al., *Sozialgeschichtliches Arbeitsbuch. Materialen zur Statistik des Deutschen Reiches, 1914–1945*, Munich, 1978

Phelps Brown, E. H. and M. Browne, *A Century of Pay*, London, 1968

Phelps Brown, E. H. and S. Hopkins, 'The Course of Wage Rates in Five Countries, 1860–1937', *Oxford Economic Papers*, 1950, 226–96

Pierenkemper, T., 'The Standard of Living and Employment in Germany, 1850–1980: an Overview', *Journal of European Economic History*, 1987, 51–74

Pribram, A., *Materialien zur Geschichte der Preise und Löhne in Oesterreich*, Vienna, 1938

Prix et salaires dans le monde. Comparaison internationale du pouvoir d'achat, Zurich, 1976

Rambsbottom, E. C., 'The Course of Wage Rates in the United Kingdom, 1921–1934', *Statistical Journal*, 1935, 639–73

Rayack, W., 'Sources and Centers of Cyclical Movements in Real Wages', *Journal of Post Keynesian Economics*, 1987, 3–21

Reichert, C., *La comparaison internationale des salaires réels*, Brussels, 1943

Richardson, J., 'International Comparisons of Real Wages', *Journal Royal Statistical Society*, 1930, 398–441

Richardson, J. H., 'Real Wage Movements', *Economic Journal*, 1939, 425–41

Richter, K., *Die Reallohnbewegung in Deutschland, England und den Vereinigten Staaten von Amerika, 1890–1913*, Würzburg, 1937

Romeuf, J., *Evolution du pouvoir d'achat en France, 1938–1949*, Paris, 1949

Rothschild, K. W., 'Langfristige Reallohn- und Lebensstandardvergleich; allgemeine Problematik und österreichisches Beispiel', *Zeitschrift für Nationalökonomie*, 1956, 423–60

Rougerie, J., 'Remarques sur l'histoire des salaires à Paris au XIX siècle', *Mouvement social*, 1968, 71–108

Routh, G., 'Civil Service Pay, 1875 to 1950', *Economica*, 1954, 201–23

Rule, J., *The Labouring Classes in Early Industrial England 1750–1850*, London-New York, 1986

Saalfeld, D., 'Lebensstandard in Deutschland, 1750–1860', I. Bog et al. (eds), *Wirtschaftliche und soziale Strukturen im säkularen Wandel*, Hannover, 1974, vol. 2, 417–43

Salaires et coût de l'existence à divers époques jusqu'en 1910, Paris, 1911

Sauvy, A., *Histoire économique de la France entre les deux guerres*, Paris, 1965–75, 4 vols

—— and P. Depoid, *Salaires et pouvoir d'achat des ouvriers et des fonctionnaires entre les deux guerres*, Paris, n.d.

Schmoller, G., *Le mouvement historique des salaires de 1300 à 1900 et ses causes*, Paris, 1904

Scholliers, P., 'A Methodological Note on Real Wages during the Inter-war Years', *Historical Social Research*, 1987, 40–50

Schor, J. B., 'Changes in the Cyclical Pattern of Real Wages: Evidence from Nine Countries, 1955–1980', *Economic Journal*, 1985, 452–68

Schwarz, L. D., 'The Standard of Living in the Long Run: London, 1700–1860', *Economic History Review*, 1985, 24–41

Sen, A., *The Standard of Living*, Cambridge, 1987

Sho-chieh Tsiang, *The Variations of Real Wages and Profit Margins*, London, 1947

Simiand, F., *Le salaire, l'évolution sociale et la monnaie*, Paris, 1932, 3 vols

——, *Le salaire des ouvriers des mines de charbon en France*, Paris, 1907

Singer-Kérel, J., *Le coût de la vie à Paris de 1840 à 1954*, Paris, 1954

Skiba, R. and H. Adam, *Das westdeutsche Lohnniveau zwischen den beiden Weltkriegen und nach der Währungsreform*, Cologne, 1974

Soderberg, J., 'Real Wage Trends in Urban Europe, 1730–1850: Stockholm in a Comparative Perspective', *Social History*, 1987, 155–76

Soecknick, M., *Die Entwicklung der Reallöhne in der Nachkriegzeit dargestellt an typischen Thüringen Industrien*, Iena, 1927

'Standards of Living of the Working Classes during the Industrial Revolution', *Population and Development Review*, 1985, 737–56

Tarlin, R. and F. Wilkinson, 'The Movement of Real Wages and the Development of Collective Bargaining in the U.K., 1855–1920', *Contributions to Political Economy*, 1982, 1–23

Taylor, A. J. (ed.), *The Standard of Living in Britain in the Industrial Revolution*, London, 1975.

Taylor, M. and P. MacMahon, 'Long-run Purchasing Power Parity since the 1920s', *European Economic Review*, 1988, 179–97

Toutain, J.-C., 'The Uneven Growth of Regional Incomes in France from 1840 to 1970', P. Bairoch and M. Levy-Leboyer (eds), *Disparities in Economic Development since the Industrial Revolution*, London, 1981, 302–15

Tucker, R. S., 'Real Wages of Artisans in London, 1729–1935', *Journal American Statistical Association*, 1936, 73–84

Vandenbroeke, C., *Vlaamse koopkracht, gisteren, vandaag en morgen*, Louvain, 1984

Van der Wee, H., *Prosperity and Upheaval: the World Economy, 1945–1980*, Berkeley, 1986

Van Zanten, J. H., 'Some Observations on International Comparisons of Index Numbers of Cost of Living and Real Wages', *Revue de l'institut internationale de statistique*, 1933, 3, 20–39

Verlinden, C., J. Craeybeckx, E. Scholliers (eds), *Documents pour l'histoire des prix et des salaires en Flandre et en Brabant*, Brugge, 1959–73, 4 vols

Von Tunzelmann, G. N., 'Trends in Real Wages, 1750–1850, Revisited', *Economic History Review*, 1979, 33–49

——, 'The Standard of Living Debate and Optimal Economic Growth', J. Mokyr (ed.), *The Economics of the Industrial Revolution*, Totowa, 1985, 207–26

Von Tyszka, C., *Löhne und Lebenskosten in Westeuropa im 19. Jahrhundert (Frankreich, England, Spanien, Belgien)*, Munich-Leipzig, 1914

Wiegand, E., 'Zur historischen Entwicklung der Löhne und Lebenshaltungskosten in Deutschland', *Historical Social Research*, 1981, 18–41

—— and W. Zapf (eds), *Wandel der Lebensbedingungen in Deutschland. Wohlfahrtsentwicklung seit der Industrialisierung*, Frankfurt-New York, 1982

Williamson, J., *Did British Capitalism Breed Inequality?*, Boston, 1985

——, 'Debating the British Industrial Revolution', *Explorations in Economic History*, 1987, 269–92

Wood, G. H., 'Real Wages and the Standard of Comfort Since 1850', *Journal Royal Statistical Society*, 1909, 91–103

——, 'Some Statistics Relating to Working Class Progress since 1860', *Journal Royal Statistical Society*, 1899, 639–75

Wright, J. F., 'Real Wage Resistance: Eighty Years of the British Cost of Living', *Oxford Economic Papers*, 1985, 152–67

Zamagni, V., 'The Daily Wages of Italian Industrial Workers in the Giolittian Period (1898–1913), with an International Comparison for 1905', *Rivista di storia economica*, 1984, 59–93

Zapf, W., 'Die Wohlfahrtsentwicklung in Deutschland seit der Mitte des 19. Jahrhunderts', W. Conze and M. Lepsius (eds), *Sozialgeschichte der Bundesrepublik Deutschland*, Stuttgart, 1983, pp. 46–65

Zehnder, A., *Die inländische und ausländiche Kaufkraft des Geldes in den Jahren 1914 bis 1922*, Konstanz, 1923

Notes on Contributors

PROF. PAUL BAIROCH, Professor at the department of Economic History and Director of the Centre of International Economic History of the University of Geneva. He studied in Paris and Brussels and has taught at the Universities of Brussels, Montreal and Paris. Publications include *Révolution industrielle et sous-développement* (Paris, 1963, 4th edition in 1974), *The Economic Development of the Third World since 1900* (1975), *Le Tiers-Monde dans l'impasse. Le démarrage économique du XVIIIe au XXe siècle* (Paris, 1971, 2nd edition in 1985, translated into six languages), *Cities and Economic Development. From the Dawn of History to the Present* (Chicago, 1988).

PROF. ISABELLE CASSIERS, part-time lecturer in economics at the Université Catholique de Louvain. Studied economics at the same university. Publications include *Croissance, crise et régulation en économie ouverte: la Belgique entre les deux guerres* (1989), 'Une statistique des salaires horaires dans l'industrie belge, 1919–1939', *Recherches économiques de Louvain* (1980).

PROF. NICK F. R. CRAFTS, Professor of Economic History, University of Warwick. Previously Fellow in Economics, University College, Oxford (1977–86) and Professor of Economic History, University of Leeds (1987–88). Publications include *British Economic Growth during the Industrial Revolution* (1985), 'Cliometrics 1971–86: A Survey', *Journal of Applied Econometrics* (1987) and 'British Industrialisation in its International Context', *Journal of Interdisciplinary History* (1989).

DR FRANK DAELEMANS, affiliated with the State Archives and the University of Brussels (VUB). Studied Medieval and Modern History at the University of Brussels. Publications include 'Tithe Revenues in Rural South-western Brabant, 15th to 18th Centuries', in *Productivity of Land and Agricultural Innovation in the Low Countries (1250–1800)* (1986), and 'Population et subsistences dans l'espace belge, XVIe–XIXe siècles', in *Evolution agraire et croissance démographique* (1987).

245

DR MARTIN J. DAUNTON, reader in History at University College London. He was educated at the Universities of Nottingham and Kent, and taught economic history at the University of Durham. Publications include *House and Home in the Victorian City: Working-class Housing, 1850–1914* (1983), 'Cities of homes and cities of tenements (British and American comparisons, 1870–1914)', *Journal of Urban History* (1988).

DR DIETRICH EBELING, graduate with the Deutsche Forschungsgemeinschaft. Previously, assistant professor at the University of Bielefeld (1979–87). Publications include *Bürgertum und Pöbel: Wirtschaft und Gesellschaft Kölns im 18. Jahrhundert* (1987) and *Getreideumsatz, Getreide- und Brotpreise in Köln 1368–1797* (with F. Irsigler) (1976/7).

PROF. JULES HANNES, Professor of Economic and Social History and Director of the Centre for Contemporary Social History, University of Brussels (VUB). Studied contemporary history at the State University of Ghent. Publications include *De economische bedrijvigheid te Brussel, 1846–1847* (Brussels, 1975), 'L'histoire sociale: problèmes de méthode et applications aux sources bruxelloises du XIXe siècle', *Cahiers bruxellois*, (1965).

DR RENÉ LEBOUTTE, conservator of the Musée du Fer et du Charbon at Liège, and General Secretary of the Société Belge de Démographie. Studied history at the University of Liège. Publications include *Reconversions de la main-d'oeuvre et transition démographique. Les bassins industriels en aval de Liège, XVIIe–XXe siècles* (Liège-Paris, 1988).

DR JAN LUCASSEN, affiliated with the research department of the International Institute of Social History and the Economic-historical Archives and Library, Amsterdam. Previously, assistant professor of Economic and Social History, University of Utrecht. Publications include *Migrant Labour in Europe 1600–1900: the Drift to the North Sea* (1987).

PROF. ERNEST MANDEL, certificated Ecole Pratique des Hautes Etudes, Paris; Ph.D. Freie Universität Berlin. He was a member of the Economic Studies Commission of the Belgian Trade Union Federation (1955–64). From 1972, professor of Political Sciences, and from 1984 director of the Center of Political Studies, University of Brussels. Among his publications are *Spätkapitalismus* (1972), *The Second Slump* (1979), *The Meaning of the Second World War*, all translated into many languages.

DR DENIS MORSA, affiliated with the Historical Department of the Credit

Communal de Belgique. Studied history at the Université Catholique de Louvain. Previously, assistant Modern History, Université Catholique de Louvain. Publications include 'Salaire et salariat dans les économies préindustrielles (XVI–XVIIIe siècle)', *Revue belge de philologie et d'histoire* (1987).

DR PETER SCHOLLIERS, Senior Research Assistant with the Belgian Fund of Scientific Research. Studied contemporary history at the University of Brussels. Publications include 'A Methodological Note on Real Wages during the Interwar Years', *Historical Social Research* (1987), and 'L'identité des ouvriers-mécaniciens gantois au XIXe siècle. Une contribution au débat sur le rôle social de l'élite ouvrière', *Histoire, économie & société* (1987).

CHRIS SCHROEVEN, affiliated to the Workshop on Quantitative Economic History at the University of Leuven. She studied social and economic history at the same university, and is working on a study of private consumer expenditure in Belgium during the interwar period.

DR L. D. SCHWARZ, lecturer since 1972 in the Department of Economic and Social History at the University of Birmingham. Studied History at Oxford University, graduating in 1969. Publications include 'The Standard of Living in the Long Run: London, 1700–1860', *Economic History Review* (1985). His book *London in the Age of Industrialisation: Economy and Society, 1700–1850* will be published soon.

DR PETER M. SOLAR, affiliated with the Workshop on Quantitative Economic History at the University of Leuven. He studied economics at Swarthmore College and Stanford University. Publications include 'Agricultural Productivity and Economic Development in Ireland and Scotland in the Early Nineteenth Century', in T. Devine and D. Dickson, (eds), *Ireland and Scotland 1600–1900* (1983) and 'A Bicentenary Contribution to the History of the Cost of Living in America' (with P. David), *Research in Economic History* (1977).

DR PATRICIA VAN DEN EECKHOUT, part-time assistant of Social and Economic History and part-time lecturer on Leisure Studies, University of Brussels (VUB). Previously, affiliated with the Department of Communication Sciences of the University of Brussels. She studied contemporary history at the University of Brussels. Publications include *De Brusselse huishuren, 1800–1940* (1979), *Bronnen voor de studie van de hedendaagse belgische samenleving* (1985).

DIRK VAN DER VEEN, co-ordinator, 'International Education', State University Utrecht. Previously, lecturer in economic and social history at the Universities of Amsterdam and Utrecht. Studied economic and social history at Utrecht. Publications include 'Bestedingen aan huur door arbeidersgezinnen aan het begin van de 20e eeuw', in P. M. Klep (ed.), *Wonen in het verleden* (1987) and 'Een onbekende enquête naar broodconsumptie in Nederland in 1890' (with B. Altena), *Tijdschrift sociale geschiedenis* (1986).

PROF. JAN LUITEN VAN ZANDEN, Professor in social and economic history at the Free University of Amsterdam. Studied economics and history at the same university and obtained his Ph.D. from the Agricultural University of Wageningen. Publications include *De economische ontwikkeling van de Nederlandse landbouw in de 19e eeuw* (1985) and *De industrialisatie in Amsterdam 1825–1914* (1987).

PROF. JEF VUCHELEN, Professor of economics, Free University of Brussels (VUB). Studied economics at the same university. Co-editor of *Economic Forecasts*. Main publications include 'The Exchange Market Announcement Effects of Belgium Discount Rate Changes', *European Economic Review* (1988). He was the editor of *Public Administration in a Modern Welfare State* (1985).

DR RICHARD WALL, senior research associate in History, Cambridge University. Studied History at University College London. Editor of *Continuity and Change*. He was co-editor of *The Upheaval of War: Family Work and Welfare in Europe, 1914–1918* (1988) and of *Family Forms in Historic Europe* (1983). Articles include 'Work, welfare and the family: an illustration of the adaptive family economy', in L. Bonfield et al. (eds), *The World We Have Gained* (1986).

PROF. VERA ZAMAGNI, Professor of economic history at the University of Bologna. Previously, professor of economic history at Trieste and Florence. Studied history in Milan, and obtained her Ph.D. from Oxford University in 1975. Publications include 'The Daily Wage of Italian Industrial Workers in the Giolittian period (1898–1913)', *Rivista di storia economica* (1985).

Index

249